HMS BRILLIANT

BRILLIANT:

Brightly shining, glittering, sparkling, lustrous,
splendid, distinguished, striking the imagination.
SHORTER OXFORD ENGLISH DICTIONARY

HMS BRILLIANT

IN A SHIP'S COMPANY

CHRISTOPHER TERRILL

BBC BOOKS

This book is published to accompany the television series entitled *HMS Brilliant* which was first broadcast in 1995.
Executive Producer: Olivia Lichtenstein
Producer and Director: Christopher Terrill

Published by BBC Books,
an imprint of BBC Worldwide Publishing,
BBC Worldwide Ltd, Woodlands, 80 Wood Lane,
London W12 0TT

First published 1995

ISBN 0 563 37184 6

Designed by Keith Watson Art Direction
Maps by Keith Watson & Ian Wellsby

Set in ITC Berkeley Bold & Medium
Printed and bound in Great Britain by Butler & Tanner Ltd, Frome and London
Jacket printed by Lawrence Allen Ltd, Weston-super-Mare

Any references in this book to horizontal and vertical measurements coincide with the official practice of all mariners and aviators to calculate distance in nautical miles, depth in metres and height in feet. Occasionally traditional naval measurements such as cables and fathoms are used.

To

Lieutenant Clive Terrill (RNVR) and Leading Wren Joan Shorter (WRNS)

AUTHOR'S NOTE

This book takes the form of a diary that records the events in Her Majesty's Ship *Brilliant* over a period of ten weeks whilst she was deployed in the Adriatic Sea off Bosnia/Montenegro helping to enforce the arms embargo on all the countries of the former Yugoslavia. Most of it is based on my own, personal diaries and notes kept whilst on board although, occasionally, I have resorted to long-term memory and sometimes, in the case of specific quotes, to transcripts of tapes recorded at the time. Every now and again I have allowed myself a measure of licence by making a few educated guesses about the unravelling of events and the inner reactions of certain people but this is only ever done to help fill the gaps of a closely observed reality. Any error of fact or misinterpretation is entirely my own and should not be attributed to individuals concerned. On two occasions I have changed peoples' names to save them undue embarassment but neither was a major player in the real-life drama that unfolded before me.

CONTENTS

ACKNOWLEDGEMENTS

This book arises from the TV series of the same name made by the Documentary Department of the BBC. My initial thanks goes, therefore, to Paul Hamann, Head of Documentaries, whose vision and energy made it possible for the project to proceed in the first place, as well as Roger Courtiour who gained the crucial, initial access to the Royal Navy. I should also like to thank Olivia Lichtenstein, my Executive Producer, for her guidance, support and friendship throughout the period of film making and book writing. I am forever indebted to Andy Willsmore and Tony Heaven, my hugely talented film editors and very good friends, who not only encouraged my writing but generously allowed me the time away from the cutting room to get on with it. Similarly, I am grateful to Trish Trufelli Stephenson and Gary McIntyre, our editing assistants, who coped magnificently with horrendous workloads and impossible deadlines, and still managed to exercise an endless good humour that sustained us all in our many hours of need. I am greatly beholden to my cameraman Chris Openshaw and my sound recordist Adrian Bell who provided great companionship, immense professionalism and loyal support during the long and sometimes arduous periods at sea during the filming. The whole project benefited from the constant back-up of our committed managment team – Andrew McKerlie, Kate Ponniah and David Julyan. Ines Cavill, my assistant producer, deserves special thanks for her unsparing efforts and tireless support in both the making of the films and the writing of this book. I have drawn enormously on her very special creative talents, sharp wits and unerring instincts as well as leaning heavily on her supreme organizational skills.

At BBC Books I received wonderful encouragement from Sheila Ableman who first prompted me to write the book and, thereafter, the most extraordinarily patient and wise editorial support from Tessa Clark. Sarah Cartwright was endlessly helpful in dealing with all my enquiries and requests. Thanks also to the design team – Jane Coney, David Cottingham, Frank Phillips and to Keith Watson for his careful and understanding approach to the book's lay-out.

Neither the films nor the book would have been possible without the generous help and good faith of the Royal Navy. I would like to thank Captain Chris Beagley and Commander Duncan Fergusson of the Directorate of Public Relations,

Navy for their help, guidance and advice at all stages of the project. I am particularly grateful to Commander Jonathan Dingle for his material contribution to the book in the form of the information boxes that supplement the text. I would also like to thank him for his fine, proofreading eye for detail as well as his friendly availability at all times of the day and night to answer the phone and deal with yet another inane question from a landlubber out of his depth in a sea of navalese. In the same vein I would like to thank my friend, and former Warrant Officer, Mike Barratt who was always ready and willing to share with me his deep knowledge of the sea and ships.

Above all others, however, I would like to thank the men and women of HMS *Brilliant*. I am grateful to all of them for allowing me and my team into their very special community and for extending to us such warm hospitality and friendship for over ten weeks at sea. Their generosity of spirit and unique wit made every day an inspiration. Many on board made a special contribution to the project but in particular I would like to extend my heartfelt gratitude to Captain James Rapp and Lieutenant-Commander Russ Harding for their trust and advice, Lieutenant-Commander Martin Atherton for his unfailing support and guidance, Lieutenant-Commander Bob Hawkins for his honesty, warmth and enthusiasm and Leading Seaman Micky Goble for his humour, good will and encouragement.

Christopher Terrill, London

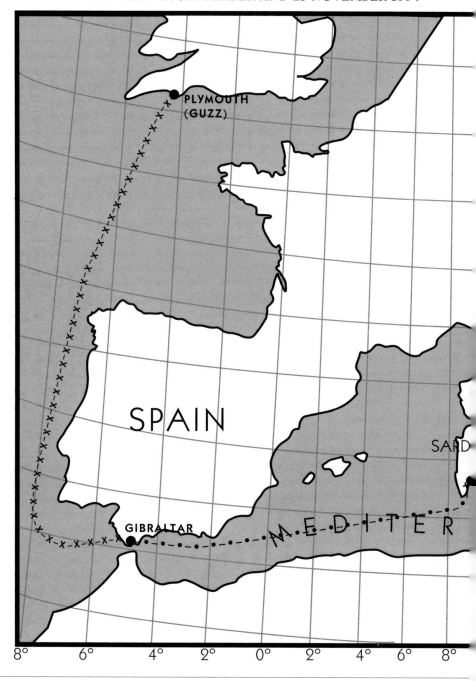

HMS *BRILLIANT*'S DEPLOYMENT
BETWEEN 24 SEPTEMBER AND 25 NOVEMBER 1994

PLYMOUTH
(GUZZ)

SPAIN

SARD

GIBRALTAR

M·E·D·I·T·E·R

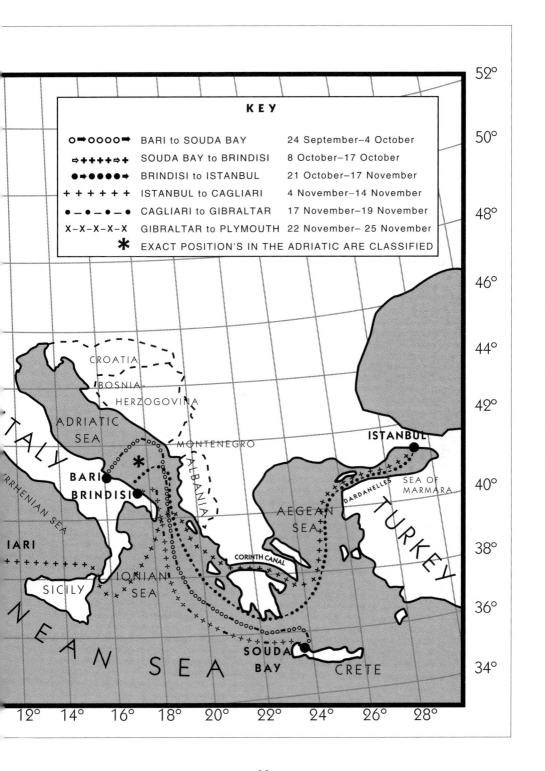

KEY

o➡oooo➡	BARI to SOUDA BAY	24 September–4 October
�]+++++➡+	SOUDA BAY to BRINDISI	8 October–17 October
●➡●●●●➡	BRINDISI to ISTANBUL	21 October–17 November
+ + + + + +	ISTANBUL to CAGLIARI	4 November–14 November
●—●—●—●	CAGLIARI to GIBRALTAR	17 November–19 November
X–X–X–X–X	GIBRALTAR to PLYMOUTH	22 November– 25 November
✱	EXACT POSITION'S IN THE ADRIATIC ARE CLASSIFIED	

52°
50°
48°
46°
44°
42°
40°
38°
36°
34°

CROATIA

BOSNIA
HERZOGOVINA

ADRIATIC
SEA

MONTENEGRO

ITALY

ISTANBUL

BARI
BRINDISI

ALBANIA

DARDANELLES

SEA OF
MARMARA

TYRRHENIAN SEA

AEGEAN
SEA

TURKEY

IARI

CORINTH CANAL

IONIAN
SEA

SICILY

NEAN SEA

SOUDA
BAY

CRETE

12° 14° 16° 18° 20° 22° 24° 26° 28°

'I NAME THIS SHIP . . .'

Sailors of the Royal Navy have a very special relationship with their ships. It is a personal relationship that involves feelings of affection, belonging, dependence and devotion. A ship is never an 'it' but a 'she' – an iron mistress who, if properly cared for, protects, fosters, nurtures and cherishes the seafarers she carries and delivers. Personified in this way it is not surprising that ships have always been given names to secure their individual identities. To launch a ship is to christen her, much as we do a baby, with joyful celebration and solemn prayer. The culminating words of the ceremony, 'May God bless her and all who sail in her', mark the climax of a *rite de passage* that symbolically anchors her soul and prepares her for the service of her country. It is this granting of a spiritual identity that belies the inanimation of wood or metal and gives a ship a special charm that no tank or aircraft has ever enjoyed. This, in turn, can lead to an immortality beyond the destruction of a ship's mere hulk. The soul of a dead ship, whether lost to the sea, the enemy or the breaker's yard, often survives in the memory of the men who served on her and sometimes, also, in the collective memory of the proud and grateful nation she defended and fought for: the *Mary Rose,* the *Hood,* the *Sheffield,* the *Coventry* have permanent moorings in British posterity.

In the 1000 years of its history the Royal Navy has chosen names for untold numbers of ships from the wooden sloops, men-o'-war and ironclads of the past to the frigates, destroyers, submarines and aircraft carriers that sail the oceans today. This, however, has not always been an easy process. Trying to agree on the right name for a ship has sometimes been as fraught and tense an exercise for the navy as it is for any parents torn over what to call their offspring. Reaching consensus has frequently taken time and involved heated and heartfelt debate. Looking down the long lists of names finally decided upon for British warships over the centuries one is amazed at the range and variety of choice. In its agonizing the Admiralty has often been imaginative, frequently emotive, occasionally bold and sometimes downright eccentric. Inspiration has been drawn from a wide spectrum of sources, some more likely than others:

Shakespeare	Portia, Viola, Rosalind.
Sir Walter Scott	Ivanhoe, Redgauntlet, Talisman.
Cities	London, Birmingham, Cardiff, Edinburgh.
Animals	Bulldog, Cygnet, Unicorn, Opossum, Fox, Fawn.
Knights of the Round Table	Sir Bedivere, Sir Galahad, Sir Geraint, Sir Percivale, Sir Tristram.
Heroic qualities	Brave, Fearless, Intrepid, Valiant, Tireless.
Weapons	Broadsword, Battleaxe.
Heavenly bodies	Sirius, Andromeda.
Leaves	Brambleleaf, Oakleaf, Orangeleaf, Roseleaf.
Apparent flights of pure fancy!	Terrible, Pickle, Snowberry, Dwarf, Flirt, Truculent, Bruiser, Candytuft, Cheerful, Truelove, Ravager, Spanker, Rollicker.

Some names, of course, are long-standing naval favourites and have been handed down through history. There have been five incarnations of *Ark Royal*, for example, twelve of *Repulse*, fourteen of *London* and thirty-nine of *Swallow*. An old name bestows on a new ship not only a ready-made reputation, but also a sense of continuity and survival – an important sense for seamen to have in the face of an enemy and the elements.*

Of the ships' names currently in use in the Royal Navy, one of the most favoured and most often used since the seventeenth century is BRILLIANT. Today HMS *Brilliant* is a Broadsword Class Type 22 frigate with Exocet surface-to-surface missile and Sea Wolf close-range air-defence missile systems but she was not always that way.

The first *Brilliant*, captured from the French in 1695, was a six-gun sloop of 60 tons that carried a crew of thirty men.

The second *Brilliant*, also a small sloop, was commissioned around 1730.

The third *Brilliant*, described as an 'armed vessel', came into service in 1755 but was paid off in 1756.

The fourth *Brilliant*, launched at Plymouth in 1757, was a 36-gun frigate of 718 tons carrying a crew of 240 men. She was very active against the French in the

---

* The Submarine Service proved an exception to the rule when it suddenly became superstitious and refused to accept the names of boats that had been lost.

Seven Years War and captured many French warships as prizes: the *Intrepide* in 1757, the *Blonde* and the *Terpsichore* in 1760 and several privateers in 1762.

She was also involved in the capture of Cherbourg in 1758 as well as the blockade and bombardment of Le Havre in the following year, helping to destroy the flat-bottomed boats and supplies which had been collected by the French for their planned invasion of England.

The fifth *Brilliant* was a 28-gun frigate, launched at Bucklers Hard, Beaulieu in May 1779. She was 600 tons and carried a crew of 200 men. This ship was involved in both the American War of Independence and the Wars of the French Revolution and Empire, seeing action against the French, the Spanish and the Dutch. She was at the forefront of the storming and taking of the French islands of St Lucia and Tobago in 1803 and also the capture of the Dutch colonies of Demerara, Essequib and Berbice in the same year.

The sixth *Brilliant* was a 74-gun ship captured from the French at Genoa in April 1814. Soon after she was added to the Royal Navy her name was changed to *Genoa*.

The seventh *Brilliant* was a 38-gun frigate, launched at Deptford in 1814. She was 1408 tons and carried a crew of 284 men. She stayed in Royal Naval service for nearly a hundred years; she became a training ship for volunteers in 1860 and in 1889 her name was changed to *Briton*. She was eventually sold in 1908.

The eighth *Brilliant* was an eight-gun cruiser (two 6 inch guns and six 4.7 inch guns), launched at Sheerness in 1891. She was 3600 tons and 9200 horsepower with a top speed of 20 knots. From 1904 to 1906 she served as the Royal Naval Reserve drill ship at Southampton. She then served in the Newfoundland Fisheries Service before being sunk as a 'block' ship at Ostend in 1918.

The ninth *Brilliant* was a 1360 ton destroyer launched at Wallsend-on-Tyne by Swan Hunter in 1930. She cost £221 638 and carried a crew of 143 men. Her armament amounted to ten main guns and eight torpedo tubes. On trials she exceeded her design speed, reaching 35.56 knots. She began service with the Mediterranean Fleet at Malta but when the Spanish Civil War broke out in 1936 she was sent to Malaga as a guardship to protect and evacuate British citizens.

At the outbreak of the Second World War, *Brilliant* was transferred to Dover for patrols in the English Channel and also for cross-Channel escort duties. A collision with a Dover breakwater in September 1939 required six weeks of repairs.

On 10 May 1940, the day the German offensive started in the Netherlands, *Brilliant* sailed for Antwerp to evacuate British citizens and, if necessary, to deny the port facilities to the Germans. Two days later she left Dover with her sister ship *Boreas* to take part in a similar operation at the Hook of Holland, but the two destroyers collided and had to put in to Sheerness for repairs.

On 25 July 1940 *Brilliant* and *Boreas* sailed to intercept enemy torpedo boats sighted off the French coast. *Brilliant* engaged them with gunfire, closing to within 5 miles of Cap Gris Nez and coming under the fire of shore batteries. The two destroyers were then dive-bombed on their way back to the British coast. *Brilliant* received two bombs on her quarterdeck. Both failed to detonate but caused flooding of the steering gear and magazines. She was towed to Chatham for repairs.

In 1941 *Brilliant* moved from the Home Fleet to the South Atlantic Command to perform screening and escort duties until 1942 when she was attached to yet another command – Force H for the invasion of North Africa. The invasion took place on 7 November and *Brilliant*'s task was close support of the landing at Beach, Oran, where she fired on Vichy French defences. The Vichy sloop *La Surprise* attempted to attack the invasion force off Y Beach but was sunk by *Brilliant* after a 14 minute gun engagement.

From early 1942, following a major refit, *Brilliant* assumed a busy anti-submarine role until the end of the war when she was given the task of escorting the many surrendered U-boats from various ports to Holy Loch where they were scuttled. Before that, on 7 May 1945, she was given the honour of escorting George VI to Jersey. She was sold on 21 February 1948 for scrapping at Troon.

History thus reveals that between 1696 and 1947 nine incarnations of HMS *Brilliant* sailed the seas of the world and fought the enemies of the realm. The ships were as fundamentally different from each other in their form and function as they were in their political and military purpose but the shared name, *Brilliant*, was the common link – a symbol that, transcending time, has led to its own tradition within the Royal Navy and one that lives on.

According to naval practice any new *Brilliant* would invariably have carried mementoes from previous namesakes on board – a battle flag, a ship's bell or paintings of famous past engagements – thereby instilling a sense of continuity in the uncertain and often dangerous world of a warship.

But whilst a name, such as *Brilliant*, passed on from ship to ship over time can provide a pedigree and, to that extent, a sense of identity, it will not actually shape a ship's character or define her 'karma'. A ship is a happy ship not because of a particular name, although pride in this can do a lot for morale, but because the collective personality of the ship's company is a happy one. Equally, a ship may be an unhappy ship because of the nature of the men aboard and the way they interact. So, what was it like to be on board any of the *Brilliants* since 1696? Were they happy ships? Who were the men who served on them? What were they like? How did they get on with each other? What made them laugh? What made them angry

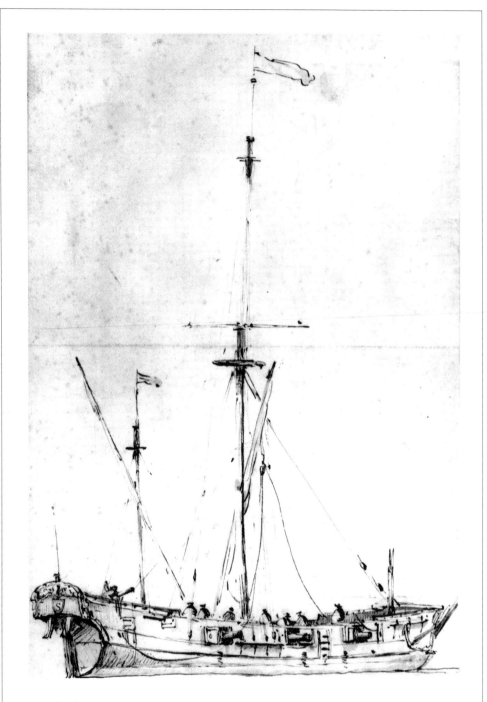

The first *Brilliant,* a six-gun sloop, captured from the French in 1695.

or frustrated? What, for example, would it have been like on the fourth *Brilliant* when she engaged the French frigates *Blonde* and *Terpsichore* in 1760. Who manned the guns? Who was the navigator? What was the bo'sun like and what sort of man was the captain? What about the fifth *Brilliant*? What was her crew like? How did they cope with the challenge of taking St Lucia and Tobago in 1803? Were the officers disciplinarians and what were the punishments aboard? And then what about the ninth *Brilliant* in the Second World War? How did the crew's morale cope with two collisions in a year or, more to the point, how did the captain's career cope with them? What was the collective mood of the ship when she sunk the Vichy French sloop *La Surprise* during the invasion of North Africa? What, on the other hand, was the collective mood of the ship when she came back to port after a long and dangerous deployment? What, at such times, was going through the minds of her crew – the gunners, the stokers, the yeomen, the seamen, the cooks and the officers?

The true spirit of any HMS *Brilliant*, whether a 60 ton wooden sloop captured from the French in the seventeenth century or an iron destroyer that escorted a king, resided in the ship's company – the community within. The men on board make up the collective heart of any ship; SOS, after all, stands not for 'Save Our Ship' but 'Save Our Souls'.

Of course, without recourse to a state of the art time-machine, pondering the nature of the community on board any of the first nine *Brilliants* is a barren exercise. The tenth *Brilliant*, however, provides more fertile opportunity. She exists in the here and now as a working warship that has seen action in the Falklands, the Gulf and, more recently, in the Adriatic off Bosnia. As tenth on the family tree, today's *Brilliant* enjoys a pedigree and the inherited identity of her predecessors; but, as with all other ships of the Royal Navy, her character is all her own and defined, not so much by tradition and name but by those who serve on her.

What follows is the record of a three-month journey taken with a 4000 ton Type 22 (Batch 1) anti-submarine frigate called HMS *Brilliant* – not on exercise, but deep into an international warzone where she was at constant risk of missile attack. On the one hand, the following chapters chronicle a voyage of unfolding maritime adventure in what is, currently, one of the most dangerous and volatile parts of the world. On the other hand, they take us on a voyage into the extraordinary lives of the men and women serving on board – hard-working and hard-playing professional seafarers who live life to the extreme. This is the inside story of today's HMS *Brilliant* – a ship of 250 souls.

'Iceman' is the code name for one of a number of classified sub-areas within Area Montenegro. 'Ethel' and 'Nancy' are the code names for two of the classified sub-areas within Area Otranto.

OPERATION SHARP GUARD

Brilliant's role in the Adriatic was as part of the United Kingdom's contribution to Operation Sharp Guard. This joint NATO and Western European Union (WEU) mission sees ships operating in support of the United Nations Security Council Resolution 820 (93), paragraphs 28 and 29.

The legal basis provided by the United Nations is vital as it gives the justification to the *Brilliant* and other ships to act to:

- prohibit all commercial maritime traffic from
 entering the restricted areas (except as approved
 on a case by case basis); and
- to use such measures commensurate with the specific
 circumstances as may be necessary to enforce the
 resolutions.

The two areas upon which these restrictions are placed are the Straits of Otranto and the Montenegrin coast. Fourteen different NATO and WEU nations have participated in the maritime interdiction operations in the Adriatic. Altogether, some 31 000 ships have been challenged during Operation Sharp Guard. Of these 3200 have been boarded and 640 diverted for inspection by NATO vessels. Other NATO ships, including HMS *Invincible* with her Sea Harrier jump-jet fighters, have been involved in the parallel operation, DENY FLIGHT, which is enforcing the no-fly zone over Bosnia. To date, the Sea Harriers of the Fleet Air Arm have flown more than 1200 sorties and 2000 hours on these missions from their aircraft carrier in the Adriatic.

The Adriatic is, however, only one of a number of areas where the United Nations sanctions against the former Republic of Yugoslavia have been sought. Whilst *Brilliant* and her sister ships have been successful in enforcing the embargo, the resolutions have been violated elsewhere, for example, on land border crossings and the River Danube.

Chapter One

BYE-BYE BARI

DAY *Saturday*	**DATE** *24*	**MONTH** *September*	**YEAR** *1994*
PLACE		*On passage from the port of Bari, south-west Italy*	
POSITION		*At 1800 41°18′N 17°00′E* **At 2359** *41°28′N 17°33′E*	

DISTANCE TRAVELLED midnight to midnight *47.5 nautical miles*

SHIPS LOG. Final day alongside in Bari. Little to report. Football team played (and lost). Sailed early at 1800 to resume duties in Operation Sharp Guard. Made passage to Area Iceman. Nuclear, Biological, Chemical Defence State – 2 YANKEE. Very calm conditions.

It is **1800** hours. Two Italian tugs, one aft and one for'ard, pull the tenth incarnation of HMS *Brilliant* carefully away from the quayside and, in a skilful manoeuvre, set the 4000 ton frigate towards open water. The Union Jack at her bow, catching a warm offshore breeze, billows as if to signal the ship's imminent departure. The upper deck swarms with hands at Harbour Stations, everybody with an allotted task and specific responsibility. From the quarterdeck the aft tug cable is unbuttoned and released from its securing bollards whilst above on the flight deck sailors line up in ceremonial order for leaving harbour – tallest aft, chin-stays down and standing easy.

On the foc'sle, just in front of the Exocet missile launchers, a cable party of ten sailors and two Wrens prepare to release the line to the for'ard tug. One amongst them is Leading Seaman (Radar) Micky Goble, a rotund, affable ex-gravedigger from Gloucestershire. He is working with surprisingly studied concentration on what to him is a normally familiar and well-practised procedure for behind a determined jaw his head is pounding like a sledge-hammer. Squinting against the piercing glare of a sinking Mediterranean sun he curses cheap Italian wine and his own tendency to excess. As the line is finally released and the tug pulls away

Goble sits gratefully on the nearest capstan. 'I'm absolutely bolloxed,'* he mutters to his amused shipmates as they fall in to their leaving harbour station – a single rank facing outboard and standing easy on the port side. Goble could not have expected sympathy for naval humour demands that a man is kicked when he is down and the more he complains the harder the kicking:

'You look like you're going to die Goble.'

'He looks like he's already dead!'

'Get fell in here you fat bastard!'

'That's Leading Fat Bastard to you!' retorts Goble as he shuffles reluctantly towards the laughing foc'sle party.

Micky Goble is not the only one on board with a thick or throbbing head. Many of the crew have taken full advantage of a three-day run ashore in Bari to relax and play in the way that only sailors know how. It has been a welcome break from the rigours of sea duty but all too short. The original plan had been to stay here for four days, until this time tomorrow evening, but yesterday a signal came in from STANAVFORMED [Standing Naval Force, Mediterranean] ordering the *Brilliant* back to sea one day early – in other words today.

This unexpectedly early departure is very unpopular with the ship's company who, because of it, are losing a whole day and night ashore along with all the accompanying delights normally associated with an Italian port town. Sailors are a remarkably long-suffering breed except when it comes to the question of time ashore. To 'Jack' that is God-given time.

Some of the ship's company tried to make the best of it last night and took the opportunity to drink as much as they could on a bar-crawl around Bari. A lot of beer and wine went down a lot of throats and many did not get to their bunks until the very early hours – if at all. That is why there are still a few lingering headaches around.

Today, most people have stayed on the ship. Apart from the ship's football team, which managed to get ashore for a couple of hours only to lose 2–1 to the local team, the rest have had to spend time gearing up for another tense period of active sea duty – one day ahead of time. Consequently, there has been a heavy mood on board all day – a sort of collective sulk though that now seems to have run its course. Sailors can make it very clear if they are unhappy about something but, then again, they are usually pretty quick to bounce back once they feel they have made their point.

---

* Sailor slang for hungover. Also 'shedded, ratted and handcarted'. For more naval slang, see Jackspeak, page 212.

'I could have done with another day just to recover,' complains Goble lining up with the foc'sle party.

'Quit mankin'* and get some Brufen** down you mate. Then get some scran,'*** suggests Able Seaman (Sonar) Ian 'Rowan' Atkinson who is standing on his left.

'I ain't eating nothing,' retorts Goble, ' 'cept bleedin' jelly.'

'Jelly?' says Atkinson looking round.

'Yeah,' grins Goble. ' 'Cos it tastes the same coming up as it does goin' down!'

Atkinson's response to Goble's hangover-humour is drowned out by the ship's siren which sounds one long, deafening blast. High on the yard-arm a row of unsuspecting Italian seagulls fly off screeching in panic. On the bridge James Rapp, captain of the British warship, nods to navigator Lieutenant Perry Stowell who quietly orders 'Set lever 40. Half ahead both engines'. Down in the engine spaces the duty stokers respond immediately and the two Rolls-Royce Tyne RM1C engines surge to 40 per cent of their combined 11 000 horsepower. The water boils at the stern and the ship slices into the Adriatic towards a classified destination 300 miles to the east code-named 'Iceman'.

It is 1847. A school of five playful dolphins, looking like cling-wrapped torpedoes, is riding the ship's bow-wave as we maintain a steady course at 15 knots in a calm evening sea. Our course is not a new one and the Adriatic, with its gentle swells and dramatic red sunsets, is now a familiar sea to everyone on board. Only the sleek, black dolphins, that love to surf on the pressure waves created by the surging warship, still hold their exotic charm for anyone on the upper deck lucky enough to see them.

HMS *Brilliant* is now four months into a seven-month tour of duty in Operation Sharp Guard – a United Nations naval blockade enforcing trade sanctions against Serbia and an arms embargo against all the countries of the former Yugoslavia. For the 210 men, nineteen Wrens and twenty-one officers on board it is hard work involving punishing duties in a high risk environment which is why intermittent runs ashore are so vital to the ship's morale.

But now with the bars and beer of Bari behind us and the secret destination of

---

* To moan, whine or complain. See also 'to drip' (Jackspeak, page 212).
** Sailors with experience of major hangovers swear by a single well-tested cure: a handful of powerful painkilling Brufen tablets which are large, pink and virtually impossibe to swallow but universally recognized as the 'sailor's best friend'. Ideally, they should be followed by several slices of dry white bread.
*** Sailor slang for food, though it can be used as a general word to refer to any mealtime. It is widely believed that a hearty scran, usually a 'full English' [cooked breakfast] is a good cure for hangovers – after the Brufen and dry bread. For more naval slang, see Jackspeak, page 212.

Iceman in front we are proceeding at Enhanced Cruising Stations – this is the normal peacetime passage state, described officially as the third degree of readiness for battle. Within an hour, however, we will be preparing to go into Defence Stations, the second degree of readiness for battle. Only when secured in this higher state of alertness will the ship be ready to enter Area Iceman. That will be sometime around dawn tomorrow. Meanwhile, though, ratings and officers alike are still brushing themselves down after the curtailed run ashore – it has taken more than a few by surprise.

In the stores office down on Three Deck Lieutenant-Commander Martin Atherton [Supply Officer] is talking to Leading Wren Fiona Sloan [Stores Accountant] about the current stock of battle bags and anti-flash gear on board. At the same time he is desperately trying to stem the flow of blood from a nasty cut in his right ear – a wound sustained no more than an hour ago at the hands of a barber trying to do a rush haircut for an officer in a hurry.

'We should have another stock-take of anti-flash gloves, overalls and . . . You don't have another tissue do you?'

'Yes sir. Here sir. We had a count up on the gloves just last week sir, but . . . 'scuse me sir, the blood's dripping on your collar sir.'

'Damn it!'

'Squeeze it sir. Squeeze it hard.'

Up one deck in the main galley Leading Cooks Mark Warburton and Mickey Nowell are rushing to get all the dishes out for the second supper sitting for the petty officers and chief petty officers who are filing in to the self-service hatch.

'God! I thought this bleeding lot were going to be ashore tonight.'

'I thought I was going to be a-fucking-shore tonight – getting bolloxed.'

'There's not going to be enough bolognese. They're all going to go for that.'

'Well, they can stuff it. They've got veggie pizza and southern fried as well.'

'Right, the vichy carrots are out, so's the sweetcorn, so's the green beans.'

'The griddle cakes are ready and so's the jam sauce.'

'The chips'll be two minutes.'

'Oi you lot! Chips'll be two minutes!!'

Immediately above the galley in the wardroom Lieutenant John O'Flaherty [Assistant Marine Engineering Officer] is leafing through a copy of yesterday's *Daily Telegraph*, obtained in Bari, whilst the ship's doctor, Surgeon-Lieutenant Richard Newton, examines the stitches in his right eyebrow.

'Not bad stitches actually. Yesterday was it?'

'Day before yesterday.'

'Who did them?'

'Some guy on the Bari rugby team had a mate who was a doctor. When can they come out?'

'In about a week. What was the score?'

'Twenty-six, twelve to us. Good game. Bit rough.'

'See the soccer team lost?'

'Prats!'

It is **1917**. Captain Rapp is at his desk going through some classified papers just brought in by his secretary, Lieutenant Liz Hall, whilst behind them his steward, Petty Officer George Cooper, is laying the table for the captain's supper. James Rapp picks up his intercom to call down to his first lieutenant, Lieutenant-Commander Russ Harding, just at the moment that there is a knock at the door.

'Excuse me sir . . .'

'Ah, Russ!' says the captain, 'I was just trying to get you in your cabin.'

'Yes sir?'

'What time are we getting into Area?'

'At first light sir, around 0530 hours – that'll be Alpha* time sir.'

'Fine and we'll be going from Relaxed State to Full Manning in Defence Watches.'

'At 0300 Alpha sir.'

'OK Russ. Let's make sure we're over there in good time.'

'Yes sir. We're increasing speed when we're out of local shipping.'

'Good.'

'Sir, I just wanted to report that we'll be securing for action at 19.30.'

'OK. Right. Thanks Russ.'

'Thank you, sir'.

'Now Liz we must signal back to the *Invincible* tomorrow about this ADEX** with her Harriers. It can't be until we're out of Area. Maybe on passage to Brindisi. Get Bob Hawkins on to that, will you?'

---

* Time in the Royal Navy is usually taken from Greenwich Mean Time which is known by the navy as Zulu time and is one of the 24 time zones that are internationally agreed around the world. Thus when the time in London is 1.00 a.m. Zulu it is already 2.00 a.m. Alpha time in most of western Europe where the clocks are normally ahead of those in the United Kingdom. When the UK goes over to Summer Time (BST) it goes into Alpha time, but happily the rest of Europe goes into Bravo time. The navy operates to a standard Zulu or Greenwich Mean Time to avoid the risk of operations starting at the wrong hour.
** Air Defence Exercise. For more acronyms, see The Wonders of Naval Abbreviation, page 218.

'Yes sir.'

'I've got a few more signals to write tonight . . . By the way, I presume the new people arrived in Bari?'

'Yes sir. Three new arrivals. Two able seamen and a Wren.'

'Right. I'd better see them for my usual welcoming speech. Fit them in in the next few days.'

'Yes sir . . .'

'*Officer of the watch sir,*' interrupts a voice from a speaker just above the captain's head.

'Captain!' replies the captain curtly into a big, black intercom.

'*At red 10, range 2 miles, I have a merchantman. I am 150 degrees on his starboard bow. His closest point of approach is 1.2 miles. I am happy and intend to stand on.*'

'Very good.'

'*For information, sir, we are otherwise clear of shipping and intend to increase to passage speed.*'

'Approved.'

' 'Scuse me sir,' ventures Petty Officer Steward Cooper as the captain replaces the intercom. 'Your soup is ready sir.'

'Fine. Right. OK. Thanks Liz. Get that one signal off to London tonight and I'll work on the others for tomorrow.'

'Yes sir. Goodnight sir.'

James Rapp selects a copy of *Golfing Monthly* and takes it to his dining-table as George Cooper comes in with a steaming bowl. 'Mulligatawny tonight sir,' he says, rocking slightly on his heels as the ship lurches suddenly forward. 'Hello. There go the Ollys sir.'

The ship has switched from the Tyne engines to her two powerful Olympus gas turbine engines. With a total of 50 000 horsepower behind her the *Brilliant* is now building up to her maximum speed of around 28 knots.

It is **1930**. Down in the operations room, the tactical nerve-centre of the ship, Lieutenant-Commander Bob Hawkins [Principal Warfare Officer] pipes the order 'Secure for action. Assume weapon state Monty.'* This is the order to arm the ship's weapons with live ammunition and to load the air-defence missiles. Gunners and seamen all over the ship respond with practised, machine-like efficiency. Wearing anti-flash hoods, gloves and overalls they first unlock the magazines deep in the belly of the ship.

---

* Weapons are loaded. Weapon state Golf means they are stowed in the magazines.

Then a whole range of different-sized ammunition is carried, hoisted or dragged to the upper deck: high velocity bullets for the 7.62 mm general purpose machine guns mounted on each of the bridge wings; armour-piercing and tracer shells for the Twin GCB 30 mm anti-aircraft guns and the two GAMBO single 20 mm mountings; six Sting Ray anti-submarine torpedoes; and twelve Sea Wolf air-defence missiles for the two launchers positioned for'ard and aft. The only missiles that are not being handled this evening are the four massive Exocet surface-to-surface missiles which are kept constantly in their pods on the foc'sle.

The ammunition is handled methodically and with respect. The gunners loading the 30 mm and 20 mm guns painstakingly thread the long belts of black-headed green shells into the magazines before locking the belts and the first shells into their muzzles. At the same time, on either side of the ship, the huge, black Sting Ray torpedoes are slowly lifted by winch and gently coaxed into their launching tubes whilst, just aft of the foc'sle, the safety G clamps are removed from the Exocets. On the Sea Wolf decks at either end of the ship teams of missile men carefully load the Sea Wolf missiles from the specially designed lifts that bring the 300 lb rockets up from the magazines on to the yellow trolleys that wheel them to the launchers. The beautifully streamlined white missiles with red trim look more like finely crafted modern sculptures than instruments of destruction. They are handled with great care and pride by the missile men who nurse them on to loading ramps before cranking them individually into the launcher. Finally, Lieutenant-Commander Fred Tulloch [Weapons Engineering Officer], signals to his deputy, Lieutenant Kevin Easterbrook, to step forward and arm the missiles by connecting them individually to their electrical launching circuits.

In the constantly darkened, windowless operations room situated below the bridge Principal Warfare Officer Bob Hawkins leans over his personal orange-glowing radar screen whilst he waits for the weapon-loading procedure to be completed. Hawkins, nicknamed 'Bosnia Bob' by those who work with him, is a deep-thinking, hard-working and dedicated officer who brings total commitment to his job. Trained as a clearance diver the navy has become his religion. He lives and breathes it but Bob Hawkins is saved from being a navy bore by the special personal qualities that stamp his work, namely a deeply felt sense of the moral responsibility of leadership, a great sensitivity to the feelings of other people, and an extrovert, madcap personality that has marked him out as a very unusual but very popular officer. Passionately proud of his specialization as a navy diver and an accomplished exponent of the diver's 'work hard, play hard' outlook on life, he is well known for an audacious, boisterous sense of fun that delights some but terrifies others. It was exactly this spirit of adventure that prompted him to broaden his credentials by training up in tactical warfare. This is his first job as a PWO [pronounced 'Pea-woh'].

At the moment he is staring intently at the pattern of tiny blips on his radar screen – the current surface picture of shipping within a 96 mile radius of the *Brilliant*. Around him his team of radar, sonar and missile operators tend to their own scanning screens, VDUs and complex arrangements of illuminated computer buttons.

This twilight zone of flashing lights, once shredded by Argentine shrapnel and small arms fire in the Falklands War,* is crammed full of electronic surveillance devices and defence and warning systems as well as the ship's own guided-missile attack system. To Bob Hawkins the operations room is the most important room in the ship. It is why she exists.

'The whole point of a warship is to go to war – or, at least, be prepared to go to war at any time. A warship is merely a floating platform for its weapons and everybody on board is there in a supporting role to those that handle and operate the weapons. Most people on a warship don't have any direct contact with the shells or missiles but they all play their part – the stokers make sure we move, the cooks make sure we eat and the seamen make sure we float. The rest is up to us here in the op's room. We, and the gunners on deck, are warriors – nothing more, nothing less. Whether we are scanning a screen for the sonar blip of an enemy submarine or pushing a button that says "fire!" we are here to kill or be killed.'

It is **2000**. Russ Harding takes the microphone from the ship's broadcast system on the bridge. He collects his thoughts, sips his tea and clears his throat before pushing the transmit button:

'Good evening. First Lieutenant here. At 0300 we go into Defence Watches in advance of entering Area Iceman where the threat from the Federal Republic of Yugoslavia, that is Serbia-Montenegro, is currently assessed as medium. However, if we have to enter territorial waters it will be a high threat environment and we would go to Action Stations. The ship must be ready for the worst case. Look hard and think hard as you leave your compartments or mess decks. Have you left them in order and secure? What would happen if we took a hit and had to pump out that space? As you know the Defence Watches routine is a hard one. Six hours on duty and six hours off round the clock. Remember, don't loiter in areas where others might be asleep. You wouldn't thank others if they woke you. The foc'sle is out of bounds as well as the for'ard and aft launcher decks. NO SMOKING AT ALL ON THE UPPER DECK!

---

* See Brilliant Under Fire, page 28.

BRILLIANT UNDER FIRE

On 19 March 1982 it was reported that a party of Argentine scrap-metal workers had landed illegally in South Georgia. Preparations began in secret to send ships to the South Atlantic and when the Argentine invasion of the Falklands began on 2 April, the Fleet was ready for war and *Brilliant* sailed south.

She had only been accepted into the navy a year earlier and over the next 107 days and nights, during which she was continuously at sea, her people distinguished themselves in constant operations. Captain John Coward, the then commanding officer, was awarded the DSO; six of his ship's company were mentioned in dispatches; and the laundryman, Leo Kang, was awarded the BEM for his courage under fire.

The ship confronted constant danger. Off South Georgia, her Lynx helicopters discovered the Argentine submarine *Sante Fe* and, in a remarkable attack, crippled her and forced her into the port of Grytviken. *Brilliant's* diving officer, Lieutenant-Commander Chris Sherman, was sent in with demolition charges to deliver the *coup de grâce*: the submarine threat to the British task force was effectively ended.

Brilliant then moved west and 12 May saw her close to the Falklands with the destroyer *Glasgow*. The ships were attacked by twelve bombers broken into four waves and *Brilliant* engaged with her Sea Wolf missiles. Two aircraft in the first wave were shot down, a third plane crashed into the sea and a fourth fell to Argentine 'friendly' fire. But the second and third waves got through and 1000 lb bombs ricocheted off the sea. One went over the *Brilliant's* flight deck, one between her masts and a third over the bridge. A few days later in San Carlos Water her luck changed. A Mirage jet attacked with cannon fire and shells swept the starboard side penetrating the op's room and three men had to be transferred to the hospital ship *Uganda* with slight injuries. Some electrical compartments were damaged, but the worst inconveniences were the shells that destroyed the officers' toilet and the wine store.

Brilliant remained at the forefront of convoy duties until the end of the war and sustained no more hits. She operated with the Special Forces and the latest technology, but also with machine guns at close quarters recalling a previous era of naval war. With an average age of nineteen, her company made a significant contribution to victory in the Falklands.

All *weapon systems are now loaded and fully prepared for action. Battle bags are to be carried at all times. My sun-glasses have gone missing. Reward for information leading to their safe return. That's all.'*

If Russ Harding had not become an officer in the Royal Navy he could have made a great career as a Radio 4 announcer or World Service news reader. He has a soft, resonant voice, flavoured with the slightest Scottish lilt, that is able to reach out to people with great but gentle authority. He uses it every night at this time to great good effect by giving masterfully ad-libbed sit. reps [situation reports] over the tannoy to the ship's company. His deadpan humour lightens the most serious of announcements.

Part of his job as first lieutenant, or the 'Jimmy', is to act as the link man between the captain and everybody else making sure of open communications between command and crew. As the captain's right-hand man he has to maintain immense authority and keep strict, even-handed discipline throughout the ship, but, at the same time, remain approachable to all and sympathetic to anyone's grievance. It is a difficult balancing act to pull off and makes the job of first lieutenant not only one of the toughest in the Royal Navy but also one of the most thankless and often one of the most lonely. The first lieutenant can never be 'one of the boys'. Even though, on paper, he might have equal rank with many other officers in the wardroom he has an added authority that requires him to live a slightly separate existence from them. A bad Jimmy who does not know his job or understand the subtle boundaries that divide his role from those of others can seriously undermine the morale of even the best appointed ships.

Russ Harding is recognized throughout the *Brilliant* as a first-rate Jimmy. He is known to be an excellent and dedicated officer with flair, initiative and a strict but fair sense of discipline. He is forgiven for his occasional quake-making temper because of his wry, dry sense of humour and rather endearing eccentricities – such as his tendency, whether on the bridge, the foc'sle or the flight deck, to be holding in his right hand a cup of hot, steaming tea, permanently poised in front of puckered lips, whilst cradling in his left hand the accompanying saucer and spoon. Harding is not a 'mug' man.

The sit. rep. finished, he sits for a while on the darkened bridge and looks out into the blackness. He can hear the voice of the yeoman talking to the bos'un's mate by the ship's wheel but he can see neither of them. The bridge on a warship is kept in total darkness at night to allow the watch-keepers' eyes to adjust to the outside.

'Somebody nick your sun-glasses sir?' says Lieutenant Tracie Lovegrove, officer of the watch, and currently a silhouette near the bridge compass.

'Yes,' replies Harding, searching with the hands of a blind man for his cup of tea momentarily put down in the blackness. 'I left the bloody things in the chart-house this afternoon. I suspect a certain navigator might have taken them hostage. I am just waiting for a ransom note unless they've been float-tested.* That will be the third time this deployment.'

'Fair game I reckon sir!' laughs a disembodied male voice from the direction of the map table.

'Thanks a bunch Yeoman. You would! Right, I'm off to get some dinner. Watch out for small fishing boats Officer of the Watch – the place is packed with them and they don't always have working night-lights. There's a cup of tea around here somewhere if anybody wants it.'

'Yes sir. Goodnight.'

It is **2358**. Officers, midshipmen, chief petty officers, petty officers, leading seamen, able seamen, Wrens and marines. Stokers, gunners, caterers, seamen, weapon mechanics, radar, radio and sonar operators, stewards, yeomen, flight engineers, cooks, nurses, regulators, writers, a club-swinger,** two dhobey wallahs*** and one civilian NAAFI-man. Throughout the ship an entire self-contained community of 250 men and women is resuming the bizarre life style that comes with the job. A sailor at sea is confined to a floating 'tin box' without even the possibility of escape. Life on a warship, especially a frigate, is all about proximity, nearness, and closeness to others, whether they would be your chosen friends in Civvy Street or not. On the one hand this can effectively bind people, boost morale and promote the common cause – those things which are the key to a proud and happy ship with a successful and spirited crew. On the other hand, proximity can mean tension, aggravation and argument, which leads to low morale which, in turn, leads to an unhappy ship. And an unhappy ship is often a dangerous ship – the one thing a warship must never be except to her enemies.

Maintaining high morale is a particular priority for any ship working in the arduous, tense, frustrating and often monotonous milieu of Operation Sharp Guard. HMS *Brilliant* is one of twenty-one warships from twelve countries operating under NATO and the Western European Union to enforce the arms embargo against the fragmented, warring countries of old Yugoslavia. The ships are divided

---

* Thrown overboard.
** Physical training instructor.
*** See Chinese Laundrymen, page 77. For more than half a century the Royal Navy has gone into ction-starched and pressedd by the efforts of the unofficial Chinese laundry entrepreneurs from Hong Kong who are invited on board by ships' commanding officers.

into two main groups. The southerly group is distributed between various designated operating areas in the Straits of Otranto between southern Italy and Albania (see map, page 18). They guard the entrance to the Adriatic by challenging and boarding merchant ships to check against any attempted gun-running to either the Serb or Muslim armies. The *Brilliant* forms part of that group every two or three weeks on a strict rotational basis. The northerly group, which the frigate will shortly be joining, is distributed between designated areas off the Montenegro coast and is responsible for maintaining a 'ring of steel' close to the Serbia-Montenegro coast – and that means close to potentially hostile Yugoslavian fighter aircraft, warships, submarines and Styx missile installations. The *Brilliant*'s mission, in this highly unstable area, will be to help stop any ships which evade the southerly group.

In just over three hours we will be closed up at Defence Stations, the second degree of readiness for battle, and about two hours after that we will assume control of area Iceman when we relieve the Turkish destroyer *Yavuz* currently on patrol there. Most people on board are now asleep though not all:

Micky Goble, still slightly tender-headed, has got his feet up in the mess he shares with an assortment of gunners, missile men and seamen. He is watching a video of Rutger Hauer and Donald Sutherland in *Buffy the Vampire Slayer.* In the background is the constant hum of the ship's air-conditioning system and the intermittent snoring of the sailors already in their 'pits'.

Up two decks in the haven of his own cabin Bob Hawkins is writing to his wife Joan and his two small sons Cameron and Jamie. He looks up from the letter, momentarily trying to think of a word, and meets the gaze of Lord Nelson from the small wooden-framed portrait he keeps on the corner of his desk. He hesitates. He picks up his diary to find out where the ship will be on 21 October, Trafalgar Day, to see if there might be a chance for a celebration. Unfortunately, he discovers that this year, on the day that everybody in the Royal Navy likes to raise a glass or three, HMS *Brilliant* will be leaving yet another Italian port, Brindisi, to go back on patrol. Hawkins leafs further through his diary to find the next run ashore after that. He stops at 31 October where he has scrawled in his famously illegible handwriting 'Arrive Istanbul'. He smiles at the prospect but then considers all the hard work in front of the ship before that, particularly in the warfare department. He returns to his letter.

Up another deck in the captain's cabin James Rapp is also at his desk. He is writing not letters home but urgent signals to various naval destinations. Some he marks 'Restricted', others 'Confidential' and a couple 'Top Secret'. He has to maintain constant communications with not only the Admiralty back in London but also, depending on contingencies, any of the other warships working in Operation Sharp Guard. Looking at the thick files of classified signals he has received over the last few months Rapp sits back and considers the frustrating enormity of the task he has been set.

This dark-haired, rugged looking man, considered to be one of the navy's real high-flyers, is preparing himself mentally for the intense pressure of command that always comes with a ship closed up at Defence Stations in a warzone. He knows only too well that the *Brilliant* is about to take position well within the missile envelope of the Yugoslavian military forces and will, consequently, present a permanent sitting target to any trigger-happy maverick with a grudge against the United Nations peace-keeping plan, especially if the political situation should deteriorate leading to a withdrawal of UN forces.

As the captain considers the complicated and highly secret rules of engagement set out specifically for this operation to help commanding officers determine at what point they would or should fire their guns or missiles in anger, his steward George Cooper looks in at the door.

'Hot drink before I go sir?'

'No thanks Petty Officer Cooper.'

'What time do you want shaking sir?'

'Better make it 04.30.'

'Alright sir. Goodnight then sir.'

'Goodnight.'

James Rapp turns off the desk light, picks up his golfing magazine and walks towards his bunk.

Meanwhile, the watch-keepers on the bridge remain shrouded in their blackness and guide HMS *Brilliant* ever nearer towards Iceman.

Chapter Two

ICEMAN BLUES

DAY *Sunday*	**DATE** *25*	**MONTH** *September*	**YEAR** *1994*

PLACE	*Area Iceman, Eastern Adriatic*

POSITION	*Classified*

DISTANCE TRAVELLED midnight to midnight *240.3 nautical miles*

SHIPS LOG. Defence Watches. Assumed Iceman duties very early on. All quiet in patrol area. Internal training for most of day – MOBEX and FLYEX. Bright Star away for fast roping. Absolutely calm throughout day.

It is **0530**. We are now on patrol in Iceman. Since we took control from the Turkish destroyer *Yavuz* half an hour ahead of schedule at 0230, the ship has assumed a full Defence Watches routine. This means that everybody works for six hours and rests for six hours around the clock, that permanent watches are kept through the high-powered binoculars on both the bridge wings in addition to constant surface, sub-surface and air radar/sonar surveillance, and that everyone carries their battle bags at all times. These white canvas bags slung around the shoulder contain the all-important anti-flash gear – hoods, gloves and overalls – that are designed to prevent the terrible flash burns that occur in the vicinity of an explosion.

Leading Steward Andy Conway is going round the officers' cabins giving them their shakes [wake-up knocks] and their early morning cups of tea. He knocks loudly on each door.

'Good morning sir. Tea sir?'

'What time is it?' groans Sub-Lieutenant Nick Cooke-Priest [Lynx Helicopter Flight Observer].

'Just gone five-thirty sir.'

'OK . . . two sugars please.'

Conway moves to the next cabin.

'Good morning sir. Tea sir?'

'What time is breakfast today?' mumbles Lieutenant Jerry Barnbrook [Lynx Helicopter Flight Commander].

'Six to six-thirty sir – same as it always is in Defence Watches sir'.

'Alright! Alright! That's quite enough lip from you Leading Steward Conway!' retorts the flight commander with mock anger. 'And keep your disgusting tea!'

The leading steward smiles and knocks at the next door.

'Good morning ma'am. Tea ma'am.'

'Just coming,' says Lieutenant Liz Hall. 'Are we in Area?'

'Yes ma'am. Since 0230 ma'am. We took over early.'

'Is the captain up?'

'Yes ma'am. PO Cooper shook him at 0430. Milk, no sugar isn't it ma'am?'

Down on the lower decks waking up is proceeding with a little less style. Normally, when the ship is at Cruising Stations, all the ratings are woken at the same time by the 'call the hands' – the high-pitched whistle of a bos'un's pipe broadcast over the ship's tannoy system. During Defence Watches, however, they are woken silently by each other according to an informal rota system based on who is going on watch and who is coming off. The sleeping areas of each mess contain five or six communal cabins or 'gulches' and each one contains six coffin-sized bunks or 'pits' stacked three high from deck to bulkhead, so the waking up procedure is complicated, sensitive and not without its risks.

'Nobby! Time to get up mate.'

Silence.

'Nobby!'

'Sod off.'

'Nobby . . .'

'Sod off.'

'Nobby. It's gone five-thirty.'

'Sod off.'

'Come on you bastard. We're on watch in half an hour.'

'Sod off.'

'Don't you want any scran?'

'No.'

A low, deliberate voice from the pit above joins the dialogue.

'Clarke! I'm trying to bleedin' rack out you gob-shite. Get up or I'll fuckin' lay you out . . .'

One rating got up of his own accord over an hour ago. It was Micky Goble. He always gets up in good time before breakfast so he can boil up a good strong brew of NAAFI tea which he always has in the same cracked, bright purple mug. He puts clingfilm carefully around the top of the mug to stop any spills* and then takes it to the isolated quarterdeck at the stern of the ship.

'The quarterdeck is about the only bleedin' place on the ship where you can be on your own – at least at this time in the mornin'. Cooped up on a ship like this you need to find some space of your own. On somethin' like an aircraft carrier there's plenty of room for everyone – 'specially those big American "mothers" the size of the Isle of Wight – but on a frigate it's practically bleedin' impossible. I come out here at silly o'clock to watch the dawn 'specially when there's an Irish hurricane** like now. Also, it's even more important to find time to be on your tod during Defence Stations because everybody gets so tense. There is just no time to relax. There's no beer. Bleedin' fridges are padlocked till we get out of Area. Somebody once said being on a ship is just like being in prison 'cept with a chance of drowning.*** He didn't know how right he was.'

Micky Goble carefully peels the clingfilm from the top of his cracked, purple mug releasing a spiral of tannin-scented steam into the cool dawn air.

'You know, sometimes I think this ship is like a little England floating around the oceans of the world. You got every type on board that you would have at home: brainy types, brawny types, nice ones, 'orrid ones. You got doctors, cooks, mechanics, sparks, chippies. You got mad scientists, village idiots, high class toffs and then a few bog-common dregs to make up the numbers . . . like the Royal Marines!'****

He takes a sip of tea.

'They gave me this mug at the Clipper – that's my local back in Guzz . . .'*****

Goble clasps the mug tightly and peers deep into the steaming brew.

'. . . I always give 'em a ring at the Clipper when we go alongside anywhere. See how they all are there – Stew, Rab, Jeff, Gerry and Taff. And see how the skittle team are doing without me – losing, I'm glad to say, when I rang them from Bari . . . Look over there! See those lights? That's Dubrovnik that is and behind those

---

* Ship's standing orders actually require mugs of hot drinks to be sealed to avoid spillages when they are carried around the ship.
** Flat calm sea.
*** 'No man will be a sailor who has contrivance enough to get into a jail, for being in a ship is being in a jail with the chance of being drowned . . . a man in a jail has more room, better food, and commonly better company.' (Samuel Johnson, Boswell's *Life of Samuel Johnson*, vol. 1, page 348, 16 March 1759.)
**** The sailor and the marine are historically and culturally very close and, because of their military interdependence, their relationship is officially one of mutual respect and trust – although no self respecting sailor or marine would ever admit to it in public! (See The Royal Marines, page 119.)
***** Plymouth. For more naval slang, see Jackspeak, page 212.

mountains is where the Serbs and the Bosnians are blasting the crap out of each other. Poor bastards.'

It is **0600**. The officers filter into the wardroom for breakfast. Nick Cooke-Priest and Jerry Barnbrook, the Fleet Air Arm helicopter crew, come in together. Before sitting down they go to the catering counter, pour out two cups of strong coffee, and consider the choice of cereals on display: Weetabix, Shreddies, Cornflakes, All Bran, Special K and muesli. Meanwhile, at one of the two long dining-tables Petty Officer Tony Lilley [Senior Wardroom Steward] is taking an order from Lieutenant-Commander Norman Boyes [Marine Engineering Officer]:

'Scrambled egg, bacon, tomato and snorkers.'

'Two sausages sir?'

'Two if it's those fat ones, four if it's the thin ones. Is it tinned tomatoes?'

'Yes sir.'

'Make it baked beans then.'

'Right sir. Rack of toast?'

'Yes please.'

Cooke-Priest with Weetabix and Barnbrook with All Bran join the marine engineering officer.

'Morning chaps.'

'Morning MEO.'

'Morning Norman.'

'Happy to be back in Iceman, eh FLOBS?'

'Over the moon old bean,' replies the flight observer with ironic sincerity.

'Cooked breakfast sir?'

'God, two whole weeks in Defence Watches . . .' says Barnbrook without hearing the petty officer behind him. '. . . and not for the last time. How long is it before we get home?'

'End of November,' says Cooke-Priest. 'Roll on!'

'Yes, I know, but how many days is that?'

'God, I don't know. How many days before we get into Devonport PO Lilley?'

'Sixty-one sir,' replies the petty officer without hesitation. 'And four hours,' he adds, looking at his watch. 'If we dock on time that is. At 1000 hours. Cooked breakfast sir?'

'Sixty-one more days without nookie!' groans Cooke-Priest.

'And four hours sir. Cooked break . . .'

'Yes! Yes! Yes! Two fried eggs on toast, bacon, tomatoes. Rack of toast. Brown.'

'Flight Commander?'

'Umm, I'll have scrambled egg on toast. That's all.'

'Thank you sirs.'

Barnbrook pushes his half-finished bowl of All Bran to one side. 'Christ, this two weeks is going to drag.'

'Never mind, Crete after this. Good run ashore that'll be,' says Norman Boyes.

'That's right. Hang-on-in-there Jerry! Souda Bay is meant to be outstanding.'

'Morning gentlemen.'

They are joined by Midshipman Christian Bamforth who, at 19 years old, is the youngest officer on board.

'Morning Bam-Bam. Don't tell us you've been trying to shave again.'

'Sit down Bum-fluff old bean.'

Casually ignoring the taunts that are the bane of any midshipman's life, Bamforth smiles sarcastically, puts down the gigantic pile of books he is carrying and joins the group.

'When's your Fleetboard* Bam-Bam?' asks Cooke-Priest sympathetically.

'Just before Christmas.'

'What have you been cramming up on?'

'Rule of the road, ops and weapons, navigation and supply.'

'You poor bugger,' says Cooke-Priest. 'Fleetboards are living hell. Ah, brekker! Thanks PO Lilley.'

It is 0800. The flight maintainers pull the Lynx helicopter from the hangar on to the flight deck at the stern of the ship. The Lynx, known as Bright Star, is folded up like a butterfly emerging fresh from its chrysalis. All four rotor blades are pulled to the back and aligned with the tail, which is itself folded into two by a hinge half-way down. Slowly, as if in response to the warming rays of the rising Mediterranean sun, the steel insect expands and starts its daily metamorphosis.

'Spreading rotors!' shouts one of the seven flight crew on board who are dedicated solely to the maintenance of Bright Star.

'Check away!'

'Pin out!'

'Walk it round!'

'Align rotors!'

In the hangar Nick Cooke-Priest, the flight observer, watches the check procedure whilst he pulls on his flying helmet and gloves and waits for Jerry Barnbrook,

---

* Fleetboards are vitally important oral examinations that all young officers have to pass if they are to proceed with their naval careers.

THE LYNX

The Lynx was originally the Westland WG13 which was designed to fulfil the army's need for a battlefield helicopter. The specification was amended in 1966 to take in the naval requirement and the following year Aerospatiale of France joined the project. The first naval Lynx flew in May 1972 and production aircraft became available in 1977 as the Lynx Helicopter Anti-Submarine Mark 2 (or HAS2). Present aircraft are Mark 8 variants and the aircraft is expected to see service until 2010.

Built around an airframe made mainly of aluminium and other alloys with advanced fibreglass mouldings for the outer structure, the Lynx has a fully laden weight of 6 tons. It is powered by two Rolls-Royce Gem 60 engines which drive a four-bladed rigid-rotor system with a relatively small disc diameter of $42^{1}/_{2}$ feet. The aircraft will climb at a normal rate of over 2100 feet per minute and cruises at 125 knots even when fully loaded. It carries fuel for up to three hours patrol flying.

In normal operations, the Lynx has a crew of two but it can be converted to carry up to nine passengers (though not in airline comfort!). A winch mounted at the starboard door can lift up to 600 lb in safety whilst about $1^{1}/_{2}$ tons can be carried as an underslung load in a cargo net.

Structurally, the naval Lynx differs from its army cousin so that it can operate safely from a pitching and rolling flight deck. The key element is a hydraulically operated harpoon which engages in a trellissed grid on the flight deck. Locked to the grid by the harpoon, the aircraft can swivel into wind for take-off or remain safe after landing in heavy seas.

During Operation Sharp Guard the Lynx was used for surface searches and transporting Royal Marine protection parties. It is also used for Sea Skua (air to surface) missile attacks and armed with Sting Ray torpedoes and Sonar buoys it becomes a potent anti-submarine weapon that can operate alone, under the control of the mother ship or in conjunction with other units. The Lynx is also well suited for logistic support, for reconnaissance and for search and rescue missions. During the Falklands War one adventurous captain used his Lynx as a fighter/bomber, with machine guns firing ahead to surprise Argentine Pucara aircraft and 'home-made' bombs for attacking transport ships!

Bright Star's pilot and Chay Robertson, today's duty flight deck officer. This morning they will be going on a routine surface search patrol of the area and then come back to pick up the marines for fast roping exercises from the helicopter to the deck of the ship. Cooke-Priest has lost count of the number of times he has assisted marine commandos down a rope on to a PVV* whilst shouting instructions to Jerry if he looks as if he is getting too near to a mast or radio cable.

Whilst he watches Bright Star take shape he considers how far he has come in the last few years. Here he is – 25 years old, a Lynx helicopter flight observer, an accomplished and respected naval officer, and a young man being given the chance to live life to the full. He is told he is good-looking, he knows he is fun-loving and thinks he is reasonably fit considering he is still a 'twenty a day' man despite seven attempts to give up during this deployment alone. He has come a long way in a short time – but it so nearly went dismally wrong. As a boy and a teenager he followed a dangerous and destructive path of rebellion and wilful disobedience. He defied authority as a matter of course and, though sent to the best schools, his complete disregard for discipline led to inevitable and repetitive 'requests to move on'. He looks back on those days with some remorse but mostly with just plain relief that he did not skid completely out of control.

'As a boy I was a wild child. And as I got older I got wilder. Then I became a real brat-packer as I discovered the delights of drinking and partying. That's what I thought it was all about – booze and girls. Especially girls. My parents sent me to Marlborough where I managed to get away with murder for a while but I was eventually caught sneaking out at night to go to meet some woman at some pub or club – I can't even remember now. I was then sent to Blundles, but I didn't improve and they sacked me as well. By the time I was eighteen I had practically zero prospects and just five O levels courtesy of a sixth-form college in Havant. Up to that time I had always rejected the idea of the Services, especially the navy, because my father was a naval officer – as a matter of fact, he was captain of HMS *Brilliant* back in the eighties – and I suppose I resented the idea that I should follow in his footsteps. If I am honest perhaps I felt I couldn't follow in his footsteps. Anyway, things changed. I changed. One day I woke up and said to myself, "The Fleet Air Arm for me" and now here I am!'

Cooke-Priest is one of those officers who everyone recognizes as a regular, genuine and stouthearted fellow. He works hard and is good at his job but he has not lost any of his social 'skills' as he can still drink most people under the table and frequently boasts the best hangover after a run ashore. Moreover, his recreational

---

* Potential Violating Vessel. For more acronyms, see The Wonders of Naval Abbreviation, page 218.

prowess does not stop at the 'private bar'. Although he sports a plummy Home Counties accent, with a particular penchant for words like 'Hurrah!' and 'Ding dong', he has a remarkable ability to mix socially with all ranks on completely equal terms – in any bar!

Fortunately for the Royal Navy, Nick Cooke-Priest's social agility is not confined to Guinness and Glenfiddick but extends into the more important realms of service, duty and command. He is a natural leader because the men respect him for what he is and they know that, whatever his background, he does not think of himself as any better than them. Sailors cannot abide pretension and soon put a stop to it – officer or no officer. Cooke-Priest always has time for his men and always has a sympathetic ear for their troubles. It is for that reason that Leading Seaman 'Swinger' Lowe approaches him now.

' 'Scuse me sir.'

'What's up Swinger?'

'It's just that I've had this letter from home sir. From the missus . . .'

It is **0900**. Micky Goble is at his place in the operations room. His job is to monitor the surface radar screen and keep a constant look-out for ships coming into the area. His eyes dart constantly over the screen, stopping every now and again as they fix on a fresh blip. Is it a merchantman trying to break the embargo? Is it a Yugoslavian warship? Is it an Albanian speedboat carrying refugees to southern Italy? Or is it merely an innocent fisherman from Dubrovnik trying to catch a few red mullet to sell at this evening's fish market?

The surface picture of activity in Iceman never stays still. It changes from minute to minute and is mostly benign. But the threat is always there and every blip is guilty until proven innocent.

'Surface to PWO,' Goble says into his headset.

'PWO,' responds Bob Hawkins immediately from his position at the central console in the darkened room.

'Newcomer on position grid, right, zero, four, one, decimal six.'

'OK. Got her. Follow her track.'

'Yes sir. Probably a merchantman . . .'

'Air to PWO!' interjects another voice on the central command channel, known as 'open line'.

Hawkins presses one of the dozens of illuminated buttons at the side of his radar. 'PWO.'

Petty Officer 'Ginger' Lowden at air radar control speaks urgently but precisely: 'Aircraft at 10 000 feet. Approaching Iceman airspace. No, repeat no, prior contact. Could be a commercial aircraft but it's not conforming. Aircraft is feet wet* and has an attack profile.'

The sweeping arm of the Marconi radar reveals the current air picture. Like the surface picture it is always busy but inevitably changes faster. Hawkins quickly searches his own command radar screen for the unannounced aircraft. Again, it is probably of no consequence but there is always the chance that it is that unpredictable maverick 'top gun' who wants to make a name for himself. Hawkins feels his heart-rate quicken as the adrenalin pumps into his bloodstream. He is alert and sharp. A good PWO has to keep his eyes on several unfolding situations at once and must continually assess the level of threat without panicking.

'OK Ginger. Got it. The Serbs have been practising on their bombing range at Bar today. Probably one of them gone astray. Request identification and to state intentions. Issue first warning to turn away.'

'Yes sir.'

Ginger Lowden switches on to the open air-traffic frequency and with a friendly but deliberate voice speaks to the offending aircraft: *'Unknown aircraft. Good morning. This is Royal Naval warship Brilliant. You are approaching us in a threatening manner. Please answer our call and turn away now. I repeat. Please answer our call and turn away now. Over . . .'*

The red-headed radarman listens intently to the random crackle of the ether. If there is no response he will give two more warning calls before Bob Hawkins puts the ship into a defensive posture.

Back on the surface radar Micky Goble has identified the newcomer on his screen as the *Adriatica*, an Italian ferry. He marks it with a reference number, sits back and presses the scan-change button that increases the reach of the radar map from 15 miles to 96. He notes the reassuring blips and code numbers that mark the other Sharp Guard ships patrolling the neighbouring sea areas. There is USS *Deyo* in one area and the Spanish ship *Victoria* in another. He glances round to Ginger who is talking again into his headset.

'Unknown aircraft. Good morning. This is Royal Naval ship Brill . . .' A foreign voice breaks through the static: *'Royal Navy ship Breelliant. I am reading you. Zis is Italian Freight Services, 707. We gain height now and turn north. Zank you. Over.'*

'Thank you 707. Roger. Out.'

Bob Hawkins nods approvingly and settles back in his high swivel chair. The real test of his skill is not so much dealing with the occasional moment of excitement but contending with the long hours of routine and monotonous observa-

---

* Indicates that an aircraft is over the sea. 'Feet dry' means it is over land.

tions that make it so difficult to maintain sharp concentration and sound judgement. The op's room keeps a round-the-clock check on threats from the air, surface and sub-surface environments – all arenas in which Yugoslavian forces operate. Leaning forward over his radar screen Hawkins quickly re-acquaints himself with the current 'surface picture' in Iceman and, not for the first time, finds himself contemplating the curiously abstract world of a modern principal warfare officer.

'Mine is no longer the world of fair winds, fresh air and sea spray enjoyed by the old fashioned gunnery officer* with his binoculars trained on the horizon, but a world reduced by technology to an impersonal black screen and phosphorescent radar signals. We are dealing with long-range warfare using long-range weapons. The most powerful binoculars in the world can only see up to the horizon but with all this gear I can see a lot further than that. And, what's more, I can strike a lot further than that. In the old days they talked about seeing "the whites of the enemy's eyes" but for me the enemy must only ever be a coordinate on my radar. As we say in the business, "If it flies it dies," and if he ever gets close enough for me to see the whites of his eyes I have failed.'

'Surface to PWO.'

'PWO.'

'New arrival – track six, one tango, mike, classified alpha, victor, victor. Southbound . . .'

It is **0945**. Bright Star is returning from a routine sea search of the area. The flight commander, Jerry Barnbrook, eases his helicopter towards the flight deck but remains over the sea on the port side. He comes to a hover and looks down to the flight deck officer who beckons him in with a wave of a bright orange glove. Flight maintainers are in their landing positions standing by for any eventuality. Landing a helicopter on the back of a moving frigate in the middle of a swelling ocean is a hazardous task and no matter how experienced the pilot the risks are always high. Barnbrook rallies all his skills and gently nudges the aircraft sideways until it is directly over the central circular grid in the middle of the deck. Slowly, in response to the flight deck officer's guiding hand gestures, Bright Star descends: 20 feet . . . 15 feet . . . 10 feet. Holding at 10 feet Barnbrook quickly readjusts his position as the orange glove indicates a slight crabbing to the left. 10

---

* The PWO of former times. The term PWO came into existence in 1975 as a response to the threat to warships from sub-surface, surface and air attack. A warship could no longer afford the luxury of closing up to Action Stations in order to defend itself; a specialist in all areas of warfare was needed on watch, at all time. And he or she is the Principal Warfare Officer.

feet . . . 5 feet. The Lynx touches down and immediately releases from her belly the mechanical harpoon that hooks on to the flight deck grid. Barnbrook gives the thumbs up. At his side, Nick Cooke-Priest grins his approval and speaks into his helmet microphone:

'Ding dong. Spot on Jerry.'

'Tickety boo! Righto, bring on the Booties.'

Six Royal Marines in full combat gear file out of the hangar and walk towards the helicopter which is waiting with its rotor blades still turning. They are wearing flak jackets over their green fatigues and have the new SA 80 assault rifles slung over their shoulders. They climb on to the Lynx one by one through the side door, helped by Cooke-Priest who has left his flight observer position next to the pilot to oversee the fast-roping exercise. This high risk procedure is practised at every opportunity; dropping marines from a helicopter is the quickest way to board and secure another ship on the high seas – something that frequently has to be done in Operation Sharp Guard to ensure that passing merchantmen are not carrying arms or ammunition. It would be safest to winch the men down but that would take too long, especially if their reception was hostile, so the only alternative is for them to slide rapidly down a rope by hand, one after the other. The record is to have all six marines on deck in 18 seconds. To achieve this requires split second timing, supreme flying skills and great courage from all concerned.

'All set Jerry. Marines in place.'

'Righto!' Barnbrook gives the orange glove the thumbs up. The orange glove returns the gesture.

'Here we go.'

With his left hand Barnbrook raises the 'collective' – a lever that initiates ascent. The rotor blades answer with a bone-shaking chant of 'Woka! Woka!' The collective comes up further and further. Barnbrook adjusts the trim. 'Woka! Woka!' The flight deck team brace themselves and lean into the massive down-draught created by the four rotor blades, now fused into a transparent spinning circle of immense kinetic energy. 'Woka! Woka!' Bright Star lifts gently from the deck, hovers momentarily, leans gently to one side, and then sweeps gracefully towards the open sea, climbing as she goes.

At around 1000 feet and 2 miles out Barnbrook turns and heads back towards the bow of the warship. From this height HMS *Brilliant* looks like a beautifully made Airfix kit embedded in a plaster of Paris sea. She looks sleek and slim but seem-

---

** A nickname for the Royal Marines. See also The Royal Marines, page 119.

ingly unmoving from an aircraft flying at 120 miles per hour. Looking down on the battle-grey frigate that height transforms into a child's toy Jerry Barnbrook always finds it strange to think that 250 full-sized people are still living on her.

'It's a really weird feeling sometimes, looking down on her. It must be the same sort of "earth from space" incredulity that strikes astronauts as they peer down on our tiny world from their orbiting shuttles or modules. It's only Nick and I and the members of the boarding parties that ever get off the ship whilst we're at sea. It's really odd thinking that at the same time as we're gallivanting around up here there's Mark Warburton down there in that tin box bashing the spuds for tonight's shepherd's pie or something; Bob Hawkins slaving over his hot radar; the Doc probably jabbing some poor sod in the arse with a tetanus injection; Tracie shouting out compass bearings to the cox'n on the bridge and no doubt big Steve Whitter training up for the next Field Gun Race* in the weights room. I mean that really is a little world down there.'

From the window in his cabin Captain Rapp looks up at the approaching speck in the sky.

'Where are they going to rope on to today?'

'The starboard bridge wing sir,' replies Russ Harding.

'Good. They need more practice coming down on to restricted spaces. The flight deck and the foc'sle have become too easy.'

'Yes sir. Some of the cattle carriers we've been boarding have virtually no flat surfaces.'

'Quite. Come on, let's go and watch this one.'

'Yes sir.'

The first to 'fast rope' will be Marine 'Spider' Webb, who sits in position at the open door of the Lynx with his legs dangling outside. He and his comrades behind him are all wearing the heavy duty black suede gloves that allow them to grasp and slide down the thick, green wool and nylon rope that Nick Cooke-Priest is preparing to throw out of the door on to the bridge wing of the *Brilliant*. The helicopter crosses the bow of the ship at about 50 feet casting a pale grey shadow that

---

* The Field Gun Race is run annually at the Royal Tournament held at Earls Court in London between naval teams from Portsmouth, Devonport and the Fleet Air Arm. It traces its origins to the naval brigades who went ashore to support the army during the Boer War. They took 12 pounder guns mounted on improvised carriages and dragged them over cliff and chasm. The modern competition encapsulates the heroic feat of these 'blue coats' through a highly stylized and fast-moving competition which tests the fittest men in the navy to their limit.

slithers across the foc'sle, over the Exocet launchers, up to the Sea Wolf missile deck and towards the bridge. The downward thrust from the rotors flattens the sea on the starboard side and throws up a spray curtain that filters the sun's rays into a fleeting rainbow.

'Rope gone!' says Cooke-Priest as he heaves the heavy green coils out of the door. The falling rope straightens into a rod that prods the deck of the starboard bridge wing. The young flight observer looks down and then, sounding like an over-exuberant commentator at the Cheltenham Gold Cup, gives a running report to his flight commander as the exercise proceeds:

'First man's on the rope, second man's waiting, first man's on the deck, second man's on the rope, third man's waiting, second man's on the deck . . .

'Come right two yards! Come right two yards!

'Come another yard. One more yard. That's good! Clear of all obstructions!

'Third man's on the rope, fourth man's waiting, third man's on the deck, fourth man's on the rope, fifth man's waiting . . . fourth man's still on the rope. Oh bugger!

'Hold it! Hold it! He's snagged on the corner of the bridge roof. Steady! Come up! Steady! Steady!'

Forty feet below Marine Chippy Norton has caught his rifle strap on a hook on the bridge superstructure. With the deck still 10 feet below he hangs on to the rope for dear life.

'Let go mate!' shouts Spider Webb from below.

'Bollocks.'

'Go on, you'll be alright mate.'

'Bollocks!' repeats Marine Norton looking up pleadingly at the helicopter.

'Steady! Steady Jerry!' says Cooke-Priest. 'Come left slowly! About one yard . . . slowly, slowly . . .'

At the same time, in the world that is a warship, Leading Cook Mark Warburton in the main galley is in fact rolling out a huge sheet of shortcrust pastry for Cornish pasties; Bob Hawkins is having a five-minute break for a cup of tea in the op's room annex; Surgeon-Lieutenant Richard Newton is in the shower; Lieutenant Tracie Lovegrove is plotting a course in the chart-house; and Petty Officer Steve Whitter is indeed on his third set of bicep curls in the weights room. They are all supremely unaware of the predicament facing the young marine dangling precariously from the helicopter over the starboard bridge wing. So are Lieutenant-Commander Norman Boyes, presently inspecting the Tyne gearbox in the for'ard engine space; Wren 'Roni' Whittaker tracking another unidentified aircraft on the radar scanner; Leading Regulator 'Pincher' Martin asleep in his pit; and Leading Steward Andy Conway scrubbing the flats* on Two Deck.

Marine Chippy Norton, of course, could not care less what anybody is doing on the ship at the moment, with the exception of those who are in a position to make an immediate contribution to his ultimate survival and bodily well-being.

'Get me the fuck down from here!'

'Hang on mate!'

'You trying to be bleeding funny, or what!?'

Jerry! Edge to the right half a yard. That's it! That's it. Another half yard . . . Keep going . . . a little further . . . a little further. Bingo! He's free! Ding-bloody-dong!'

Marine Chippy Norton descends the final 10 feet on the rope and plants his rubber-soled bush boots firmly on the deck.

'Fourth man's on the deck, fifth man's on the rope, sixth man's waiting, fifth man's on the deck, sixth man's on the rope, sixth man's on the deck.

'Nice one Jerry!'

'Tickety boo!'

Bright Star wheels round to the left and heads south in order to make her landing approach to the stern of the ship. On the starboard bridge wing Chippy Norton leans against the gunwales, looks out towards the mountain ranges of southern Bosnia and whispers to himself through clenched teeth:

'Fuck a bleedin' duck!'

It is **1359**. James Rapp looks up at the brass clock above his desk. He is in his cabin leafing through the personnel files of the three new ratings who joined the ship in Bari and who have been told to report to him at 1400. At exactly the moment the second hand completes the hour a set of gunner's knuckles knocks at the door with impressive punctuality.

'Come in!' shouts Rapp over the roaring air-conditioning system.

Three young ratings in freshly ironed Number Eights** step smartly into the captain's day cabin and line up, stiffly at-ease, facing the starboard bulkhead. The captain walks over to them, attempting to relax his naturally stern features into something he imagines looks more avuncular, and starts the 'captain's briefing'.

'Right. Names first I think. You are Able Seaman . . .'

'Broughton sir. Ops.'

---

* Floors.

** A working rig: dark blue trousers and light blue shirt.

'And you ?'

'Rimmer sir. Gunner.'

'And you I've already met. It's Wren . . .'

'Wolstencroft sir. Radar.'

'OK. Well, erm, welcome on board. I always like to meet everyone who joins the ship just to say one or two things. First of all, what I always stress is that you must very quickly develop a really good knowledge of the ship. Broughton, you've served once before on the *Brilliant* and you've been on the *Battleaxe* so you already know the Type 22s. But you other two must work hard on this because only when you know the ship will you be a safe member of the ship's company, and only then will you be able to contribute in areas other than your own specialist areas. Alright?'

'Yes sir.'

'Yes sir.'

'Yes sir.'

'The other thing is that you are all members of a single team. Just because you are all able rates and I've got four rings on my shoulder does not separate us but combines us. It just signifies that we've all got our part to play. You are just as important as everybody else on the ship because you all have your duties to perform and if you don't perform them well you not only let yourself down but also your shipmates. Understand?'

'Yes sir.'

'Yes sir.'

'Yes sir.'

'Good. Finally, just remember an effective ship is, erm, generally speaking a happy ship. So work hard whilst we're at sea – we've got a tough job to do out here – and then you can feel that you've earned your runs ashore when we go alongside. OK. Any questions?'

'No sir.'

'No sir.'

'No sir.'

'Good luck. Dismiss.'

It is **1700**. The club-swinger,* otherwise known as 'Clubs' or Leading Physical Trainer Dave Mynett, is writing with chalk on one of the bulkheads on the boat

---

* Swinging clubs was the traditional way of keeping fit on board ships – hence the name club-swinger which today is often shortened to the more colloquial 'Clubs'.

deck. As he does so the young blond Yorkshireman talks over his shoulder to a small group of ten sailors and two Wrens in sports rig.

'Right you lot. Listen up an' watch. We're goin' to start wi' arms, go on to ab's and finish wi' legs. Yer exercises in each group are writ up here alright. Whilst we're in Defence Watches we can't use the flight deck so we're stuck with the boat deck – that's just the way it is, so quit drippin* an' jus' get on wi' it. There ain't much space so watch yer selves OK? Hello, hello what's this then . . .?'

Petty Officer Steve Whitter joins the group with a sheepish grin only to be greeted with a howl of derision.

'Dearie me, shipmate!' grins Dave Mynett. 'Bit late I think Stevie boy! Down you go. Gimme twenty press-ups. Go!!'

The group cheers loudly and counts out loud as the huge and popular petty officer, famous for representing the Portsmouth field gun team two years in a row, starts pumping his immense frame up and down on oak-tree arms.

'Twenty! Nineteen! Eighteen! Seventeen! Sixteen . . . !'

As the count continues another body surreptitiously joins the back of the group and hopes he is not seen.

' . . . Three! Two! One!'

'Well done, Stevie mate,' laughs Mynett. 'That'll teach you to be a Pompey sailor on a Devonport ship!'

The club-swinger then slowly folds his arms, raises a quizzical eyebrow and casually aims an X-ray gaze towards Lieutenant Steve Boynton, the ship's communications officer, now hiding behind a torpedo tube.

'Good evening sir.'

'Ah! Sorry I'm a bit late Clubs . . .'

'Watch broken is it sir?'

'Meeting with the skipper actually Clubs . . .'

'Too bad! Gimme thirty squat thrusts! At the double sir – if you please!'

'Thirty! Twenty-nine! Twenty-eight! Twenty-seven . . . !'

As the count continues amid guffaws and belly laughs a huge orange-red sun on the port side of the ship sinks low over the western horizon dramatically back-lighting the billowing cumulonimbus that now crowd the evening sky. Shafts of dying sunlight pierce and penetrate gaps in the giant storm clouds, emerging to form a gigantic fan of exploding pink light that colours the immediate world of the lone British warship. Her flaking battle-grey war-paint, designed to blur the ship into the steely colours of savage oceans, suddenly takes on the unlikely hue

---

* Complaining. For more naval slang, see Jackspeak, page 212.

of cherry blossom. Momentarily, it is as if the gentle gender of the ship has insisted on shrugging off the ugly livery of war to expose and celebrate her suppressed femininity. The surreal picture of pink Exocet launchers on the front of a pink frigate sailing on a frothing sea of rosé wine is ideally completed by the ludicrous sight of pink sailors in shorts counting backwards.

'. . . Six! Five! Four! Go on sir, get those legs right back! Three! Two! One!'

The lieutenant kicks out the last squat thrust of his punishment, gets up and bows low to the delighted applause of all around him.

'Let that be a lesson to you sir,' grins Mynett. 'Remember you lot, there's no ranks at circuits – except mine!' He claps his hands, punches the air and barks his orders: 'Right! Pair up shipmates. First one does the exercise whilst yer oppo* gives encouragement. Then change round. OK. First off gi' me thirty seconds each of wide-arm press-ups, tricep-dips, snakes and bear-walks. Go!'

Half the assembled group drop on to the deck to start their gruelling session. The other half stand over their partners and scream encouraging abuse:

'Push it! Push it! Go on! Puuuush it you prat!'

'Chest to the deck! Chest to the flamin' deck!'

'Make it hurt, drongo!'

'Up, down, up, down! Keep it goin'!'

'Call that a fuckin' press-up?!'

The voluntary evening circuit session is a sacred ritual attended by only the most devout fitness freaks. They are known around the ship as the 'fitties' and are thought of as being more than slightly barmy as they press up, pull up and squat thrust with an evangelical zeal.**

'Three! Two! One! . . . Right change over. Come on! Come on! Come on! Don't hang around!'

The 'shouters' swap with the 'doers' as the dying sun sinks below the horizon changing the ambient colour from cherry blossom to red rose. The club-swinger, warming to his task, promptly broadens his grin and raises the stakes:

'Just remember, shipmates – it's a case of mind over matter . . . I don't mind and you don't matter!'

It is **2000**. The junior rates and senior rates have had supper and are now either sleeping or working according to their watch. On the bridge the watch-keepers peer into the darkness in front of them, whilst outside on the upper deck bridge

---

* Opposite number. For more naval slang, see Jackspeak, page 212.
** 'Clubs' runs another session at midday for the less inspired who glory in the title 'huffers and puffers'.

wings two gunners peer deeper into the same darkness through fixed, high-powered binoculars. High above, on the apex of the ship's superstructure, the constantly revolving radar scans everything the human eyes cannot see. Down below, the op's room remains fully manned, fully alert and fully prepared for a long night in Iceman. In the wardroom a few of the officers toy with the remnants of their apple crumble and chat about the likely impact of the new rucking laws on the flow of international rugby. Meanwhile, one deck above, Captain Rapp is in his cabin being served the second course of his supper by his personal steward.

'Cornish pasties tonight sir.'

'Thank you Petty Officer Cooper.'

'Peas and cabbage sir?'

'Thank you.'

James Rapp spoons some Colman's mustard on to the side of his plate, shakes a gesture of pepper over the vegetables and then sets about his pasty. Every night he eats alone. This is not because he shuns the company of his officers but because commanding officers in the Royal Navy always do eat alone. It is a long-held tradition emanating from the idea that a captain is the figurehead of the ship and, therefore, needs to stand apart and a little bit above the rest of the ship's company.* It is tempting to dismiss this as a hangover from an 'upstairs, downstairs' class system but many argue that it does successfully underpin the command structure on board a ship. Furthermore, with the captain in his cabin the wardroom remains the strict preserve of the officers. It is their haven and sanctuary where they can relax, do what they want and say what they want.** James Rapp fully understands and endorses the messing tradition that seats him alone on his own high table.

'Some people call it the "loneliness of command" but I think that living up here on my own adds to my ability to lead. Some captains are different. They like to laugh and joke with their officers and try to be friends with everybody. I don't see that as the best way to manage a ship's company. You need to stand apart and give a positive firm lead so that they know where they stand and have a direction to follow. And as for being lonely myself – that's something I've got well used to.

---

* The Royal Navy is different in this respect from most other navies. In the United States Navy, for example, the captain is the president of the wardroom and so always eats with his officers.

** A commanding officer in the Royal Navy is only ever allowed into his ship's wardroom at the express invitation of the officers (except when he is serving on a minor war vessel like a minesweeper where, because of size, he shares the facilities). Otherwise, rules are fairly relaxed although the first lieutenant is always the president of the wardroom and has the final say in how it is run. The saying is that a wardroom is run on the principle of 'one man, one vote' – the Jimmy is the man and his is the vote!

'This is my third command now and whilst I recognize the personal benefits of fellowship and camaraderie that come with communal messing at least I can live entirely my own routine in entirely my own space . . .'

James Rapp is the only person on board to have his own suite of rooms [a living room/office or 'day cabin', a bedroom or 'night cabin' and a bathroom], his own personal steward and a window. His cabins are comfortable, though Spartan in their decor. The regulation colour scheme is Ministry of Defence cream and green, the only insinuation of homeliness being a [cream and green] floral design to the seat covers and some [cream and green] tassles on the wall lampshades. Rapp has customized the day cabin slightly by putting up a watercolour seascape and a couple of oil landscape paintings on two of the bulkheads. His night cabin has more warmth and intimacy, largely because of the photographs of his wife, Ann, and two young daughters, Rachel and Hope, displayed on the chest of drawers next to his bed. On the wardrobe opposite is a crayon drawing of many colours with the message 'To Daddy, love Rachel' followed by a string of 'X's' and on the bed itself lies a present from both his daughters in the form of a small teddy bear dressed as an aviator – a reminder of his own naval specialization.

Rapp's identity as husband and father is kept locked like a precious treasure in the privacy of his night cabin. There and there only does he allow himself the luxury of contemplating and savouring the soft memories of those he has left behind – memories that all sailors take to sea with them, whether they be four-ring captains or junior stokers.

Outside his night cabin Rapp reverts to the austerity and, some would say, coolness that mark his style of command. He is ruthlessly efficient with a relentless eye for detail that can sometimes upset people. He certainly does not suffer fools gladly and is quick to castigate anyone who does not meet his own exacting standards. For these reasons, James Rapp is convinced that living apart from others is an essential prequisite to sound and objective naval management. Just occasionaly, however, when he is off his guard, he reveals a surprising softness behind the titanium-hard exterior.

'. . . when I'm at sea there just isn't time to be lonely really. But, I suppose, if I'm honest, the time I might feel a little out on a limb is when we go alongside. If we are visiting somewhere, some foreign port, everybody runs ashore with their messmates and sometimes I feel oh, I'd like to go out with other people, but then I suddenly think – who? There is no one else in my mess . . . It's just a burden that comes with command.'

THE FLEET AIR ARM

This branch of the Royal Navy began in the dawn of aviation. On 10 January 1912, Lieutenant Charles Samson flew a Short biplane from the foc'sle of HMS *Africa* and proved naval flying was possible. This led to the birth of the Royal Naval Air Service on 1 July 1914. When, four weeks later, the navy's first airborne launch of a torpedo took place at Calshot, near Southampton, a fundamental change in naval warfare had begun.

By the start of the First World War, the RNAS had seventy-one aircraft patrolling from Dover to Rosyth. Number 2 Squadron RNAS operated BE2 bombers and launched Britain's first strategic bombing raid on Germany on 22 September 1914 carrying 20 lb Hales bombs.

In 1915, HMS *Ark Royal*, the first ship to be completed as an aircraft carrier, was in action against the Turks in the Dardanelles whilst on the Western Front 1 Squadron RNAS was employed in anti-Zeppelin operations. On 7 June 1915 two giant German airships were destroyed, the first in air-to-air combat, by Sub-Lieutenant Warneford VC whose method of attack was to toss small bombs from his cockpit on to the Zeppelins.

It was the Second World War, however, that saw the blossoming of carrier aviation and the supremacy of even unsophisticated single-engined aircraft over battleships. This was most powerfully demonstrated on 11 November 1941 when twenty-one ancient Swordfish biplanes of 815 and 819 Naval Air Squadrons from HMS *Illustrious* attacked the Italian fleet at its base in Taranto. Three battleships were sunk or disabled and the Italian navy's threat to the Allies was ended.

Taranto Night is still enthusiastically celebrated by the Fleet Air Arm to recall the skill and bravery of those pilots. It also marks the arrival of naval air power as a strategic weapon free from land-based politics and airfields. The continued importance of this has been seen in the Falklands, the Gulf and most recently the Adriatic where Fleet Air Arm Sea Harriers, Sea Kings and Lynx have all played significant roles. The laconic wit and imperturbability of the FAA aircrew, engineers and support staff whilst regularly flying in appalling weather from postage-stamp flight decks, mean they view the rest of the world with a certain disdain and are not to be confused with the RAF!

DAY *Monday*	**DATE** *26*	**MONTH** *September*	**YEAR** *1994*

PLACE	*Area Iceman, Eastern Adriatic*

POSITION	*Classified*

DISTANCE TRAVELLED midnight to midnight *169.9 nautical miles*

SHIPS LOG. Remained on patrol in Iceman. Quiet day at first but then a reported embargo breaker enlivened proceedings in late afternoon. Bright Star launched in SUCAP role with live MK 46 torpedo and Sea Skua missile.

It is **1355**. Micky Goble is at his radar consul in the op's room. He is about to hand over his watch and is busy describing the current surface picture through his headset to his relief, Leading Seaman Jason Allan, sitting opposite. Coming through their headsets simultaneously is voice traffic between a female radio operator on the Belgian ship *Wandelaar* and the American ship *Deyo*.

'. . . OK Jase, three tracks of interest at the moment. Track six, one, seven one. . .'

'. . . *Hello Deyo, hello Deyo. This is Wandelaar . . .*'

'. . . Cor! Have you heard this Belgian woman on here . . . sounds like a cross between Marlene Dietrich and Mariella Frostrup. Pure sex . . . !'

'Come on Micky – get on with it you idiot!' says Jason Allan raising his eyes to the deckhead.

'Hold on a sec,' says Goble, switching through on the intercom dial to the air surveillance team: 'Hey fellas. Tune in – I've got a real 0898 voice on the line . . .'

'Micky!'

'OK! OK! . . . all you've got is one fisherman in your sequence right – just outside 12 miles tracking zero, two, three, speed seven . . .'

'. . . *Deyo from Wandelaar we would like to confirm time of your RAS with Stromboli . . .*'

'Oh yes. Marry me! Marry me!'

'Micky!!!!'

'Alright! Alright! A man can dream can't he . . . ?! At four, fox trot, uniform at position grid zero, four, one, decimal five . . .'

A few yards away at the master console in the middle of the room Bob Hawkins and the second PWO Lieutenant-Commander Paul Metcalfe are briefing Wren

Stephanie Wolstencroft, the radar operator who joined the ship in Bari.

'You'll be joining the surface surveillance team Wren Wolstencroft but we do have all three environments to deal with. Anti-air warfare dealing with aircraft and missiles, anti-submarine – there is at least one submarine we know they can deploy – and of course anti-surface warfare dealing with their frigates and enemy patrol boats.'

'I see sir. Are they coming very near us at the moment?' asks the young Wren with dispassionate interest.

'Not really,' answers Metcalfe. 'On the surface side we've had a deployment of Russian designed patrol boats sniffing around occasionally. They have a significant missile capability but they know that we track them as soon as they come out of harbour . . .'

'Then there's the aircraft,' breaks in Hawkins. 'We've also had at least two periods of intensive training by the Yugoslavian Airforce involving up to twenty aircraft carrying out all kinds of training missions. They come out to sea towards the edge of their territorial waters which is something we have to watch. We have to track them and if they come towards us we go through the warning procedure. If they kept coming we would deal with them.'

'Have you ever seen them sir? I mean from the upper deck.'

'Nobody in this ship has actually seen any Yugoslavian units since we've been here. They've always been over the horizon. As far as I recall the closest the Yugoslavian aircraft have come to us is about 30 miles. That's right isn't it Paul?'

'Yeah. Although they once came as near as 3 miles to the *Nottingham*.'

'Oh Christ, yes! That caused some excitement as well,' says Hawkins as he turns towards a familiar figure squeezing his substantial frame down the narrow gangway towards the door out of the op's room.

'Ah, Leading Seaman Goble. Going off watch?'

'Yes sir.'

'Get some shut-eye then. Don't start watching your *Star Trek* videos.'

'Don't knock the Trekkies sir. For we shall inherit the earth!'

'Even more reason to catch up on your sleep then. It's a tiring job running a planet so I'm told.'

'Yes sir,' smiles Goble broadly, revealing the gap where a former front tooth once stopped a flanker's boot on a Gloucestershire rugby field. 'Don't worry – I'll get to my pit sir. But I'm goin' to get some scran first and then the leading regulator* is goin' to cut my hair.'

---

* A ship's policeman'. He works to the master-at-arms (see The Master-at-Arms, page 167).

'OK. See you tonight.'

'The idea fills me with great joy sir,' says Goble leaving.

Hawkins laughs and turns back to the young Wren. 'Right, Wren Wolstencroft. Leading Seaman Goble there will be your surface picture supervisor incidentally. He's a bit of a comic but he's a good radar-man. You'll learn a lot from him.'

'Yes sir.'

'And don't forget – come and ask me or Lieutenant-Commander Metcalfe here anything you don't understand. Alright?'

'Yes sir.'

Hawkins has to maintain a certain level of pressure on his op's room team. He knows that tension and adrenalin provide the impetus for concentration that is so vital in their current surveillance role. But he also knows that the need for concentration has to be balanced with the necessity of maintaining morale and not wearing the team out. Exhausted, miserable people are dangerous people and the responsibility of a PWO is to ensure that everybody always has some spare capacity so they can easily increase their performance when the chips are down. It is a difficult balance to achieve because if people are too relaxed there is a danger that the three-picture compilation of air, surface and sub-surface environments will break down and potential threats will be missed. It is precisely for this reason that Hawkins and Metcalfe place so much value on people like Micky Goble, who are not only first-rate observers, trackers and plotters but who are also, by sheer strength of personality, major morale boosters.

It is **1535**. Down in the gunners' mess 'Pincher' Martin, the leading reg., is standing over Micky Goble with a monstrous pair of Whal electric clippers.

'What do you want then mate? Number one or number two?'

'Can you do it sort of shaved to the scalp on one side, leaving long wispy strands on the other side with the back cut into irregular, straggly tufts?'

'No I bloody can't.'

' 'S funny. That's what you did last time you bastard!'

'Belt up you fat git!' grins Pincher Martin as he switches on the clippers. They sound disconcertingly like a dentist's drill.

'Come on. Make up your mind. Number one or number two?'

'Number two. Number one's a lobotomy isn't it?'

Martin changes the cutting attachment on the clippers and then proceeds to thin out Goble's already thinning stack. Holding his tongue between his teeth in great concentration, he moves the buzzing clippers backwards and forwards over the radar-man's head in regular sweeping motions.

'Pincher – it feels like you're Hoovering my head!'

'Shut up!'

'At least you're using clippers now. Last time it was a knife and fork wasn't it?'

Martin ignores the quips and continues Hoovering. He does all the haircuts in the mess, charging £1.50 a head with 50p going to charity and £1.00 going to him. The word around the ship is that his booming business is due not to any innate talent for *coiffure*, but because, as leading regulator, he has the authority to tell people when to get their hair cut.

'There you go. All finished.'

Goble shakes his head, stands and looks into a bulkhead mirror.

'Jesus H Christ! What's this? The Bosnian '94 tour style so I'll blend in if I go ashore?'

'Don't you like it?'

'I didn't think it would be that short! I look like Buster Bloodvessel!'

'You did say a number one didn't you?'

It is **1735**. Jerry Barnbrook and Nick Cooke-Priest are in the cockpit of Bright Star. They are preparing to go on another routine surface search of the immediate sea area and are finishing the long series of instrument checks that precede any flight. The rotors are turning and Barnbrook is increasing his revs for take-off. As the deep throb of the powerful twin Rolls-Royce Gem engines increases to an ear-splitting scream the flight deck officer raises the orange glove to indicate 'all clear for take off'. Barnbrook's left hand reaches for the lever to alter the pitch of the rotor blades and convert their power to downward thrust when the radio in his headset spits out a sudden and shocking order.

'*Action Lynx! Action Lynx! Terminate take-off . . . Load two live Sea Skuas!* This is not an exercise! This is not an exercise!*'

The flight commander immediately reduces the power of the engine and then looks at his flight observer in amazement.

'What in the name of Christ . . . !'

Captain Rapp, informed over his private tannoy of a brewing emergency in the vicinity, has rushed from his cabin to a buzzing op's room to get an immediate briefing from Paul Metcalfe, the duty PWO. Metcalfe talks intermittently as he

---

*A Sea Skua is a medium range, air launched, sea skimming guided missile carried by the Lynx helicopter. Although specifically designed for use against small to medium-sized patrol boats, its explosive warhead is sufficiently large to pose a real threat to larger craft. Using semi-active homing, it is guided by the Lynx's Seaspray radar.

tries to listen to bursts of frantic radio traffic passing between vessels positioned about 30 miles to the south-east.

'Sir! The situation seems to be that . . .' Metcalfe suddenly cups his hands to his headset.

'. . . *point zero one, this is nine, nine zero. The Croatian is firing again . . . the Croatian is firing!*'

'*This is point zero one . . . we don't copy . . . say again . . . say again . . . !*'

'Sir . . . the Dutch frigate *Jan van Brakel* on a bearing 267 is being fired upon by . . . I think it is three Croatian gunboats . . .'

He breaks off again.

'. . . *the smuggler is coming round behind us. He is using us as a shield from the gunfire . . . !*'

'. . . *nine, nine, zero. Copy affirmative . . . !*'

'. . . but there seems to be an Italian smuggling boat involved as well. It could be that the gunfire is being aimed at that. The situation is not clear yet, sir, but the USS *Deyo* is down there talking to the *van Brakel* and we have brought the Lynx to immediate readiness . . . for SUCAP.'*

'. . . *point zero one. The boat is trying to escape . . . request assistance!*'

'Jerry and Nick briefed?' asks the captain coolly.

'Being briefed now, sir.'

'Skuas?'

'Yes sir. Two. Going on now.'

'Good! . . . And link up with the Deyo as soon as possible.'

Out on the flight deck the aircraft maintainers have wheeled the low-slung yellow trolleys that cradle the Sea Skua missiles out to the waiting Lynx. Quickly and efficiently they hoist the blue and grey projectiles up to the launching arm of the helicopter on the port side. The air crew look out to their left incredulously – they have never taken off on an attack mission with live ammunition before. Within seconds the deadly missiles are hooked up, wired up and primed. The maintainers scuttle back to the hangar and wait. Bright Star, rotors spinning, waits. Barnbrook, head spinning, waits. Cooke-Priest, stomach churning, waits. Everybody waits . . .

'*Action Lynx! Action Lynx! Alert Zero . . . Proceed quickest!*'

'*Roger!*'

The orange glove gives an immediate thumbs up. Bright Star rises, hovers briefly and then accelerates seaward. The symmetry of her diminishing silhouette

---

* Surface Combat Air Patrol. For more acronyms, see The Wonders of Naval Abbreviation, page 218.

against a reddening southern sky is distorted grotesquely by the missiles bulging at her side.

In the op's room James Rapp and Paul Metcalfe watch Bright Star's departure on the video screen above the command console. Then as they look down to study the radar surface picture of the area their concentration is broken by the sound of a lugubrious American voice coming through on their headphones from one of their NATO sister ships, the USS *Deyo*:

'Four, four, zero. Brilliant. This is point zero one, err, we are sat right by the Jan van Brakel. We have a sit. rep. Do you read?'

Metcalfe switches to 'transmit' and responds immediately.

'Point zero one. This is four, four, zero. Roger, copy.'

'This is point zero, one. We have a situation with three boats . . . err, two are armed Croatian police boats and they are in pursuit of a third vessel which is suspected of being an Italian flag smuggling vessel . . . err, named Mikia. The Croatian police boats fired upon the Italian vessel which moved behind the Jan van Brakel and has requested permission to surrender to her and to be turned over to the Italian authorities. Permission for that has been denied. Err, request that you contact Italian authorities err, to get Italian naval vessel or coastguard into the area. Over.'

'This is four, four, zero, one. Roger. Copy. We will action your request immediately, re Italian authorities. Please confirm that Croatian police activity was directed towards this other vessel and not towards the Jan van Brakel. Over.'

'Err four, four, zero, one, this is point zero one. That is affirmative. Over.'

'This is four, four, zero. Roger, many thanks. Have the three boats disappeared or are they still in vicinity of Jan van Brakel? Over.'

'This is point, zero one. The Croatian police boats are returning to Dubrovnik. That has been confirmed by radio with Dubrovnik. The Italian vessel is motoring near the Jan van Brakel approximately one hundred yards off her starboard bow. Over.'

'This is four, four zero. We're awaiting answer on Italian support. I'll keep you informed. Glad to hear all safe and all clear. We can bring back our helicopter. Zero one south general copy out.'

'Four, four, zero. This is point zero one. Adios! Out.'

It is **1827**. Bright Star has returned from her sortie and is now safely folded away in the hangar. Barnbrook and Cooke-Priest are perched on the now empty missile arm of the helicopter and chatting animatedly to Chief Petty Officer Alan 'Basher' Bates, the aircraft engineering artificer in charge of the flight maintainers.

'It was amazing,' says Cooke-Priest brushing a hand through his thick, dark red hair. 'To be honest Basher, my heart leapt into my mouth when it happened. I mean, there we were, one minute just sitting there ready for a routine flight and the next moment you and the guys were rushing to get the live Skuas out . . .'

'That's right sir. The blokes got a surprise an' all. The order came down from the op's room an' some of 'em was just standing there saying "Did they say live?!!". I said "Yes – real 'bang-bangs' – get on with it!"'

'They did well Basher,' nods Barnbrook. 'The Skuas were on bloody fast!'

'Yeah, once the blokes knew it wasn't a wind-up they pulled their fingers out. What were you feeling like in the driver's seat sir?'

'Bloody odd. I mean that was the first time we had ever taken off with live weapons. For all we knew we were going up to fire them off at someone. It was a weird feeling. Right out of the blue . . .'

'Ding dong. It was a gob-smacker! You know some people go through an entire career without ever taking live bullets up . . .'

The aviators are interrupted by a familiar voice echoing over the tannoy:

'Good evening. First Lieutenant speaking . . .'

Russ Harding is giving his regular evening sit. rep. from the bridge.

'. . . after a little bit of excitement this evening we are now back in the centre of Iceman about 15 miles to the south of Dubrovnik and now carrying on with the normal patrol. What started out today as a very routine day in Defence Watches ended up in a near emergency involving Croatian police boats and an Italian smuggler. This set us from routine operations to a heightened alert state that involved loading two Skuas on to Bright Star. Thankfully, they were not required. However, it serves as an example of how unpredictable the operations up here can be. Well done to all of you involved in that incident. The Croatian police boats have now cleared away and the Italian smuggler, for a while hiding behind the Jan van Brakel, we believe has headed off towards Montenegrin territorial waters. Unfortunately, because of this incident we were not able to land on any mail today as we had hoped. I know this is a disappointment to many of you as we have not had a lot of luck with our mail drops recently but I hope we can put this right soon.

'Looking ahead to tomorrow, the main event of the day is the visit by Admiral Sir Michael Layard, the Second Sea Lord and Commander-in-Chief, Naval Home Command. Admiral Layard is coming out here to see all RN units in area. He has specific responsibility for personnel matters and as he goes about tomorrow he will want to meet as many people as possible and to hear your views and, no doubt, he will have information for you. He is coming out from Naples tomorrow morning by an Invincible Sea King and is being winched down at approximately ten-thirty . . .'

Chapter Three

ONE LUMP OR TWO, SIR?

DAY *Tuesday*	**DATE** *27*	**MONTH** *September*	**YEAR** *1994*
PLACE	*Area Iceman, Eastern Adriatic*		
POSITION	*At 0600 Classified At 2359 37°08'N 20°42'E*		

DISTANCE TRAVELLED midnight to midnight *194.5 nautical miles*

SHIPS LOG. Remained on patrol in Iceman. Admiral Layard, the Second Sea Lord, arrived by Sea King. Continues calm and sunny.

It is **1028**. The thunderous roar of the 12 ton Sea King helicopter from HMS *Invincible* now hovering over the *Brilliant's* flight deck, reverberates around the entire ship. The huge aircraft, too big to land on the back of a Type 22 frigate, hangs in the air and slowly winches down its cargoes – first, a cardboard box full of spare parts ordered by the weapons engineering officer; second, a new 'man-size' nylon dummy for 'man overboard' exercises; and third, the Second Sea Lord.

Admiral Sir Michael Layard descends jerkily on the helicopter's vibrating winch-wire. Suspended from the powerful, throbbing flying machine over the lurching deck of a warship and being buffeted by a 'down-draught from hell', the sea lord looks more like a helpless rag doll than the second most powerful man in the Royal Navy. He touches down gratefully, shrugs off his harness and walks quickly towards the extended hand of Captain Rapp who is there to meet him.

It is **1042**. The Second Sea Lord, more relaxed and slightly less windblown, is sitting with James Rapp in his cabin. As they chat Steward Stuart Conder comes in carrying a silver tray with a pot of tea and a plate full of ship-made shortbread.

'So, how long have you been out here now James?'

'Coming up for five months now sir.'

'Not always in Defence Watches, I hope.'

'Oh no, we spend half our time in Defence Stations and half down in the Otranto Straits doing boarding operations . . .'

Stuart Conder breaks in.

'Sugar sir?'

The admiral shakes his head.

'Shortbread sir?'

'Ah, yes. I'll try some of that. Thank you.'

The captain continues. '. . . we do boarding operations on the merchantmen coming into the Adriatic.'

'Board and search, eh?'

'Yes, and up here in Iceman we keep an eye out for anybody who might have sneaked through. We would board here too if we found a violator but mostly it's just a waiting game. You heard about the excitement we had yesterday afternoon?'

'Yes I did. You weren't involved with that were you?'

'We sent our Lynx off with two Skuas. That was when we thought the *Jan van Brakel* was being attacked . . .'

'Fun and games, eh?'

'Absolutely. There was quite a major flurry of activity actually. By the way, I don't know if you know but Admiral Cooke-Priest's son is on board . . .'

'Colin Cooke-Priest?'

'Yes. Nick, his son, is the observer on the Lynx.'

'Is he really? No, I didn't know that.'

'I think Nick learnt a little yesterday, when he suddenly discovered that, in all possibility, he was flying into action.'

'Yes, yes, yes. Well, goodness me. I'll be blessed.'

The Second Sea Lord puts down his teacup and brushes some shortbread crumbs from his lap.

'Right! Better get a move on and meet some of the troops because I've only got a short slot before the helo comes back to get me at 1230. So who's first?'

It is **1110**. The Commander-in-Chief Naval Home Command, Chief of Naval Personnel and Second Sea Lord, Admiral Sir Michael Layard, KCB, CBE is sitting in the chief petty officers' mess just opposite the main galley on Two Deck. The chiefs have gathered to ask the visiting VIP some straight questions about their and their men's future in the modern Royal Navy.

'Alright, you chaps. I am the Second Sea Lord and directly responsible for your well-being as members of the Senior Service. I don't get a lot of opportunities to come into the front line like this so when I do it is hugely valuable to me. OK! I'm sure you would like to have a go at me about bees in your bonnets so who's got the first question?'

'Yes sir, I've got a question.'

'And you are . . . ?'

'Gregory sir. Op's room supervisor.'

'OK. And your question?'

'Redundancies, sir. A lot of the men reckon they're gonna be sold down the Swanee before long. Especially in the warfare branch.'

'OK, let me explain something to you. One of the most important aspects of my job is to recruit and train and make sure that the right numbers and quality of people are around. And this is all against the backdrop of having had to reduce numbers since 1990 and to go on doing so up to the turn of the century. At the same time I need to keep an eye on our manning requirements in operational theatres like this one, regeneration and also to look after ship-to-shore ratios. This is all proving very tricky as you might imagine.'

' 'Scuse me sir.'

'Yes.'

'Robertson sir. Master-at-arms.'

'Yes Master.'

'I think most of it, sir, is all down to one problem. We haven't got enough people to do the jobs that are required of us. You have to keep your front line running, which is your ships, but soon there won't be enough of us to run the ships.'

'That's right,' breaks in Basher Bates, the flight air engineering artificer, 'and we're being given more and more of these policing jobs all around the world.'

'Listen,' beseeches the sea lord, 'the philosophy of "front line first" hasn't changed. In fact, it is what drove the defence cost studies. All the manning, drafting and appointing philosophies are based on making sure that the front line is priority. But that does mean we have got to be sensible about who does what jobs and how. Undoubtedly, there are some jobs that can be streamlined. And other jobs that can be combined. This will mean, in some cases, after appropriate cross-training, that one man will be able to do the jobs that two men are currently doing. Logically, this must mean that some people will end up without a job. I do not believe in hiding that fact and I will tell any man the same thing.'

The Second Sea Lord looks at his watch and refers to a list he has taken from his inside pocket.

'Right! A couple more questions and then I must move on to . . . let me see. Yes, yes, yes, the op's room for a chat with the chaps there . . .'

It is **2325**. Micky Goble is on watch again at the surface radar position in the op's room. He is in pensive, nostalgic and melancholic mood.

'I used to enjoy this work. Still do. But I don't think I'll be doin' it for much longer somehow.'

'Why's that then Micky?' asks his oppo, Wren Stephanie Wolstencroft.

'The Second Sea Lord popped in today for a chat and, being a bloke in the know, he told me it might be an idea to look for another job.'

'What?' says the Wren.

'Straight up! He was on about this "leaner manning" and the combining of operators and maintainers. You know, instead of having one bloke to operate the radar and another to maintain it they're now goin' to have one poor sod to do the lot. But then there's an even poorer bleedin' sod who's out on his ear. Guess who? They're looking for the youngsters now because the kid out of school is a better investment on the cost o' training. Honest, Steph, he told me he reckoned I was too old at twenty-nine to do the cross-training. You know, "Thanks a bunch! Bye-bye, and leave your gas mask and your ID as you go out the door". I mean there's plenty of matelots who would love to get out but really I don't want to go. I like the navy . . .'

Goble pauses and then, holding his head to one side, smiles his gappy smile and points to his headset.

'Listen to Upper Deck comms. The gunners have got bored again!'

Up on the port and starboard bridge wings the two duty gunners manning the high-powered binoculars are relieving the tedium of staring into darkness for hours on end by singing to each other over their headsets. By switching in to their channel Goble adds a bizarre musical accompaniment to the tracking traffic in the op's room. Tonight it is Wet, Wet, Wet's 'Love is all Around':

'*Track five, zero, two, four . . . classification pending . . .* I feel it in my fingers, I feel it in my toes . . . *four, foxtrot, uniform, range of seven, seven, one, four . . .* Love is all around me, and so the feeling grows . . . *tracking zero, two, four, speed ten . . .* You know I love you, I always will . . . *pappa, charlie, tango, this is delta, eight, uniform, over . . .* My mind's made up by the way that I feel. There's no beginning . . . there'll be no end. . .'

Up in the pitch darkness of the bridge wings the singing gunners, 'Scouse' Milburne and 'Brum' Westwood, hear a click on their headsets followed by a chuckling voice from the op's room:

'Hey, lads. Don't give up your day jobs!'

DAY *Saturday*	DATE *1*	MONTH *October*	YEAR *1994*

PLACE	*Area Iceman, Eastern Adriatic*

POSITION	*Classified*

DISTANCE TRAVELLED midnight to midnight *164.9 nautical miles*

SHIPS LOG. Patrol Area Iceman. Some Yugoslav air activity south of Dubrovnik. Mail drop and RAS with Stromboli. Fine and settled. Visibility good.

It is **1100**. The ship is buzzing with the prospect of a mail drop by an American stores helicopter from the Italian mainland today. The last mail drop was cancelled because of the *Jan van Brakel* affair on Monday and the one before that was cancelled because of 'procedural contingencies'. Letters from home assume an epic importance to sailors at sea. To receive them is a major event to be savoured and celebrated. Not to receive them, however, is a major non-event to be protested and lamented. It is for these reasons that everybody on board is depending on the mail being dropped today.

The flight deck duty watch are lowering the perimeter safety rails in preparation for the supply helicopter's arrival.

It is 1123. Lieutenant Liz Hall, the captain's secretary but also one of three trained flight deck officers, is today sporting the orange gloves, and it is with one of these that she points out to sea. Far out on the horizon a black speck is moving steadily towards us. Watching it approach is to see it foetally transform from a speck to a dot; from a dot to a spot; and from a spot to a shape. The shape is undoubtedly that of a helicopter but to a squinting, straining eye the conformation seems oddly twinned. Double rather than singular. Could it be two helicopters approaching?

Minutes later the shape assumes deafening substance, revealing itself as a twin-rotor US Navy Sea Knight that eclipses the very sun with its immensity. Everybody on deck, safe behind the silence of their ear 'duffs', prepares for the winchman to lower the anticipated treasure of chocolate bars and billets-doux. The Sea Knight pilot, one of only two 'big 'copter' women pilots in the American Navy, skilfully manoeuvres the monster aircraft directly over the stern of the British frigate and waits for the orange glove to give her the thumb. Left a little,

HMS *Brilliant.*

Fast roping exercise by *Brilliant's* boarding party from Bright Star on to the flight deck.

Sub-Lieutenant Nick Cooke-Priest, Flight Observer.

Officer of the watch,
Lieutenant Tracie Lovegrove.

Bob Hawkins and Micky
Goble observe a surface radar
in the op's room.

Leading Cooks Mickey
Nowell and Mark Warburton
in the main galley.

Leading Seaman Micky Goble.

Previous page: The ship's company.

Captain James Rapp, Commanding Officer.

Lieutenant-Commander Russ
Harding, First Lieutenant.

Lieutenant-Commander Bob
Hawkins, Principal Warfare Officer.

Left: Chief Petty Officer Alan 'Basher' Bates, Aircraft Engineering Artificer.

Above: Lieutenant Jerry Barnbrook, Flight Commander.

Bright Star is landed on the flight deck.

left a little. 'Thumbs up!' The winchman pushes four, big blue mail bags to the gaping cargo door in the side of the hovering Sea Knight . . .

It is **1208**. The ship's central broadcast system bursts into voice:

'Mail is ready for collection. Mail is ready for collection. Mess deck leading hands report immediately to master-at-arms' office to pick up mess mailies.'

Within minutes a dozen leading hands are queuing for their and their ship-mates' precious bundles. Chay Robertson, the master-at-arms, and Pincher Martin, the leading regulator and freelance barber, shout out the mess deck names and hand out the piles of buff and white envelopes, packages and parcels:

'3G Port – Gunners, come and get it! 3H Port – the Wrennerie* . . . 3H Port – Wrennerie! Come on, jump to it lassie! 2N Port – Stokers. Grab this lot. Whole bloody bag for you guys. All sports pages** I'll bet . . .'

It is **1217**. All over the ship, officers, sailors and Wrens are tearing envelopes, cutting string or opening boxes:

In the gunners and radar mess, Micky Goble is reading a letter from Hannah, an old Wren friend who has written to ask him to be a page boy at her wedding next year; in the Wrennerie, Roni Whittaker is on to the third page of a twenty-six page letter from her boyfriend, Paul, a leading cook at HMS *Drake*, the naval shorebase in Plymouth; in the cooks' mess, Mark Warburton's eyes are filling with tears as he looks at the confirmation photographs of Kathryn, his eight-year-old daughter, sent by his wife Jacki; in the sports store, Dave Mynett is looking curiously at a small, fluffy, pink pig sent to him by his fiancée Marianne; in the wardroom, Fred Tulloch is disappointed to find that the chocolate sent by his wife has melted and lined the inside of an entire extra-large Jiffy bag; in the flight office, Nick Cooke-Priest is wryly considering a message from his long-suffering girl-friend, Georgie, who has written in cut-out letters stuck on a gigantic sheet of paper the ultimatum: 'WRITE OR I WILL TELL EVERYONE YOU'RE GAY!'; and in the chart-house, navigator Perry Stowell, who this time has received no letters, grimaces at the ribbing he knows he will get for being a 'Billy-NO-Mail'.

---

* Female ratings have no special provision on board ship other than their own mess deck which, contrary to rumour, is not fitted out in chintz but is identical to that of their male counterparts. Men are not allowed in that accommodation save in an emergency or when on duty. There are separate female heads [toilets] and bathrooms. See also Women at Sea, page 145.

** The romantic or sexy sections of a letter from a lover. Usually highly explicit, these are greatly valued by sailors on a long deployment. Particularly fruity sports pages have been known to be passed round or even lent out for a fee. Classic or vintage ones have gone down in naval legend and brought their owners great and lasting prestige.

In his darkened cabin on One Deck, Bob Hawkins, mercifully off duty from the op's room for a few hours, is fast asleep and dreaming of playing football with his sons, Cameron and Jamie, in their back garden in Devon. As he sleeps, Leading Steward Andy Conway quietly slips a thick white envelope under the door. On the back of the envelope which has a Devon postmark is the deliberate handwriting of a child:

Lieutenant-Commander 'Daddy' Hawkins,
HMS *Brilliant*,
B.F.P.O. 237.

It is **1544**. Lieutenant Tracie Lovegrove is officer of the watch on the bridge and she is feeling very anxious. The *Brilliant* is making her final approach to the 8000 ton Italian supply ship *Stromboli* to take on fuel oil. Close manoeuvring for a RAS, a replenishment at sea, is a hazardous procedure and nerve-racking for the officer at the helm. What makes it worse for Lovegrove is that Captain Rapp is on the bridge to oversee the approach to *Stromboli* and to observe how she gets on as he will be the one eventually to decide whether she gets her watch-keeping 'ticket' – a sort of seagoing driving licence. Right now, she is filled with trepidation but she is determined that the guts that have sustained her over the last five months in this rather unforgiving world of men are not going to desert her now. As the *Brilliant* approaches the *Stromboli* from the stern on the port side, the tall, slim, 28-year-old brunette reflects on the path that brought her into the Royal Navy.

'I was half way through a PhD in applied physics at Edinburgh University and heard that the navy was going to send women to sea. I couldn't get it out of my mind and eventually summoned up the courage to go for a preliminary interview which went very well. But then came the really hard part. I had to phone mum and dad to tell them I was quitting my PhD immediately to go to sea in warships.

'They were shocked to say the least. Their first reaction was to fly up to Edinburgh to talk me round to my senses, but they soon realized that I was adamant and so gave it up as a lost cause. Now, they love it. They're as chuffed as anything. They came to my passing out parade and mum, of course, was in bits'!

'Two cables, and closing ma'am.'

'Roger. Steady on course 241. Set lever at 40,' says Lovegrove, bowing down to look through the prismatic eye-piece of the ship's compass.

'You'll come in too wide at 241!' barks James Rapp from the commander's chair on the right-hand side of the bridge.

Lovegrove bites her lip. ' Aye, aye, sir. Steer 235 Quartermaster.'

Lovegrove looks over to the captain who says nothing. She carries on with an outward coolness that conceals her inner turmoil. She knows she can do the job but Captain Rapp, with his photographic memory and preoccupation with detail, always makes her nervous. But, then, he makes a lot of people nervous. He is the ultimate perfectionist and expects everybody else to be the same. In his determined bid to get the best out of people, both for their own sakes and for the sake of the navy he loves so much, he can seem unbending and, sometimes, undermining. Lovegrove knows that there is no captain better qualified to guide, teach and advise her but she just wishes he would give her a little more space.

Lovegrove positions the *Brilliant* immediately astern of the *Stromboli* and gets ready to move up. At this point both ships are virtually side by side and doing 14 knots in the same direction. The next trick is to keep their bows pointing slightly away from each other so that the force of the sea moving between them pushes them constantly apart.

A mistake of only a degree or two in the heading of either ship could lead to a collision and potential tragedy.

'Half a cable, ma'am!'

'Very good, lever 40 . . . Captain, sir. The ship is ready to RAS. Permission to inform the *Stromboli* by hoisting Flag Romeo for close up.'

'Make it so. Close up and take us in, officer of the watch, the MEO's* thirsty!'

'Aye, aye, sir. Yeoman, Flag Romeo – close up.'

'Very good ma'am.'

Lovegrove glances over her bow to the Italian supply ship that is now no more than 150 feet away, slightly forward of the *Brilliant* on the port side. She then looks down to the sea raging between the two ships before giving the final order to nudge up the final few yards so that the oil hoses can be hoisted across for the refuelling.

'Lever 80, steer 236.'

Four thousand tons of British frigate surges forward at the young lieutenant's command, accelerating towards the 22 knots necessary to get through the tanker's pressure waves and to find a safe spot from which to replenish.

'Steer 235 . . . steer 234. Easy. Steer 235.'

Lovegrove judges the moment and calls for the speed reduction 'Lever 20!' and the *Brilliant* settles. At this power setting the ship will only do 6 knots so she needs to be ready to increase again: 'Lever 50. Steer 236.'

The manoeuvre is complete. James Rapp says nothing but Lovegrove peeks over and is certain he is nodding his head – ever so imperceptibly.

Outside on the port side upper deck the RAS crew are in place. Two riflemen,

---

* Marine engineering officer. See also Who's Who (Official Job Titles page 216).

one aft and one for'ard, aim their automatic rifles towards the Italian supply tanker and fire. Two piercing reports echo in the watery valley created between the two ships and two bright yellow projectiles soar from one side to the other. The rubber missiles pull long lengths of nylon twine behind them which are quickly gathered by the Italian sailors who pull on them frantically. The twine pulls over thick hemp rope which, in turn, pulls over wire cable and soon the two ships are substantially linked.

Now, using the cable wire, the *Stromboli* sends over massive heavy-duty hoses through which she can pump the tons of diesel oil the *Brilliant* needs to sustain her in her continuing patrol and eventual passage to Souda Bay in Crete.*

In the cavernous engine spaces deep in the bowels of the ship the stokers prepare to take on the fuel. Overseeing the procedure is Lieutenant-Commander Norman Boyes, the marine engineering officer. Boyes, though an officer, came through the ranks and was a chief petty officer engineering artificer until 1986 when he applied for and was given a commssion. Now he is in charge of fifty-five stokers of whom he is fiercely protective. Perhaps because of his own experience as a stoker, he believes them to be the unsung heroes of any ship and all too easily forgotten unless something goes wrong:

'Nobody loves a stoker! It's because we're never seen and inhabit this mysterious underground netherworld full of pipes, dials, pistons and oil leaks. They all take us for granted. I mean, we're responsible for the obvious things like the engines that drive the ship through the water but we're also responsible for the production of water through the desalination plants that produce two tons of fresh water per hour, the electrical generators, the sewage plants, the air conditioning – the list is endless! Of course, there are more glamorous positions, like in the op's room or on the upper deck with the gunners, but you try running this ship without the stokers. They only realize we're here when something goes wrong and we have to fix it.'

For Norman Boyes, the engine spaces with their gas turbines, electrical generators, massive gearboxes and drive shafts is a sort of paradise of mechanical wonder to which he is totally committed and in which he is completely at home:

'If you think of the ship as a human body then the bridge, I suppose, represents the eyes, the op's room is the brain and nervous system and the engine room is the heart and the muscle. And diesel oil is, of course, the blood!'

On the upper deck the fuel hose from the *Stromboli* rams into *Brilliant's* RAS liquid 'receiver' just aft of midships and promptly begins to pump fuel. In the

---

* During Operation Sharp Guard the *Brilliant* refuelled every four or five days.

for'ard engine space 'Tug' Wilson, the chief stoker, checking the fuel flow, watches the arms on the tank dials quiver as the diesel flows in. Boyes watches on with the same excitement he feels every time the ship refuels. He maintains a boy-like fascination with engines and has amassed a remarkable 'did you know' collection of ship-engine trivia with which he likes to test peoples' concentration spans at cocktail parties.

'Did you know that our Olympus engines are the horsepower equivalent to sixty-nine Ford Escorts or fifteen Porsche 911s . . . ? Did you know that when we are on full power we use 369 gallons of fuel for every mile whilst your dear old Ford Escort would do 14 000 miles for the same amount . . . ? Did you know that on the Tyne gas turbine engines we average 247 feet per gallon whereas on the powerful Olympus engines we do no more than 14 feet per gallon!'

It is **1705**. The RAS over, Tracie Lovegrove has returned exhausted to her cabin. Perching on her bunk she reaches for her Wren officer's cap and pokes her index finger under the curved side brim. She hooks out a concealed Wispa chocolate bar which, with delicious, wide-eyed anticipation, she proceeds to unwrap very, very, slowly. Wispa bars are a rare and prized commodity on the ship at the moment as the NAAFI stores ran out over three weeks ago. Some are to be had on the black market and Lovegrove managed to negotiate a single bar this morning, through a certain wide-boy missile man who is known to have his sources. It had cost over four times the current shore-side market value but Lovegrove reckons she deserves a treat after her watch on the bridge this afternoon.

'It went pretty well in the end but the pressure is outrageous. Sometimes, when it gets really bad with people running around snapping and growling at you, I start not to enjoy it and wonder "Do I really need this?". Mind you, I would never show the others if I was phased or upset. I never cry in public, never. If something has upset me badly this is my sanctuary in this cabin. I might come and have a cry here but then I go out and nobody will know any different. It's difficult being a woman in a man's world because a lot of the men are still getting used to the idea. It's new for them and it will take time before the idea of women at sea is accepted completely. A warship is still very much a male bastion. They let you join in some parts of life on board but it's impossible to get into their male bonding thing – you know, the boarding-school rough and tumble of wrestling and water fights. If you do try and join in they all stop, and say, "Oh! Are you getting hormonal again?" So, sometimes it's just me on my own with a little help from nutty!'*

---

* General naval term for chocolates and sweets.

It is **1900**. One by one the heads of department file into the captain's cabin for the nightly command brief. There is Martin Atherton, supply officer, Fred Tulloch, weapons engineering officer, Bob Hawkins, principal warfare officer, Russ Harding, first lieutenant, Norman Boyes, marine engineering officer and Jerry Barnbrook, flight commander. Each takes his regular position around a small wooden table near the captain's desk on which Petty Officer George Cooper has placed seven glasses of orange cordial for their refreshment.

James Rapp waits for everybody to settle and then motions Nick Cooke-Priest who is waiting at the door to give the nightly meteorological report.

'Good evening sir, gentlemen . . .' says Cooke-Priest, leaning a weather chart against the nearest bulkhead. 'This is the situation from 1200 Zulu today until 0600 Zulu tomorrow morning. We have got this low of 1012 millibars clearing away to the east and this high of 1024 being replaced by this low of 1014. This will change the shape and type of the frontal system which will then start moving away to the south-east. Visibility will be good sir, and the sea state will remain 1 to 2. So fairly decent conditions once the front is through us tomorrow. Thank you sir, gentlemen.'

Cooke-Priest goes out of the cabin and makes way for Leading Seaman 'Wiggy' Bennett, electronic warfare director, to give the latest intelligence report that is gleaned daily from a number of classified and non-classified sources.

'Captain sir, gentlemen. It's been relatively quiet on and under the water today sir. All Yugoslavian submarines and frigates have remained in port over the last twenty-four hours. One patrol boat conducted a routine coastal patrol and then returned to port. Air activity, on the other hand, has been busy again sir. There were seventy-one tactical flights across the region and one episode of bombing practice on the southern ranges. In the actual conflict, sir, according to the press, UN aircraft were hit by small arms fire at Sarajevo airport. The airport went on alert following the incident, sir. The Russian special envoy has urged the West to lift sanctions on the Serbs without imposing conditions . . .'

It is **1906**. As the command brief continues the rest of the ship has settled into the usual Defence Watches evening routine. As always, half are on watch and half off. Those off watch are asleep or relaxing in their mess decks. Of those in the mess decks, some are playing cards and some are playing Uckers* whilst others have

---

* A fast-moving naval variation of the old family game of Ludo, played on a highly coloured board (see Lower Deck Traditions, opposite).

LOWER DECK TRADITIONS

Traditions on the lower deck have been changing as fast as society itself in the last 25 years. Until 1970, rum was still flowing, some ratings had still slept in hammocks and a personal bucket was about the most useful item a seaman could own on board, used for laundry, washing and the secret stowage of grog.

Messes did not have televisions, so film nights when 16 mm projectors showed spliced-together cuttings of the saucier moments from a dozen movies, were the height of entertainment. The living environment, improved in the newer Leander-Class frigates, remained austere and in the face of such adversity there were traditions and often unpleasant initiation rites to break the regimen.

These traditions have now almost all departed and are unlamented. The one that has remained is the most light-hearted, yet the most keenly fought. To some it might appear a child's game. To others it will remain a lifelong obsession. It is 'uckers', the very singular and highly refined half-cousin of Ludo. Uckers is played on a board that is a mess-made, but unbelievably serviceable, hardwood replica of the Ludo design. The circular pieces are usually carefully fashioned from painted metal or hardwood to be an inch in diameter and of pleasing weight. They must also sound right when banged down.

Moves may resemble Ludo but anyone who adopts a simplistic style is accused of 'Ludo playing' in tones of great disparagement. The subtleties are in the extra rules, for pairs playing with 'blobs' and 'mixy blobs', for attacking opponents through 'suck backs', 'blow backs' and 'side swipes' and for dealing with cheating by 'timber shifting', 'number rolling' and 'six-throwing bastards'. The ultimate sanction against blatant cheats is to 'up board', a toddler's tantrum tactic much admired by artificers, which involves scattering the board, the pieces and the players to the four corners of the mess.

The game remains firmly alive with sailors of every rate and station, rivalling even the video and CD players that have their own corners in each mess – and would probably provide one of the few recognizable features of life for someone who last served at sea in the 1960s.

tuned in to the ship's closed-circuit television system which tonight is showing *EastEnders, Big Break, Tomorrow's World* and *Pop Quiz*.* A few 'hardies' are pumping iron to a tape of Elvis Presley hits in the small exercise room next to the Sea Skua magazine and a handful are thumbing through books in the ship's library (neatly kept by the education officer at one end of the main dining hall).

Of those on duty, many are scrubbing and cleaning in preparation for the imminent inspection of the mid-section of the ship by the captain in two days time. These regular inspections, called 'captain's rounds', involve the minutest scrutiny of every nook and cranny. If anywhere is not up to standard questions are asked and heads can roll.**

On Two Deck, just for'ard of the wardroom, Leading Steward Andy Conway and Wren Steward Viv Worrall are on their rubber-gloved hands and well-worn knees scraping and scrubbing the old, stained ME7 polish off the blue coloured flats. Watching them with an amused grin is PO George Cooper who is leaning casually against the wardroom galley door having a cup of tea.

Viv Worrall, with her hair tied up in a bun except for one long strand that has fallen over her face with the exertion of scrapping and scrubbing, raises her voice caustically.

'Is that you George?'

'Yes.'

'Yeah, I thought I smelled Essence of Skunk.'

'Come on Viv. Scrub for England!' retorts the Geordie PO.

'Abso-fuckin'-lutely!' says Andy Conway, 'Or else we might be blown up by a Serb missile and then we'd all sink and die in a boat wiv' dirty floors. Don't warrant finking about does it? What you up to then George?'

'I'm just waiting for the command brief to finish so I can set the skipper's supper.'

'Dinner!' says the blonde Wren, brushing back the strand of hair from her face before attacking the flats again.

'What?'

---

* Videotape recordings of British television favourites are flown out regularly with the mail drops. Sailors can also provide their own video entertainment and play it independently on their mess deck video machines. Blue movies are referred to euphemistically as 'training films' or 'recognition vids'.

** Captain's rounds' never involve inspecting the whole ship at once. They are staggered around different parts during the term of any particular deployment. Hence mid-section rounds, aft-section rounds, for'ard-section rounds, mess-deck rounds, etc. The first lieutenant, however, inspects mess decks, heads and bathrooms each evening out of Defence Watches; it is a two-way process for not only does he see the ship but ratings can see him and make known any defeats or difficulties.

'Dinner! He would call it dinner, not supper, 'cos he's posh and you're jus' dead common you are . . .'

'Ere, George,' says Conway holding up his hands to show off his bright yellow rubber gloves, 'What do you reckon to me Marigolds then. I fink I'd look better in pink meself . . .'

It is **1952**. The command brief is still in session. Normally it would be over in three-quarters of an hour, after each officer had given a brief report on his department for that day, but this evening the captain has returned to the question of the embargo itself.

'. . . and judging from the intelligence reports the Serbs are putting up a hell of a lot of aircraft at the moment. How many was it yesterday, Bob?'

'Over a hundred sorties sir?'

'Exactly. So the question we're being asked is "Where is all the aviation fuel coming from?" '

'Well, it's a valid question sir,' says Russ Harding. 'It's very worrying to think it might be getting through the sea blockade.'

'I don't think it is,' breaks in Hawkins. 'It's got to be coming in over land.'

'Yes, I agree,' says Barnbrook, 'but what's the difference anyway if we have to lift the embargo . . . ?'

'I don't know how many of you heard the World Service today, but Malcolm Rifkind has said that any pressure from any quarter to have the arms embargo lifted would raise a large question mark over the deployment of troops in Serbia. And apparently the Muslim-Serb president, Alija Izetbegovic, has actually removed his original demand for the embargo to be lifted and that's relieved some of the tension that's been building up recently. And it does reinforce the fact that we'll continue to enforce the embargo . . .'

'Yes sir,' interrupts Hawkins, 'but it could get very tricky if we're told to enforce the embargo on just the Serbs and not the Muslims. That's what the Americans would like but how would we apply it? How could we ever prove that any one ship was taking its cargo to the Muslims and not the Serbs before it was too late . . . ?'

It is **2135**. Lieutenant-Commander Martin Atherton, the supply officer, exhausted by his day, exhausted by Defence Watches and exhausted by the extended command brief walks thankfully into the solitude of his cabin. Grateful for some peace at last, he lies back on the bunk and reaches for his book, *The Theatre of Protest and Paradox* by George E. Wellwarth. In the background, playing on his portable CD player, is the sound-track of *The Piano* by Michael Nyman. Atherton thumbs through the book on developments in avant-garde drama. He stops at a section on 'the drama of alienated youth' about the playwright Shelagh Delaney and starts to read. On the shelf behind his bunk there is an extensive library of books that betrays wide-ranging and catholic tastes: *Four Quartets* by T. S. Eliot, *England, My England* by D. H. Lawrence, *The Intellectuals and the Masses* by John Carey, *Music and the Mind* by Anthony Storr, *Venice* by Jan Morris, *West of Sunset* by Dirk Bogarde, *An International Directory of Terrorism and Espionage* . . .

If there is such a thing as a typical naval officer Martin Atherton is not he. His background is academic and his early ambitions were aimed at success in the arts. A graduate in English Literature at Oxford, he started a PhD thesis on the role of Shakespeare as an inspiration to composers of opera and committed himself to a career in academia. But then something occurred which was to change his life forever – the Argentinians invaded the Falklands.

'I remember it was the night the *Canberra* sailed from Southampton and I was watching it on the TV with some friends. As I watched I remember thinking to myself, "I wonder if I could cope with that experience". I considered that perhaps my background and training to date was so protected that I couldn't. I said out loud to my friends that I wondered whether I could actually go to war to which one of them replied, "Well, why on earth should you want to? That's for the marines or the para's to do. It's for them to enact it whilst it's for us to sit here and debate the rights and wrongs of it all." I was then suddenly struck with the absurdity and the fragility of such a fragmented view of society – that some people "do" and others "think" . . .'

For Atherton it was the realization that he had come to a critical crossroads in his life. Suddenly he sensed a terrible danger of being forced to live out a life that he felt morally wrong and also of being imprisoned in an environment that was constraining his spirit. He was overcome with the idea that if he did not reach out and grasp exactly that experience of life that his peers considered so far out of his reach then he was not in ultimate control of his destiny.

'I was then faced with an inescapable and inevitable decision. I needed to embark on some sort of journey, a personal odyssey, and experience a psychological adventure that would liberate me from the introversion and selfishness of academic life. It was immediately a very exciting idea because it held out all kinds of promise and it seemed by then inevitable that this "calling", if you like, was to the sea. I mean I was born in Liverpool and ships had been part of my childhood. I remember my grandfather taking me down to the pierhead there and pointing out all the ships and telling me stories about all the things that had happened to him when he had been at sea. I somehow associated all that with the business of being an adult – of having to make a journey, and that journey had to be with the Royal Navy. I wanted to be of use, you see. At university I wasn't of use to anyone but in the navy I could fit into a larger community, which is what this ship is. And I have found that being in the navy is the most marvellous way of extending your capabilities towards other people. You find that people complete each other. We complement each other, we make up for each others' deficiencies, we depend on each other – both in times of peace and war. There is an old phrase about "a ship of souls" – many disparate souls but united symbolically in a very clear, common cause and it is a great joy to feel part of that. I mean, here we are on the *Brilliant* in the middle of the Adriatic, within missile range of potential enemies, and all we have to depend on is each other, 250 very distinct but very able people. Maybe a ship like this is a model, a paradigm for the way all societies should be – and then perhaps there would be no wars and, therefore, no need for warships . . .'

Martin Atherton has a remarkable strength, even toughness of will, but also an astonishing gentleness of spirit – a combination that inspires confidence and trust in both his fellow officers and the ratings. Everybody likes and respects this friendly, genuine, but enigmatic officer. On the other hand, few know what really drives him, few realize the nature of the journey he has embarked on, and few know his personal philosophy:

'I don't know very much about philosophy but I do know a bit about poetry and there is a wonderful line in Tennyson's 'Ulysses' where he talks about the old man setting out again on another journey. He says that, "his course is set to sail beyond the bounds of all the western stars until he dies". The idea of constant exploration and discovery is what excites me. I look to the navy to continue to challenge and surprise me. I hope it will, I believe it will.'

DAY *Monday*	**DATE** *3*	**MONTH** *October*	**YEAR**	*1994*

PLACE	**On passage from** *Area Iceman, Eastern Adriatic*

POSITION	**At 0600** *Classified* **At 2359** *37°08'N 20°42'E*

DISTANCE TRAVELLED midnight to midnight *404.3 nautical miles*

SHIPS LOG. Departed from Iceman at 0620. De-weaponed and commenced fast passage to Souda Bay, Crete. Cleared missile envelope by 1130. Captain's mid-section rounds this a.m.

It is **0620**. The 3000 ton Spanish frigate SNS *Andalucia* arrived half an hour ago to take over our duty in Iceman and to release us for a few days break in Crete. The main contact was by radio but she was sighted briefly about 6 miles off our port bow when she flashed a greeting in morse code from her upper deck signal lamp:

ICEMAN IS OURS. GOD SPEED TO SOUDA BAY. HAVE FUN.

We flashed back a 'Thanks and farewell', opened up the powerful Olympus engines and have now set course for the southern Aegean Sea. Although no longer on patrol, everybody remains vigilant as the the ship will be within range of the Serbian shore-based missiles until about 1100. Until then we must remain closed up at Defence Stations.

It is **0715**. Down in the aft section of Two Deck is a steamy space known as the dhobey palace.* Leo Kang, known as the dhobey wallah or Number One, is busy ironing shirts, trousers, overalls and socks. This small, industrious Singaporean has been on the *Brilliant* since she was commissioned in 1974 and is famous amongst generations of ratings for his razor-sharp creases, starched collars and explosive temper. Although he has a cabin of his own he spends nearly all his time in the dhobey palace which he shares with his assistant, another tiny Singaporean with a fixed smile and thick glasses, known only as Number Two or, inexplicably, 'Scouse'. Together, they wash, dry, iron and press the ship's company's clothes all day, every day, in foul weather and fair, in peace and at war.** It can be lucrative as they have guaranteed custom and charge per item according to a published tariff, but profit margins are not always enough to placate the moody Number One dhobey. This morning, with a mountain of work and a face like thunder, Leo is clearly on a short fuse. Number Two, sensitive to his boss's mood swings, has ducked behind a wall of hanging washing for a bit of peaceful sock sorting.

Suddenly, a rating arrives at the door with a huge bundle of washing. It is an unsuspecting Micky Goble.

'Watcha Leo mate, can you . . .'

'NO!'

'Eh?'

'No can do all dhobey! Too much! TOO MUCH!'

'I ain't got much . . .'

'Steam pless bloken!'

---

* See Chinese Laundrymen, opposite.
** Leo Kang has dhobied at Action Stations in the Falklands War and the Gulf War and was awarded the British Empire Medal for bravery under fire.

CHINESE LAUNDRYMEN

For most folk the end of January is significant only to pay off Christmas bills. For the ship's laundryman and his assistant Number Two Dhobey, it is the most important day in the calendar: Chinese New Year. On board ship, even in operational conditions, great lengths are taken to mark the significance of this event.

The captain will often invite the dhobeymen to his cabin for a glass of wine. The wardroom and other messes may do the same. Highly stylized presents are given, offered in a traditional way to guarantee good fortune: they must be money, in new notes handed over in special red envelopes with the traditional good wishes spoken in Cantonese.

There is a scale to giving, which reflects the position of the donor and also the value of the service that the dhobeymen have given over the past year. While most members of the ship's company pay a fixed rate for their overalls, shirts and smalls, some key people in the life of the laundry are not charged for their washing. By tradition the captain (for allowing the unofficial workers on to his ship), the marine engineering officer (who is usually the laundry officer and responsible for supplying the steam and hot water essential for work), the supply officer (for helping the laundrymen send their money home and assisting in the administrative details of their lives) and, generally, the master-at arms (for his help in regulating laundry practise) receive a nominally free service.

It is the custom for the 'free'-laundry users to place money to reflect this service in the red envelopes. The laundry officer will advise the captain how much to give – it is rarely less than three figures. The two heads of department and the master-at-arms give proportionate sums. It all goes to Number One dhobey, who puts an amount aside for Number Two. Number Two will also receive small tokens of esteem from the officers and messes unless they like having their buttons crushed.

All this will go when Hong Kong is returned to the Chinese in 1997. For the time being, however, in many ships Number One dhobey will remain second only to the captain as the highest earner on board – though undoubtedly the hardest worker.

'You what?'

'Steam pless bloken!'

'Come on Leo. I've only got a couple of shirts and a pair of trousers . . .'

'NO! NO! NO! Evly time we go run ashore you come too much dhoby!'

'Leo . . .'

'Bling little evly day! Not too much all same time!'

'But . . .'

'Steam pless bloken! Steam pless bloken!'

'I don't need . . .'

'GO AWAY! TOO MUCH DHOBEY! GO AWAY . . . STEAM PLESS BLOKEN!'

'Daft Chink!' whispers Goble under his breath as he heads back to his mess deck. At the first bulkhead door he bumps into Dave 'Clubs' Mynett who is carrying an even larger bundle of dhobey.

'Hiya Micky. Gone to collect your dhobey?'

'Er, yeah. That's right.'

'How's Leo this morning?'

'Oh, he's fine actually.'

'Not blowin' his top?'

'Noooo! Noooo! He's in a really good mood – did all my stuff on the steam press for no extra charge. Jus' go in there an' ask him mate . . .'

It is **0830**. Chay Robertson, the master-at-arms, knocks at the captain's door.

'Come in.'

Robertson, a tall, imposing Scot with the bearing of a sergeant major in the Guards, steps into the commanding officer's cabin, stands to attention and salutes smartly. 'Sah! Mid section ready for your rounds, sah!'

James Rapp returns the salute. 'Very well Master. Let's proceed.'

The two men walk out of the cabin, past the op's room and down the ladder to One Deck, then along the main passage towards the mid section. On their way they pick up the large retinue of officers and chief petty officers that will follow the captain on his rounds like a conga line at a Mardi Gras carnival.

Throughout the mid section on One Deck and Two Deck sailors and Wrens rush around, frantically doing bits of last-minute polishing and dusting. Then, as they hear the shrill whistle of the bo'sun's call herald the approach of the captain and his conga line, they freeze to attention. The inspection is minute, exhaustive and critical. The captain looks into every corner, crack and crevice with a narrow beam torch. The master-at-arms runs his finger along every flat surface from deck to deckhead inspecting for the slightest sign of dust. Behind them the first lieutenant and the conga line make copious notes on what is being said, noticed and ordered for a 'rescrub'.

'Bit of grunge down here, Master,' says the captain, pointing his torch behind the photocopier outside the writers' office.

'Really, sah,' replies Robertson, bending down to look for himself. 'You're right sah! Grunge!'

The conga line makes a note.

'It needs redoing.'

'Re-inspection sah?'

'Yes, tomorrow.'

The conga line makes another note.

The party moves on down the passageway towards the mid-section storerooms.

One deck below, on Two Deck, ratings are waiting for the captain and his retinue to arrive. At the moment the sound of the bo'sun's whistle is still some way off so everybody is relatively relaxed. The huge Petty Officer Steve Whitter and Leading Seaman 'Pax' Paxford are looking into the radio room they have spent an entire week cleaning, scrubbing and polishing.

'What a waste of bleedin' time,' says the iconoclastic Whitter. 'I mean we've 'ad over a week in Defence Watches when we was meant to be on a flamin' war footin' in case we got 'it by a Serb rocket or summat and what do we do? Polish the fuckin' ship.'

'A clean ship is a fightin' ship is what they say.'

'Bollocks! Rounds is all about the skipper givin' everybody grief. He's comin' round so everythin's got to be gleamin', scrubbed and put away. It ain't normal. It ain't how the ship would normally be is it?'

'Join the navy and be a scrubber!'

'He'll walk in wiv' all that lot followin' 'im, he'll walk round seein' what he can pick us up on so we 'ave to do a rescrubbin'. Basically it's bullshit. BBB, bullshit, buckles and braid.'

It is 0930. The captain's rounds are continuing and are likely to last for at least another two hours. In the main galley, which is in the aft section of the ship and so spared today's inspection, Leading Cook Mark Warburton is busy preparing lunch. On the menu today is corned beef pie, chicken and vegetable curry, liver, bacon and sausage casserole and seafood pasta, with baked and boiled potatoes, leeks, carrots and baked beans. As he rushes between oven, hob and cutting-board he talks fast in a broad Black Country brogue.

'It don't matter to us cooks whether the captain's comin' to inspect the galleys or not. This place 'as always got to be "shipshape" as the sayin' goes. I mean this place is always workin' isn't it? People 'ave always got to eat even if we're at war – an' it don't matter whether the queen's comin', the pope, or a hundred bleedin' admirals, we've still got to get the grub out or there'll be a bleedin' mutiny . . .'

He starts to slice up large, bloody calves' livers into thick strips.

'. . . This job ain't just about filling bellies it's about keeping morale high. Jack ain't got much goin' for him at sea, especially in Defence Watches, so he looks forward to his scran. And if it isn't up to scratch he lets you know it. Never mind about captain's rounds – us cooks are the only ones on board who 'ave their work quality-tested three times a day, 365 days a year!'

Mark Warburton is a sparky, plain-speaking Midlander who joined the navy 19 years ago when he was sixteen. He was actually born in Sheffield but grew up in Derbyshire where the only jobs available were in the coal pits.

'I didn't fancy the mines so I joined the navy. All my cousins and friends went down the mines but they're all out of work now. Mines 'ave all closed down. So I reckon I made the right decision putting on the blue suit but I'll be glad when me time is done. It's not what it was in the navy. I mean they used to be cryin' out for people to join up and then they would train you from scratch – teach you everythin' you wanted to know about ships, damage control, fire fightin', ropes, knots – everythin'. But now they've got very choosy an' only take people with O levels an' GCSEs so you've got youngsters comin' in as senior rates 'cos of their bleedin' exams who can order people like me around . . .'

Warburton turns and calls out to another cook on the other side of the galley.

'Ain't that right Mickey?'

'What's that?'

'I was just sayin' about all this lot comin' in with all their exams an' everythin' but no common dog'.*

Mickey Nowell, a 37-year-old leading cook from Nottinghamshire, walks over with a gigantic pot of seafood pasta which he puts on a burning gas ring next to an even bigger pot of simmering chicken curry.

'Oh yeah! They've got all the qualifications but they've never had a ship before. They have to take charge of people like myself who's had nine ships and they don't have a clue . . .'

'Exactly!' interrupts Warburton. 'They can tell you how many pickles there are in a jar but they can't get the bloody lid off! And then you try and show them the ropes, tell 'em what it's all about, and they don't want to know.'

---

* Common sense. For more naval slang, see Jackspeak, page 212.

'Yeah, but that's the same with the junior rates as well. I mean in the old days if my hooky* said "Jump!" I would say, "How high?" but now with me and Mark both being hookies and we say "do something" to these youngsters they just look at us and say "Why?".'

'An' I'll tell you summat else. When we first joined an' we didn't do somethin' right we'd get a clip round the 'ead. An' we learnt fast. Today, if you touch 'em you're up on a bleedin' charge!'

'It's all changed since the Falklands really.'

'Yeah, well I'd leave tomorrow if I could. Like a bleedin' shot! How's the curry goin' there Micky?'

'Fine. Spuds need some salt though . . .'

It is **1046**. The captain and the conga line are nearing the end of the mid-section inspection.

'That's a bit of an eyesore, Number One,' says the captain looking at a stain on the flats at the bottom of one of the mid-ship companionways.

'Yes sir. It's certainly not up to standard,' replies the first lieutenant.

'It needs to be stripped right back. Get all that polish off and scrub it down.'

'Yes sir. Master, we need that done again from scratch.'

'Yes sah! There's a certain sailor I'll be talking to about that sah!' says the master-at-arms narrowing his eyes with intent.

'Right,' says the captain. 'And we need to make sure that anybody carrying hot drinks around has clingfilm around the top of the mug. These stains are the result of constant spillages. It's unhygienic and it's dangerous if anybody slips.'

The conga line nods its heads in a chorus of affirmation and writes purpose-fully on its notepads.

The captain walks through another door to inspect the last space of the rounds. Steve Whitter jumps to attention and salutes.

'Radio space ready for inspection, sir!'

'Very good Petty Officer Whitter,' says James Rapp, returning the salute and peering up at the gigantic weapons engineering mechanic. 'Any problems in here?'

'No sir.'

'Managing to get in the training?'

'Yes sir. Doin' me best. Weights when I can and circuits with Clubs every day.'

'Are you doing the field gun again next year?'

'Hope so sir.'

---

* Nickname for a leading hand.

As the captain talks to the giant petty officer he scans the room with his ever-searching eyes.

'What's that?'

'Wot's wot sir?'

'That!' says the captain, pointing to a corner.

'It's a parrot, sir.'

The captain walks over to a brightly coloured explosion of feathers with two beady eyes that is sitting on a perch suspended from an emergency fire pipe.

'Er, that's to say, sir, it's a toy parrot . . . wot talks.'

'Talks?'

'Yes sir. If you switch it on 'ere sir, like this, and talk to it, it repeats wot you say in a sort of parrot-like voice, sir.'

'Really?'

'Yes sir. It's a kind of a mascot. 'Ave a go sir. Jus' say summat to it.'

The captain looks round uncomfortably to an intrigued conga line and then bends tentatively towards the petty officer's parrot.

'Er, hello.'

'Er, hello.'

'Goodness . . . !'

'Goodness!'

'That's quite extraordinary . . .'

'That's quite extraordinary!'

'Yes sir.'

The conga line smiles.

It is 1147. The captain has finished his rounds and is back in his cabin for a debriefing with the first lieutenant. The master-at-arms is in the regulator's office reprimanding the nervous-looking junior rate responsible for the flat at the bottom of the mid-section companionway.

'It was a perishin' mess!'

'There was no time . . .'

'I don't want excuses sailor. I'm just telling you it was a perishin' mess!'

'Yeah, well . . .'

'You need to change your attitude . . .'

'But . . .'

'. . . and organize your time better. Raise your standards fast, sailor, or you'll be in trouble!'

'I . . .'

'Just remember PPPPPP!'

'Eh?'

'Prior Planning Prevents Piss-Poor Performance!'

Back in the Two Deck radio room, Steve Whitter talks to his parrot:

'Captain's rounds . . . ! Wot a load of bollocks . . . !'

'Captain's rounds! Wot a load of bollocks!'

It is **2000**. The ship's state of battle readiness has been reduced from Defence Watches to Enhanced Cruising Stations. The ammunition has been unloaded from the weapons on the upper deck and the ratings are in their mess decks relaxing, for the first time in ten days, with a tin or two of beer. Nobody ever drinks during Defence Watches but now the ship is out of Area the padlocks have come off the mess deck fridges. The boxes of ammunition that were being lugged around all afternoon between the missile and gun decks and the magazines have now been swapped for boxes of MacEwan Export, Budweiser and Special Brew. The ship's mood is transforming as the tension of Defence Watches diminishes.

As the mess decks sit back with their tins of beer Leading Steward Andy Conway unlocks the grill over the spirit shelves behind the wardroom bar to the cheers of the officers present. Meanwhile, Russ Harding has gone up to the darkened bridge where he picks up the microphone for the ship's central tannoy system.

'Good evening. First Lieutenant speaking. We are now well en route to Souda Bay in Crete. We've had a busy week in Montenegro with some excitement but, as usual, a lot of the tense routine patrolling. We saw an increased amount of Serb air activity which makes us a little concerned as to how they are getting their fuel. As for today I know the captain is generally very pleased with the effort that went into rounds – particularly as most of the work had to be done in Defence Watches. So, well done.

'The weather in Crete is fine so it should be a good run ashore. But remember this – your behaviour must be of the highest standard. The Greeks take a very dim view of people who drink too much alcohol and particularly those who interfere with the Greek flag. Recently three Canadian sailors were sent to prison and fined $2000 for removing a Greek flag from a mast near their ship. Hire a car if you want to but remember there is a ship's ban on hiring motor bikes or scooters. You all know about the fatalities that have occurred within Sharp Guard units over the last year. If you go into town at night don't go alone, and that's particularly important for the girls. Make sure there's someone with you and avoid the dark back streets late at night. And finally, enjoy yourselves. That's all.'

Chapter Four

ON THE STREET IN CRETE

DAY *Tuesday*	DATE *4*	MONTH *October*	Year *1994*

PLACE	*On passage to Souda Bay, Crete*

POSITION	At **0600** *36°34'N 21°38'E* At **1200** *35°00'N 25°50'E*

DISTANCE TRAVELLED midnight to midnight *195.3 nautical miles*

SHIPS LOG. A busy day arriving in Souda Bay. Excellent weather. Agents came aboard to organize stores and Greek money for run ashore. Leave granted at 1800. Spirits high.

It is **1405**. The *Brilliant* glides out of the softly swelling Sea of Crete, past the imposing headland of Akrotiri and into the pond-calm waters of Souda Bay. The upper deck is alive with harbour station hands, no longer in their drab, blue Number Eights but in a bright, light tropical rig. The white cotton shirts and neatly pressed shorts seem to reflect the holiday mood of the ship as she approaches the beckoning finger that is her jetty. The Greek harbour master, embarked from his pilot boat, helps Perry Stowell, the navigator, guide the ship to her final mooring position.

As the *Brilliant* edges sideways into the jetty, thick securing ropes are hurled from either end of the ship to a gang of moustachioed Greek harbour hands who wrestle briefly with the coils before expertly tying them off around large, black fastening bollards. Micky Goble, with the foc'sle party on the bow, gives a friendly wave to the two Greeks on the head rope and then turns to Wren Ginny McHale standing on his right:

'It's bleedin' amazin' Ginny!'

'What's that Micky?'

'Four thousand tons of surging British warship tamed by a handful of Greek peasants and a couple of bits of string at either end . . . !'

The foc'sle party turns towards the point of the bow where a rating is pulling on the hoisting rope of the jack staff. Slowly, a furled bundle of material emerges from a white canvas sack. As it is pulled higher it partially loosens and unfolds as it catches the wind, but then tugs violently at the containing sack which seems insistently and stubbornly to restrain it. The rating on the rope pulls harder and further until the angry, flapping material is finally freed and allowed to wave strongly and patriotically in the warm Mediterranean wind.

'Best bleedin' flag in the world that!' says Micky Goble, looking up at the Union Jack* with pursed lips.

It is **1436**. On the flight deck at the stern of the ship the much bigger White Ensign has been hoisted on the ensign staff and it is under this flag that the first duty watch now musters. This is the skeleton crew that will look after the ship – especially her security – whilst in harbour. At all times armed sentries are posted on the upper deck whilst inside the ship an anti-terrorist squad remains constantly on alert. As the sentries take their positions a mobile crane lowers a steep metal gangway on to the the flight deck from the quayside. This is rapidly secured to allow a crowd of besuited men carrying briefcases to come on board. These are the local chandlers, supply agents, always the first on board any visiting warship once she is docked. There is an agent for everything: food replenishment; money exchange; telephone connections; car hire; tourism; recreation and sport. As the smiling businessmen, grateful to any navy that brings them such potential bounty, set foot on the flight deck various members of the ship's company are there to meet them and greet them. Martin Atherton, the supply officer, steps forward with hand outstretched to Nico Balassis, an old friend and the best 'fixer' in Greece.

'Marteen! Good afternoon! It is a pleasure and a delight to see you again. My goodness! But you have lost weight. My dear chap you are working far too hard!'

'Hello Nico. Good to see you too. It's funny – I was just about to say that you've put on weight so business must be good.

Balassis laughs heartily and continues to shake Atherton's hand with the energy and gusto of an all-in wrestler. He then puts his arm around the shoulders of the lieutenant-commander and walks with him to the wardroom to discuss the ship's needs and his prices.

It is **1507**. Sitting around the wardroom dining-table the various agents talk fast and furiously to their opposite numbers from the *Brilliant*. Some are talking about day trips to the south of the island whilst others talk about temporary golf club memberships. One group is talking about the best and cheapest cars for hire and

---

* The Union flag [Union Jack] is raised on the jack staff [the flag pole at the ship's prow]when alongside in harbour or at anchor. The flag and jack staff are struck [lowered] when the ship proceeds to sea.

others are discussing international telephone credit cards. At one end of the table Clubs Mynett is talking excitedly to a tall, athletic young man in a tracksuit about local sports facilities whilst at the other end Nico Balassis, spooning a fifth sugar into a cup of tea, gesticulates balletically with his free hand.

'Marteen. We have a problem with the phones. Normally we would have connected you to outside lines even as we speak. But we are currently suffering a one-day strike of the telephone people so today we can do nothing. But tomorrow, I promise the *Brilliant* will be connected so your people can all phone their dear loved ones. I hope that will be alright Marteen.'

'Well, Nico,' replies Atherton with a resigned smile, 'have you ever heard of the word "mutiny" . . . ?'

Back on the flight deck a tall Geordie petty officer caterer called Bryan Elliot is going through a long list of food supplies for the ship's stores with a Greek supplier whose limited understanding of the English language surpasses only his understanding of the English palate.

' 'Scuse plees. Thees! What ees thees?'

'Marmite.'

'Eh? No understan'.'

'Marmite! It's a spread. You know . . . on your bread. Very salty . . .'

'Ah, salt! Yes we have. Plenty salt . . . ! You put on your bread?'

'No! No! Never mind. What's next on the list?'

'Yes. What is thees plees?'

'Ah, that's Weetabix.'

'Wootobox?'

'Weetabix.'

'Ootibix?'

'Weetabix, man! Double U, Double E, Tee, A, Bee, I, Ex!'

'You put on bread . . . ?'

It is **1618**. The Royal Naval officer asks the taxi driver to wait and then walks slowly towards the large limestone archway. As he goes through he notices an old gardener turning on an outside water tap. He stops and watches as the spurting, dripping faucet feeds a long, green hose that snakes away towards gently undulating and beautifully manicured lawns. He continues to watch as moments later dozens of sprinklers hiss and spin into action, hurling out transparent veils of water that cascade into the sun-dried grass. The officer continues to walk around the edge of the garden and then, avoiding the water sprinklers, he weaves his way towards one of many long ranks of marble headstones. He stops at the first of hundreds in the line and reads the inscription:

Sailor. Died 1940. Known only to God.

Bob Hawkins is in the tranquil grounds of the Souda Bay War Cemetery which inhabits a wooded terrace cut into a hillside overlooking the bay. Wherever and whenever he can Hawkins comes to pay his respects to his naval forebears:

'I always make a point of visiting war cemeteries where Britons are buried – especially sailors. Seeing these graves puts a lot of things into perspective for me about the navy and about Britain as well. It's very important for all of us to remember these people because it's thanks to them that we enjoy the life style and freedom that we do today. They fought and vanquished a terrible evil in Europe which we too easily forget these days. I'm one of the shrinking number of people who actually had parents who were involved in the Second World War – my father was a signalman in the Royal Navy – and so I feel a very real responsibility to remember the people who sacrificed their lives for us. Places like this are very moving . . .'

Hawkins walks pensively along the endless line of headstones that mark the resting-places of British servicemen who lost their lives in the defence of Crete against German forces in 1941.* Every few paces he stops to read an inscription, paying particular attention to the ages:

'Able Seaman, aged 19 . . . Sub-Lieutenant, aged 23 . . . Leading Seaman, aged 21 . . . Lieutenant-Commander, aged 24. God, a two-and-a-half striper at twenty-four! Lots of promotion in war – that's for sure. Coming to places like this really reminds you of your own mortality and that there's always a chance that it could happen to you. I didn't go to the Falklands and I haven't been in a campaign yet – I hope I never have to – but if you've never really thought about having to die for your country when you volunteer for the armed forces, then perhaps coming to a war cemetery is a timely reminder that it could happen to you.'

Hawkins walks into the small chapel of rest to sign the visitors' book and to leave his own personal message of remembrance. He then wanders to the edge of the cemetery, redolent with the scent of jasmine and honeysuckle, and looks out over the calm waters of Souda Bay, once the scene of such terrible carnage. Far below, in the evening haze he sees the comforting outline of his own ship, HMS *Brilliant*, moored safely, intact and at peace. He turns, puts on his sun-glasses and beckons the waiting taxi driver.

---

* Many of the 32 000 Allied soldiers, sailors and airmen in Crete at the time had been evacuated from the mainland as the Germans pushed south into Greece. With their superior air power, however, the Germans then invaded Crete and pushed the Allies back to the sea to await evacuation. The navy lost three cruisers and seven destroyers.

It is **1845**. Dave Mynett, in shorts, singlet and Adidas trainers, jogs down the gangway to the jetty and sets off for his first run on dry land since leaving Bari. He starts slowly and a little unsteadily as he knows it will take a few miles to find his shore-legs but he is grateful to feel solid ground under his feet at last. It is not easy keeping really fit on a warship – especially on a frigate where there is no real space to run. He does not find it difficult to maintain muscular strength because of his regular circuits and the iron-pumping in the weights room but it is hard to keep up the aerobic fitness essential for long distance running. Mynett is keen to maintain a good cardiovascular condition as he desperately wants to win the famous Rock Race in about six weeks time when the *Brilliant* puts into Gibraltar on the way home to Plymouth. This extraordinary race, run only by sailors, goes from the quayside to the very top of the Rock of Gibraltar. Just to make it is an achievement but to win it is the stuff dreams are made of.

As the lean, young club-swinger heads away from the *Brilliant* he sees coming towards him others of the ship's company who have already ventured outside the port gates. First he passes a group of Wrens loaded down with carrier bags full of crisps, sweets and chocolates.

'Hey girls. You'll get fat eatin' that lot!'

'Up yours Clubs!'

Next he passes Leading Seaman Jason Allan walking back hand-in-hand with his fiancée Wren Alex Sparrow, exercising a temporary freedom from the 'no touch' rule that applies on the ship.

'Yer goin' the wrong way shipmates. The nearest hotel's that way!'

'It's full up!'

Finally, he passes Petty Officer Ginger Lowden who is returning from his own training run.

'Give up Ginge. The Rock Race is mine!'

'Dream on Clubs!'

Mynett passes through the gates of the port, stretches out his pace and heads up towards the distant hills of Khania. The bounce in his run is a clue to his character: extrovert, outgoing, happy-go-lucky – typical of most naval club-swingers whose main responsibility, apart from the general fitness of their ships, is morale on board.

'We're the bleedin' Red Coats of the Royal Navy we are. I mean people think I don't do nothin' 'cept sport and play around but they don't realize what it would be like on board if there was no club-swinger. I do my hardest to motivate people, get 'em smilin', you know. If I see someone lookin' miserable I'll go and pep 'em up in no time. It's me job. Thing is I'm never allowed to be unhappy meself which can be a bit of a strain at times. But, when all is said an' done I am bloody proud of my job jus' like I'm bloody proud to be in the navy – not just any navy, but the Royal Navy. An' whilst I'm about it, I might as well tell you I'm bloody proud to be British. I know it's old-fashioned to be proud of things like that these days but I don't care. I am what I am – I ain't goin' to change. Actually, you'll find a lot of the matelots think the same way, although they won't always admit it. I mean bein' a sailor on a British warship would be pretty bleedin' daft if you didn't believe in yer country an' flag an' that wouldn't it?'

The Yorkshireman from Barnsley accelerates along a gravel path, jumps across a small stream and then slides down a grass embankment to a dusty road. He turns left, follows the road for about 2 miles and then finds himself on a busy main road full of rush-hour traffic. The pavement is pot-holed, cracked and eroded so, like a cross between a marathon runner and a tightrope walker, he does his best to run along the narrow strip of kerbstones, occasionally losing his balance and putting one foot into the puddled gutter. To protect his eyes from the glare of the headlights he holds his right hand to his eyes as if in a constant salute to the oncoming traffic which is now thickening into a jam. After about 15 minutes he comes to an intersection which he sprints across to avoid more drivers coming from the left, but not without provoking a chorus of angry car-horns in the process.

'I've run all over the world now. Everytime we get alongside – I don't care where it is – I get out the old trainers and off I go. I love the travel. Seein' all the weird an' wonderful places around the world. I've been to lots of good places . . . lots of piss-poor ones an' all!'

It is **1942**. Dave Mynett is back on the ship and towelling down in the PT store. This small room next to the aft Sea Wolf missile deck is full of sports equipment. A racing bike hangs from the deckhead on the left whilst straight ahead there are deep shelves full of rugby shirts, football shirts, boxing gloves, hockey sticks and basketballs. To the right there is a small desk in front of a bulkhead that displays several photographs, all of the same pretty, smiling brunette. On one a message has been written: 'Darling Dave. I miss you lots. Come back soon. XXXX.'

'Aye, it's a great life in the navy but it plays merry-bloody-havoc with your love life. Any sailor with a serious relationship – wife, girlfriend, whatever – is goin' to have problems. From that point of view it's a flamin' nightmare job. Especially now that deployments are gettin' longer with all this policin' type work that we have to do and, remember, we've got a lot fewer ships these days.'

Mynett pauses to look at the photographs above his desk and grins broadly.

'Marianne's a great lass an' no mistakin'. . . . deserves better than a friggin' matelot!'

He kisses the air in the direction of the photographs and then claps his hands.

'Right! I'm off for a shower then I reckon I've earnt a few beers!'

It is **2035**. Strange whooping noises and high-pitched, gargled screams echo down the passageway on Two Deck in the aft section. From a hatchway marked Three P Port a shadowy figure with long black hair, dressed only in a loincloth, feathers and beads emerges with wide, staring, unblinking eyes. The figure drops to its haunches, raises a double-bladed hatchet and lets out three piercing yelps:

'Yiiiiiiiiiiip! Yiiiiiiiiiiiip! Yiiiiiiiiiiiiip!'

Another figure emerges – this one with a single feather in its plaited hair and grotesquely painted with body and face paint. Then another appears with a headband and a glinting drawn dagger. They gather and as they wait for more of their band to squeeze through the narrow hatch they start a jerky, hopping, circular dance to the rhythm of an ape-like chant:

'Ooogh, ooogh, ooogh, ooogh! Ooogh, ooogh, ooogh, ooogh . . .'

Up on the flight deck, Micky Goble has taken over sentry duty. With his SA-80 assault rifle slung over his shoulders he stands in front of the closed hangar doors and leans against a lectern that supports the large, duty logbook in which he must record the events of his watch. From on top of the logbook he takes a white paper bag, spreads the top, and offers it to his fellow sentry, Wren Stephanie Wolstencroft.

'Sweet?'

'Oooh, thanks Micky.'

Gratefully, the small, plump Wren dips her hand into the bag, takes out a small, tightly wrapped rectangle and starts to unwrap it.

'Jesus!' says Goble 'Eight hours on a flamin' flight deck when everybody else has gone to get bolloxed . . .'

'Never mind, you'll get your chance tomorr . . . Micky – you bastard!' screams Wren Wolstencroft. 'This is a bloody condom!'

Half a dozen of the feathered, body-painted figures creep warily along the dimly lit passage on One Deck, past the wardroom and towards the stern of the ship. Behind them, struggling in vain, they drag two whimpering, pale-skinned captives dressed only in white lace underwear and stockings. The band moves silently and swiftly, but just as they reach the airlock doors that open to the flight deck a voice rings out behind them.

'Intruders stop!'

They spin round and from the dark shadows at the end of the passageway they see six guns raised threateningly towards them – five long-barrelled silver pistols and one rifle.

On the flight deck Wren Wolstencroft tosses the partially unwrapped condom back in the white paper bag of free-issue prophylactives that are always made available to any of the ship's company going ashore. Micky Goble watches her, shaking his head in disbelief.

'Hook, line an' bleedin' sinker!'

'Ha, ha. Very funny I'm sure.'

'Five more seconds and you would've been chewin' it! An' I don't think the M.o.D supply the flavoured variety . . . !'

'Yiiiiiiiiiiiiiiip! Yiiiiiiiiiiiiiiiip! Yiiiiiiiiiiiiiiiiiip!'

The feathered figures rush screaming on to the flight deck dragging their hostages behind them. Close behind are their heavily armed pursuers.

'Hands up!' they shout in unison. 'You can't escape! Hands up or we shoot!'

'Yiiiiiiiiiiiiiiiip! Yiiiiiiiiiiiiiiiip! Oooogh, ooogh, ooogh, ooogh . . . !'

Micky Goble moves quickly and purposefully towards one of the scantily dressed hostages who has fallen to the deck panting.

'Oi! Get off my deck. An' by the way your left tit's slipped!'

The hostage springs up, thrusts a hand down a deflated D cup and pulls out a soft red balloon.

'Oh, no! I've got a leak!'

'It may seem like a stupid question,' says Goble casually, 'but why are you silly bastards dressed up as cowboys and Indians? And, I realize this may be an even stupider question, but why have you got two Royal Marines dressed up in women's underwear?'

'We're going into town,' says a cowboy, holstering his Rowdey Yates repeat action six-shooter.

'Oh! All is now abundantly clear!' retorts Goble with dramatic over-emphasis.

'We jus' felt like a laugh,' says an Irish Indian chief called 'Mickey' Rooney, peering through long, straggly pigtails made of frayed rope dyed with boot polish. 'We thought we'd go out as a mess an' do summink different – you know, dress up like. So I'm the chief, these are me braves, them's the fuckin' palefaces and those two are their whores who we captured. Come on you lot. Let's go. See you Mick!'

Cowboys and Indians file past the flight deck sentries and head down the gang-way to the unsuspecting clubs and pubs of Souda Bay. The last to go down are the marines, Spider Webb and Chippy Norton, with their bright red pouting lips, mascara, suspenders and padded bras.

'The Royal Marines . . . lean, mean fightin' machines!' muses Goble out loud. 'Look and bleedin' wonder Steph.'

Lighting a cigarette he goes over to lean against the rails and survey the unlikely scene on the jetty – marauding, yelping, half-naked sailors waving wooden hatchets being chased by Lone Ranger look-alikes and Royal Marine commandos bursting out of borrowed, Wrens' lingerie.

'Makes you proud to be British, don't it?!'

It is 2330. Having soon discovered that Souda Bay after dark has little to offer the discriminating reveller, most members of the ship's company have found their way to the nearby resort of Khania. This pretty, historic port town, built on top of ancient Kydonia, spreads all the way down to the edge of a small harbour full of colourful Cretan fishing and sailing boats. Along the harbour front are brightly lit, open-air restaurants, cafés, and bars whereas further back, in the winding narrow alleys that lead up the hill, there is a multitude of clubs, pubs and discos.

Captain Rapp, Russ Harding and Chay Robertson, the master-at-arms, have taken seats at an open-air restaurant right on the water's edge. The two officers have ordered taramasalata to start, followed by lobster and prawn Creole and are waiting for the master-at-arms to make his choice from the menu. He is tempted by one of the more familiar dishes such as fish and chips, but thinks better of it.

'Very good choice sah's. I think I'll have the same. Yes, indeed. Very tasty I'm sure.'

Further along the curved harbour frontage, outside a bar dotted with green and white umbrellas, Petty Officers Tony Lilley and 'Kiwi' Belben, with more than a few beers inside them, have decided it would be a very good idea to pulverize each other.

'Come on then! Come on you wanker! I'll knock yer fuckin' block off!'

'Oh really . . . ?!'

'Yeah! You bleedin' space cadet!'

'Just fuckin' try it . . . !'

Belben swings a left hook. Lilley ducks and counters with an uppercut. Belben side-steps and rallies with a right jab. Lilley dodges and moves in for a bear hug. The two, locked in a twirling, crushing embrace, go red, then purple, then stop.

'Bugger this for a game of sailors!' says Lilley exhausted.

'Yeah. Bollocks to it. Want a beer?'

'I'll have a lager mate.'

A hundred yards away, in one of the narrow side-streets behind the harbour front, at a club called The Trapeze, a few of the officers have joined some junior rates for a drinking and bopping session. In the centre of the room, hanging seductively about 6 feet above the dance floor, is a black trapeze. Currently on it, hanging upside down by his legs, and trying to drink a bottle of San Miguel beer to the thumping rhythm of 'Celebration' by Kool and the Gang, is Nick Cooke-Priest, the flight observer. Fellow officers and ratings are cheering him on whilst Jerry Barnbrook, the flight commander, has decided to make the feat a little more test-ing by giving the inverted sub-lieutenant a hearty shove from behind. Cooke-Priest splutters, sprays everyone beneath him and is instantly dragged to the ground in a fit of helpless laughter. Meanwhile someone, having deliberately poured Drambuie over the length of the bar counter, has set light to it. White tongues of flame dance along the marble surface as sailors shout and sing their approval. Tumblers of flaming Drambuie, called 'Thunder and Lightnings', are now passed around a group of officers at the bar – the rule is that the flames have to be blown out and the alcoholic fumes inhaled before the liquid is drunk in one, rapid and unhesitating swallow. The officers line up and one by one step forward to throw the blazing liqueur to the back of their throats.

'Go on sir! One swift movement remember!' shouts a leading stoker hanging from the vacated trapeze.

'Three, two, one . . .' Gulp. '. . . Hurray!

'Three, two, one . . .' Gulp. '. . . Hurray!'

'Three, two, one . . .' Gulp. '. . . Hurray!'

Lieutenant Keith Blount steps forward to take his turn. He grasps the flame-topped tumbler and stands poised . . .

'Three, two, one . . .' 'Oh, fuck!' '. . . HURRAY!!'

A cheer of enormous approval goes up as a slight hesitation in technique sends the burning liquid everywhere except down the lieutenant's throat.

'Christ almighty!' says Blount, cupping his hand to a deeply reddened mouth. 'I've fucking burnt myself!'

All around him sailors and officers howl with delight.

Not far away at a small, waterside taverna, a group of stokers and gunners are hap-pily sipping ice-cold lager and tucking into huge plates of exotic Mediterranean fruits. Suddenly they become aware of some excitement on the far side of the harbour.

'What's going on over there, shipmates?' says a stoker levering a huge piece of melon into his mouth.

'Can't really see . . .' replies a gunner sucking noisily on a sweet fig and reaching for a bunch of grapes, '. . . just a lot of laughing and shouting.'

'It's not our lot is it?' says another stoker looking over as he sinks his teeth into a succulent prickly pear.

'Nah,' says the gunner, who has stood up to have a better look. 'Not ours. It looks like some gi-normous women have stripped off to their undies and are jumping into the harbour.'

He sits down to resume his attack on the grapes.

'Not our girls. Too bleedin' big . . .'

The two drenched Royal Marines hoist up their knickers, adjust their bras and get ready once more to take a header into the harbour. An audience of inebriated cowboys and Indians shouts slurred encouragement.

'Go on Schpider. Jump, jump, jump, jump, jump . . . !'

'In yer go Chippy old son. One more time for England. GO! GO! GO!'

Waiting only to thump their chests and yodel like a couple of transvestite Tarzans, the marines hold hands, run, leap and plunge into the glassy, black water of the harbour. They bob up laughing and swim back to the edge. As they pull themselves out, dripping in their now transparent lace underwear, they come face to face with an elderly gentleman of military bearing who has stepped forward to confront them.

'Am I led to believe that you two are Royal Marines?!'

'Er . . . yeah.'

'By jove! Real bootnecks!'

'Eh?'

'Did you hear that, Ruth? Booties. By jingo!' says the elderly gentleman, turning to his wife who has clearly decided to sit this one out on a nearby wall.

'Yes dear,' she replies resignedly. 'Very nice dear.'

'Delighted to meet you both,' he says, offering his hand to the soaked marines. 'My name's Gwyn. I'm from Cardiff and I used to be a Royal!'*

'You were a bootneck?' says Spider shaking the Welshman's hand warmly.

'Ah, well! Back in the Dark Ages don't you know! And your names?'

'I'm Spider and this is Chippy.'

'Splendid!'

'Were you in the war sir?'

'Oh yes, rather. Engagements all over the place. Got torpedoed off Sicily, went and got sand in my boots in North Africa, bit of stuff in the Dutch Islands. Never

---

* Royal Marine. For more naval slang, see Jackspeak, page 212. See also The Royal Marines, page 119.

got here though – it was all occupied by the Germans you see. Joined up when I was seventeen. My father hated it. Most wonderful time I ever had!'

'It's bloody marvellous this bootneck thing,' says Spider Webb, looking up at the tall ex-marine with misty-eyed admiration.

'Yeah, and only bootnecks can understand it,' agrees Chippy Norton. 'It doesn't matter about age does it? Once a bootneck always a bootneck.'

'So, you chaps are with the frigate up at Souda Bay eh? Sailors still the scum they always were?'

'You said it sir! And bloody Jack reckons himself so superior.'

'Well, remind them of a bit of history. Tell them that marines were originally put on board ships to protect the officers from the undisciplined rabble that had been press-ganged into the crew. In those days the marines were the only professionals on board.'

'Still are sir.'

'I say, Ruth,' says the old man turning to his wife, 'I wish you'd get one of these frilly bra numbers like this young man's wearing . . .'

It is **0140**. Still on guard on the flight deck, Micky Goble lights the last cigarette in his packet, inhales deeply and blows smoke at the stars.

'It's gettin' a bit parky Steph.'

'Yeah, want a cuppa!'

'I'd kill for one.'

'I'll go down the Wrennerie and get us some.'

'Stout woman!'

Wren Wolstencroft heads into the ship on her tea run just as Bob Hawkins, returning from a night in Khania, climbs a little unsteadily up the gangway. At the top he stands briefly to attention before stepping on to the deck where Goble salutes him by coming to attention himself and slapping his rifle held diagonally across his chest.*

'How's it going Leading Seaman Goble?'

'OK thanks sir. They're coming back in dribs and drabs.'

'Any officers back, yet?'

'Oh, yes. Sub-Lieutenant Cooke-Priest came back a little while ago with the doctor, Lieutenant Newton, looking a little the worse for wear. Somehow they

---

* When officers return on board it is a custom of the service that they should salute the White Ensign which embodies the person of Her Majesty. That mark of respect is returned by the quartermaster or, in his absence, the bosun's mate who will either salute the officer in the conventional manner or, if armed, will slap his rifle in such a way that his hands are close to his weapon.

managed to do the tango all the way up the gangway whilst singing "I Did It My Way". For some reason the Doc insisted on salutin' the ship's bell and then I thought he was goin' to collapse but Sub-Lieutenant Cooke-Priest helped him inside.'

'Oh dear. I don't think I'm quite that bad am I?'

'Positively sober in comparison, sir.'

'No other dramas then?'

'Well, we had a right one earlier on when weapons engineering mechanic Carfew returned.'

'What's he been up to?'

'Listen to this. I wrote it up . . . you'll love it!'

Goble reaches for the logbook, opens it and leafs through to the relevant page.

' "At 2150 WEM Carfew returned to the ship after sustaining an injury to the anal region. Apparently, while ashore Carfew sat on a wall where a metal spike . . .'

'Oh, no!' grimaces Hawkins with painful expectation of the inevitable.

'. . . "shot up his bum." '

'Poor bugger!'

'. . . "With profuse bleeding he was taken to the sickbay and treated by MAQ* Jacqui Quant." I bet she was over the blinkin' moon with that little injury.'

'Bit of excitement for you anyway.'

'Well, the officer of the day was informed so there's nothin' for me to worry about now. It's more WEM Carfew's problem than mine.'

'What time are you off duty?'

'0830 sir.'

'Good luck.'

'Yeah, they'll all start rolling back soon. And I mean "rolling".'

'Good night.'

'Night sir.'

Bob Hawkins goes off to his bunk. Goble watches his breath condense in the chill night air.

Leading Seaman Micky Goble is in some respects an unlikely looking sailor. Chubby and balding, he walks with the rolling shuffle of a veteran prop forward, sports the beer belly of a veteran hooker and talks with the nasal twang of a scrum half who has had his nose kicked once too often. But looks can be deceiving because, apart from being a first-rate radarman, Goble is an electric personality with a dynamic sense of humour, and a veritable superman when it comes to building and sustaining morale. If he was not a committed matelot it would be

---

* Medical assistant (Queen Alexandra's Royal Naval Nursing Service).

easy to see him succeeding as a stand-up comic on the tough Northern club-cir-cuit, giving as good as he got and a regular encore. But Micky Goble is a commit-ted matelot – for him the navy became a vocation.

'When I left school at sixteen in 1981 I did a number of bizarre jobs from gravediggin', to hod-carryin' until I landed the ultimate mellow number workin' at a monastery. It was Prinknash Abbey in Gloucestershire and I ran a small market garden that sold fruit, veg, and flowers. I loved it and the monks were great – especially Brother Harry who listened to the Sex Pistols while he did his gilt let-terin'. But then I just woke up one day and said to myself, "Hold everythin' I'm goin' to join the navy!". My father had been in the mob and my brother too – in fact Russell was on the *Ardent* when she went down in the Falklands although he bobbed up eventually and came home. So I went to the recruitin' office where they told me if I didn't have a sense of humour then I might as well forget the navy as a career. I thought "Great! Sounds like a good laugh!" That was twelve years ago and it's been fantastic, though now of course, we're all waitin' to hear about redun-dancies which is worryin' me sick. But they were right about the sense of humour. You've got to laugh or you'd go bonkers cooped up in a tin box with a load of loonies, morons and imbeciles – and that's just the officers!'

Micky Goble rubs his hands in anticipation as Wren Wolstencroft returns with a steaming hot mug of tea. He takes a grateful sip of the warming brew but then a noise on the jetty steals his attention.

'Oh no. That's all I need!'

'Who is it?'

'Bloody sailors! That's who it is.'

Goble and Wolstencroft look down on the jetty and watch as a crowd of their singing, swaying shipmates try and negotiate the steep gangway.

'Look at that!' says Goble with a smile. 'Here is your classic example of Jack on shore – the wobbly man!'

'They'll never make it up here,' says Wolstencroft.

'They'd better or we'll have to report them. My rule is if they can make it up the gangway on their own steam, peg 'emselves in, and walk into the ship without fallin' over then they're OK. If not, then they go into the book and we get a sentry on 'em. It's for their own good, because otherwise they could roll over, be sick in their sleep and choke to death. And if they die then we're in the crap. Right, this first lot looks like they're goin' to make it up here . . . Evenin' all.'

Two sailors, arm in arm and attempting a duet of 'Together We Are Beautiful', meander over to a board of names at the back of the flight deck to stick a peg in by theirs to indicate they are back on the ship.

'Together . . . we are . . . beautiful! You must agree . . . we're beautiful . . . !'

'Micky!'

'OK guys, better get below . . .'

'I can't find my name!'

'It's there you blind git! Look!'

'That's not my name!'

'Really! Well, it was this mornin'.'

'I think . . . we're beautiful! Oh so beautiful . . . beautiful!'

'Go on get below or the officer of the day'll be up here.'

'We're pissed Mick!'

'You amaze and astound me. Now get the fuck below!'

Goble helps the sailors to peg in and then turns back towards the gangway to see Chippy Norton, in his now tattered women's underwear, trip off the gangway and reel haphazardly towards him.

'Micky! Do you want to suck my fuckin' tits or what?!'

'Oh, my life!'

'Don't you like me?'

'I think you're lovely mate.'

'No you don't!' shouts the marine running to the other side of the flight deck to climb astride the guardrail. 'I'm goin' to jump in!'

Goble sprints over and pulls the young marine back from the edge of the ship and a 40 foot fall into the lapping water. 'You ain't goin' anywhere Royal 'cept to yer bunk!'

'OK, OK. I'm goin'. Hey unhook me bra, Mick.'

'Micky! Come here quick!' shouts Wren Wolstencroft. 'This one's out cold!'

Goble hurries over just in time to see big Steve Whitter staggering up the gangway with an unconscious sailor slung over his shoulders.

'I'ts alright Mick. I've got 'im safe.'

'Looks like he needs a fuckin' embalmer!'

'He'll be alright.'

'Get him down to his bunk. I'll alert the duty rating in his mess to look after him.'

'Cheers mate.'

Whitter carries his groaning burden into the ship as Goble reaches for an internal phone.

'Hello . . . yeah, it's the flight deck . . . Whitter's comin' down with someone for you . . . yeah, absolutely rat-arsed! Completely bolloxed . . . keep your eyes on him alright . . . yes, every fifteen minutes go and make sure he's on his side and

DRINK AND DRUNKENNESS

'Popping the cork' has recently been reintroduced as an acceptable means of relaxation for junior ratings: wine may now be taken on the lower deck along with beer and cider. There is a sense of *déjà vu*, however: sailors were living on wine, beer and grog 500 years ago. This was because basic victuals were so bad, and water so foul after a few days at sea, that alcohol was the only salvation. At the start of a voyage, beer would be the staple. Normal stocks lasted for about a month, even when issued at the rate of up to a gallon per man per day. When the last of the beer was gone, captains would authorize the issue of wine. One half-pint of wine was deemed the equivalent of the beer issue.

When it ran out, rum – 'grog' – was issued. By 1747 the noon measure was fixed at one gill of navy rum mixed with three gills of water (and, sometimes, lemon juice and sugar). The supper allowance was the same without the frills. One gill was enough to render mellow most seamen, but many saved the lunchtime tot till supper.

It was 1957 before Section 28 of the Naval Discipline Act defined a person as drunk if he is 'unfit to be entrusted with his duty or with any duty which he might reasonably expect to be called upon to perform or behaves in a disorderly manner or in a manner likely to bring discredit upon Her Majesty's Service. Every person subject to this Act who is drunk whether on duty or not shall be liable to imprisonment for a term not exceeding two years or any less punishment authorised by this Act.'

No one goes to prison for being drunk, even on duty, but the power is an indication of just how seriously the abuse of alcohol by those on duty is viewed. Attitudes to shoreside drinking are rather more relaxed but, even so, someone who brings discredit on the service through irresponsible behaviour when he or she is out for a drink will be firmly disciplined – usually by a significant fine.

Those found drunk on duty are never tolerated. For ratings, reduction in rank and detention for 28 days or more are almost inevitable. Officers who get drunk on board a warship can face a court martial which may result in fines of the order of £700 to £1000 and if an officer is drunk on duty he or she will usually be dismissed from the Royal Navy.

not on his back. If you have a problem let me know and I'll have to get hold of the officer of the day . . . cheers mate.'

Goble replaces the phone with a smile. 'He was skunk drunk that bloke, absolutely helpless . . . Hopefully that'll be me tomorrow night!'

It is **0335**. Smiling broadly and groaning softly Surgeon-Lieutenant Richard Newton is lying flat on his back on the floor in the wardroom. Kneeling over him is the flight observer, Nick Cooke-Priest, carefully putting a fresh blade into a Gillette Contour razor. He is talking to the doctor in soothing, relaxing tones.

'There, there. Go to sleep, Richard. Go sleepy-byes . . .'

'Worragh wooooriggh bluggggh,' replies the young doctor with conviction.

Carefully, Cooke-Priest leans over the supine medico and, as a punishment for his failure to stay vertical after a drinking session, gently starts to shave off his eyebrows.

'Ding dong Doc!'

'Wiiiiirggggh aaariiiigh huuurra . . .'

DAY Wednesday	DATE 5	MONTH October	YEAR 1994
PLACE	Souda Bay, Crete		
POSITION	35°00'N 25°50'E		

SHIPS LOG Relatively busy morning. Hull checked by divers and stores brought on board. Captain ashore. Phone lines connected. Afternoon and evening most of ship's company ashore.

It is **0753**. Lieutenant Steve Boynton, as officer of the day, takes his position next to the first lieutenant and the captain on the flight deck. They stand at ease in a line facing the ensign staff at the stern where a signalman stands ready with a folded White Ensign – the St George's cross with a Union flag in the top left quadrant. At the bow, another signalman stands ready with the Union Jack.* This is the

---

* Strictly speaking the Union Jack should only be referred to as such if it is being flown from a jack staff at the bow of a ship. At all other times it should properly be referred to as the 'Union flag'.

ritual of 'colours', the ceremonial morning hoisting of the ship's flags that happens whenever and wherever she is in port.*

It is 0755. The shrill whistle of a bo'sun's pipe pierces the morning stillness. A signalman at midships hoists a green and yellow pennant, known as the 'prep flag', to the top of the main mast. This is the signal for everybody involved in colours to close up** and means that there is five minutes to go before the ensign and jack are to be hoisted. The duty watch reports to the officer of the day: 'Five minutes to colours, sir.'

It is 0759. The signalman lowers the prep flag to half way down the halyard and gives it several jerks. This is the signal that there is one minute to colours. The duty watch reports again: 'One minute to colours, sir'. The three officers come smartly to attention.

It is 0800. The prep flag is lowered completely which prompts the final report to the officer of the day: 'Colours, sir.' Steve Boynton replies, 'Make it so.' At the corner of the flight deck a rating strikes the ship's bell eight times after which the order is given: 'Pipe the Still.' One long, even call is made on the bo'sun's pipe and the ensign and jack are hoisted as the officers salute. Once at the top of their staffs the flags are both tied off and another pipe pipes the 'Carry on'. On the last note the officers bring down their salute and the colour party is dismissed.

The ship is now ready to start the day.

It is 0905. The telephone engineers have been aboard and connected the ship to two outside telephone lines. One of the lines has been connected to a telephone outside the wardroom and is reserved for official business and officers' use. The other line has been fed to a telephone located outside on the upper deck and is for the general use of ratings.

It is on the upper deck telephone that Wren (Radar) Roni Whittaker is presently dialling 044, the international code for Britain, followed by 752, the area code for Plymouth. She completes the number, hears a ring and waits impatiently for someone to answer.

'Hello, Devonport, how can I help you?'

---

* The flags are struck every evening at sunset.
** Take your positions in readiness, for example; 'Close up for Action Stations'.

'Can I speak to Leading Cook Britter, please? In HMS *Drake*.'

'*Hold on a minute please . . .*'

Roni Whittaker phones her boyfriend whenever she can, especially now after four months away at sea. She has found it difficult being a woman on board a warship and is longing for home and her friends, especially Paul Britter. It is not the work in the op's room she minds, or even the constant scrubbing and cleaning, but it is the unforgiving male environment that has begun to erode her morale and undermine her confidence.

'I come from Portsmouth so I have always lived close to the navy. Then when they announced that Wrens were going to sea I thought that would be something different so I applied. My first ship was the *Fearless*, which was alright because it wasn't operational, but the *Brilliant* has been completely different. Because we are on deployment the workload is much greater and you always feel that you are resented by a lot of the men. I think they feel this is a man's world and that we are in the way. It'll take a long time for them to get used to Wrens at sea – if ever. My boyfriend, Paul, was actually on this ship – that's how we met. Having him on board was terrible. It was one of the hardest things I have ever had to cope with because the environment of a warship doesn't allow a show of emotions. When we were on board we just had to be regular shipmates, no different from anybody else. Then, on shore we could be normal and "lovey-dovey" for a while, but then the next day back to being shipmates again. It was pulling me in two. I actually prefer it this way with him being far away. I feel closer to him this way.'

'Hello.'

'Hi! It's me!'

'*Roni! I'm so pleased it's you. When did you get in?*'

'Oh, we got in yesterday but there were no phones until this morning. I've got all your letters . . .'

'*I've got all yours as well. I'm really missing you.*'

'I'm missing you too.'

'*Listen, you know my sister Claire has been going to the fertility clinic?*'

'Yeah.'

'*She's had four pregnancy tests now and they're all positive.*'

'Oh, excellent! I'm so pleased for her. Send her my love.'

'*I will.*'

'I got your letter about going there for Christmas . . .'

It is **1056**. Nick Cooke-Priest is dialling a number on the officers telephone as Bob Hawkins comes up behind him.

'You going to be long Nick? I need to call Joan and the boys.'

'No, I hope not.'

'God you look terrible!'

'Yes, I feel quite atrocious, thank you.'

'What time did you go to bed last night?'

'I haven't the faintest idea. All I know is I had far too many Drambuies. Not as many as the Doc though . . . Have you noticed his rather tufted eyebrows?'

'Hello,' says a woman's voice from the telephone receiver.

'Hold on Bob,' says Cooke-Priest, putting his hand over the mouthpiece. 'I've got through.'

'OK. After you with the blower. Then you should put yourself out of your misery with a bullet old chap.'

'I might have to after this call, actually . . . Er, hello. Is that you Georgie?'

'Nick!?'

'Hi! How are you?'

'Why the hell haven't you phoned before?!'

'Ah, well . . . you see, it's been, mmmm, really busy. I was going to phone in Bari, but we had to sail early because mmmmm, you know, the er, the orders changed and everything. And, er, yes, that's it really – we had to sail early . . . So, how are you keeping?'

'Hold on! I want to know, how long were you there in Bari?'

'About two days but I, er, had lots of duties and things so, er . . . how's work going?'

'Two days!'

'Eh?'

'Two whole days and you didn't phone once!'

'I did try actually, I did. You were engaged.'

'So, why didn't you keep trying? And what about writing? How about a letter?!'

'Absolutely! I'm in the middle of one at the moment actually. A really long one. . .'

It is **1103**. Micky Goble has got to the front of the queue for the flight deck telephone and after two attempts has got through to a number in a village in Gloucestershire.

'Hello, Dad!'

Whenever Goble gets a chance he phones the father with whom he still lives when he is in England. They are very close, especially since his mother died in 1993. At that time he was serving in the Gulf on HMS *Brazen* and he remembers only too well the terrible day he got the news that his mother had fallen seriously ill and that he had to return home immediately. Overcoming his intense fear of flying he took off in the ship's Lynx helicopter to shore and then flew home only to arrive too late to say goodbye.

'Hello son! How are you? Where are you?'

'Fine thanks. I'm in Crete. How's everyone at home? How's our Russ?'

'He's fine. Doing nicely. Working on his house.'

'How's Chipper?'

'He's very well. Always looking around for you of course.'

'So he's alright then? Getting his walks?'

'Yes, yes. Every day. By the way, are you going back to the Gulf next year?'

'Yeah, October 95 in theory. 'Cept I might be on Civvie Street by then.'

'What?'

'The Second Sea Lord came on board and basically told me to get another job – and a hell of a lot of the others in the op's department. Apparently, by the end of 1996 they're goin' to batter us down by 50 per cent.'

'Oh dear.'

'Needless to say I'm pretty gutted.'

'Don't worry about it too much Michael. Things change you know. Hey, listen – I'm thinking of coming down to Plymouth to meet you when you come home.'

'Really! That'd be great Dad. We're comin' in in the mornin' so come down the night before . . .'

'I'll have to find some digs.'

'Go and stay at the Clipper in Union Street. Go in and make yourself known to Geoff – big blond bloke with a moustache. Tell 'im who you are and he will look after you . . .'

It is **1110**. Bob Hawkins smiles broadly as his wife answers the phone in their house in Devon.

'Hello.'

'Hello darling!'

'Hello darling! Hey Cameron, Jamie – it's Daddy on the phone. Bob talk to the boys first. They're so excited. Here's Jamie.'

'Alright . . .Hello, Jamie!'

Bob Hawkins is constantly torn between his love of the navy and his love of his family. He sometimes finds it difficult to reconcile his highly developed sense of duty and loyalty to his ship with his deep-felt concern for the welfare and happiness of his wife and two small sons.

'Being away from the family is something every sailor has to deal with in their own way. In some ways I prefer it when I am really stretched at work because then I am so concentrated that I don't have time to dwell on how much I miss my family. My wife and I have got used to dealing with the seperation – you know, because we are both adults, but I do miss my two boys very painfully at times. I will always remember the first time my sons ever cried when I went away and I don't mind admitting that I did exactly the same thing when my back was turned. It was a very poignant moment to say the least. But, that's navy life.'

'Hello Daddy!'

'Hello sweetheart. How are you? What have you been doing?'

'We went to buy a toy. Mummy bought us a toy. An Action Man. Then we had lunch at McDonalds. I had Chicken McNuggets. Cameron had a cheeseburger. I don't like cheeseburgers. When are you coming home?'

'At the end of November darling.'

'Is that soon?'

'Well, it's before Christmas.'

'Oh, good! Here's Cameron now . . .'

'OK. Bye-bye Jamie. Love you . . . Hello Cameron.'

'Hello Daddy! I did badminton.'

'Hello darling. You did badminton? That's good. But how's your maths?'

'I did hockey as well. I scored a goal.'

'That's good, but how is the maths going . . . ?'

'Here's Mummy now. Love you, Daddy!'

'Love you too, Cameron . . .'

'Hello Bob.'

'Hello darling.'

'So, how are things with you?'

'Incredibly busy in the op's room. We've just been in Montenegro which is non-stop surveillance. We're now in Crete for a few days before we go out into the Otranto Straits for boarding operations for about ten days. That'll be absolute non-stop as well. Still, with this experience under my belt I should be a step nearer to my own command.'

'That would be marvellous darling, wouldn't it? Oh, by the way I had a thing from your insurance people about your No Claims Bonus. And we seem to have a bit of damp in the hallway . . .'

Chapter Five

WATCHMAN NINE ZERO

DAY *Saturday*	**DATE** *8*	**MONTH** *October*	**Year** *1994*

PLACE *Southern Ionian Sea*

POSITION At **1200** *36°06′N 22°47′E* At **2359** *37°58′N 20°13′E*

DISTANCE TRAVELLED midnight to midnight *242.43 nautical miles*

SHIPS LOG. Sailed from Souda Bay. Fast passage north to Otranto. Stopped for hands to bathe. Passage to Area overnight. Weapon State Olly.

It is **1245**. The bow of the ship is cutting through the white-capped waters of the Ionian Sea at a rate of 22 knots on a northerly heading. We are making good time to the Straits of Otranto where we are due to take control of Area Ethel at first light tomorrow morning. Once in area the *Brilliant* will take her place in a line of NATO warships that permanently guard the narrow straits between Italy and Albania, enforcing the trade embargo against Serbia and the arms embargo against all the countries of former Yugoslavia.

Although not as tense as patrolling in Area Iceman with its constant risk of missile attack, standing guard over Ethel will be exhausting, taxing and unremitting as every merchant ship passing through the straits has to be monitored and many actually intercepted, boarded and searched.

The *Brilliant* departed the jetty at Souda Bay this morning at precisely 0802. The ship's company were, to a man and a woman, sorry to leave. Everybody seemed to enjoy Crete with all it had to offer a shipload of exhausted British sailors: warm weather; good food; good drink and friendly people. There were no arrests by the local police or street fights to deal with so the master-at-arm's temper remained unperturbed and the ship's lock up undisturbed. But everybody is now looking not only a little jaded from their merry-making but also utterly forlorn at being back at sea – something that has not gone unnoticed by the captain who has called the first lieutenant to his cabin.

'Russ, everyone's looking so incredibly washed out and miserable . . .'

'Yes sir. A combination of "the day after the night before" and being back at the coal-face I think, sir.'

'Unquestionably. That's why I was just looking out at the sea-state. There are a few breaking crests out here but I reckon it would be pretty calm nearer to land. Any sharks about . . . ?'

It is **1250**. Russ Harding picks up the microphone to the ship's central broadcast system:

'Good morning. First Lieutenant speaking. As most of you realize the weather up in the Adriatic is starting to deteriorate with the passing of the summer so it is likely the conditions are going to get a little colder and rougher than we have been used to for a while. However, for now the weather remains good and the sea calm. So, it is intended, in about half an hour, when we are in the lee side of the island of Kitra, to stop the ship for a "hands to bathe" . . .'

It is **1325**. The ship has come to a stop in the middle of a gently swelling, dark blue sea. The big, rope scrambling nets have been secured over the port side and the Gemini rubber speedboat with its engine running and carrying two coxswains has been lowered carefully into the water from the midship boat deck. Having pulled away from the *Brilliant* in a wide arc it has now taken up a position just off the port bow from where its crew waits and watches with great expectation.

Russ Harding, from his position on the port bridge wing and stirring a cup of tea, looks around and checks all is ready before making the announcement everybody has been waiting for over the upper deck tannoy:

'This is the First Lieutenant speaking. Hands to bathe may commence!'

All the way along the port side of the ship sailors, Wrens, chiefs, petty officers and officers step to the edge and peer down to the water 30 feet below. From the bridge wing itself, some 50 feet above the water, 'Bosnia' Bob Hawkins climbs on top of the enclosing bulwark, curls his toes over the edge and holds both his arms directly out in front of him, palms down. After a pause of no more than two seconds the principal warfare officer lets out the piercing rebel yell of 'Yaba daba doo!' and hurls himself headfirst off the ship in a plunging, endless dive towards the lapping waters far, far below. Everybody watches in wonder as the plummeting lieutenant-commander disappears into a frothy white explosion of sea spray before they themselves start to jump, leap, spring, skip and dive lemming-like towards the beckoning waves.

'Hands to bathe' is a bizarre naval tradition that temporarily transforms a warship into a diving platform in the interest of ship's morale. Today, with the

Mediterranean summer on the wane and in an attempt to cheer up a hungover ship with a bad case of back-to-work blues, the command has made the considered decision to delay passage for an hour so that everybody can enjoy a last burst of the holiday mood. It seems to have been a wise decision.

Sailors and Wrens of all ranks hurtle into the briny whilst others, dripping and hair-flattened, climb back up the scrambling nets with the sole purpose of leaping straight back in again; from behind the Sting Ray torpedo tubes a yodelling cook jumps off in full working uniform, complete with white chef's hat; from the upper deck gangway a line of seven stokers joined hand in hand take a running, shrieking jump over the edge; and in the water below a circle of bobbing sailors look up in terror as Big Steve Whitter holds his nose, shuts his eyes and launches into space from just in front of the 30 mm cannon. Everybody is laughing.

Everybody, that is, except the coxswains in the Gemini, who keep a vigilant watch on all those in the water in case of emergencies, and sharpshooter Kiwi Belben posted on the upper deck with a high velocity rifle to look out for sharks.

Micky Goble watches everything from the for'ard Sea Wolf missile deck sipping tea from his purple mug and shaking his head with incredulity.

'You wouldn't catch me doin' that – no way! If I can't touch the bottom I'm not interested. There are things in that water that crawl up your bum and have wild parties and there is nothin' you can do about it. No fear! Me? I'm happy to stay up here havin' a fag, a cup of tea and mellowin' out.'

From the bridge door Captain James Rapp watches on with satisfaction, knowing that the mood of his ship will be much improved and so, therefore, will her efficiency for the hard tasks ahead.

DAY *Sunday*	DATE *9*	MONTH *October*	YEAR *1994*
PLACE	*Otranto Straits, Adriatic Sea*		
POSITION	Classified		

DISTANCE TRAVELLED midnight to midnight *294.18 nautical miles*

SHIPS LOG. *Fast passage to Area Ethel. Small Albanian powerboat in middle of ocean had run out of fuel – suspicious. Gave assistance but informed Albanian authorities. Assumed all duties in Area Ethel mid-morning after relieving HDMS Olfert Fischer.*

It is 0758. The ship is approaching the southern boundary of Area Ethel and has stopped to investigate a small powerboat adrift and without power. There is no radio contact but frantic hand signals from the three men aboard the wave-buffeted vessel indicate that help is wanted. This is not the first time the *Brilliant* has had to stop and help stricken powerboats, essentially pleasure craft, stranded in the middle of the Adriatic, sometimes far outside their own territorial waters. The suspicion is always that they are up to something illegal, probably smuggling, but no contraband has ever been found.

The further suspicion is that once they have broken down they realize they are probably going to be found by a Sharp Guard warship and so they throw anything illegal overboard.

The powerboat now on our port beam is without power and drifting fast to the south. The *Brilliant* turns to port in a tight circle in order to keep abreast of the lame vessel.

Captain Rapp watches the procedure through his binoculars from the bridge and talks impatiently to Russ Harding:

'I'm fed up stopping to help these chaps. They're obviously up to no good but we'll never be able to prove it. Send the Pacific over with some men and see what their problem is.'

'Yes sir. They're probably Albanian as we're just inside Albanian territorial waters.'

The Pacific rubber speedboat, larger and more powerful than the Gemini, is lowered by ropes and pulleys from the boat deck into a fast-running and deeply swelling sea. With a throbbing roar from its powerful outboard engine it cuts a white frothing swathe through the waves before picking up enough speed to skim the crests in a leaping, thumping and soaring semi-flight towards the dead powerboat. The *Brilliant* continues to encircle the stranded craft at about 6 knots.

The captain, still looking through his binoculars, sees the Pacific pull alongside the powerboat and then watches as the crew of both boats gesticulate animatedly towards each other. It is no more than a minute before the Pacific is heading back. Moments later the news is radioed up to the bridge that the craft is out of petrol but seems empty of cargo.

'Right,' says the captain. 'Send them over fifty gallons of fuel and a boarding officer. They're still just in Albanian territorial waters and I bet they're up to mischief, so I want to get sufficient information to be able to provide a comprehensive sit. rep. to the authorities. I want to know nationality and some idea of what they say they're doing, where they have been and where they're going.'

'Yes sir,' replies the first lieutenant.

It is **0816**. The Pacific revs its engine and launches itself once again towards the fuel-dry powerboat. This time Lieutenant Kevin Easterbrook is on board carrying translation cards in Italian, Albanian and Serbo-Croat. The tall, dark young weapons engineer, who doubles as a boarding officer, tucks his feet firmly into the heavy rubber toe straps, grasps the inboard safety lines tightly with both hands and braces himself against the impact of the bucking boat as it soars and crashes on to succeeding waves like an angry, kicking stallion at a Wild West rodeo. On the upper deck of the *Brilliant* quite a crowd have gathered to watch the unfolding drama. Everybody has got an opinion about what the broken boat has been up to:

'Obviously a smuggler. Why else would you get a powerboat this far out?'

'Yeah! Could be guns . . .'

'Nah! Reckon it's refugees comin' out of Albania.'

'Or just about anything going into Albania.'

'Or Italy. Albanians make a lot of fags. Could be black market fags . . .'

'Well we should arrest 'em or jus' leave 'em there to fend for theirselves. They're jus' small fry.'

'Don't be stupid! Mariners can't ignore other mariners in trouble – whatever they're up to.'

'I bet whatever they were carrying has gone over the side.'

'Hope it wasn't refugees then!'

'Hey, look there's another boat comin' up behind 'em!'

'It's another flamin' powerboat . . .'

It is **0838**. Kevin Easterbrook has returned and gone straight to the bridge to report to the captain:

'Enjoy your trip out there?' asks James Rapp with an amused grin.

'Yes, yes sir,' replies Easterbrook, soaked to the skin and shivering. 'It fairly wakes you up!'

'OK, so what did you find out?'

'Well sir, the three guys on the broken-down boat spoke no English at all – only Albanian. We passed over the petrol but that didn't seem to do any good and then this other boat came up. They were friends of theirs and they indicated that they had come to tow them back to Albania. There was no indication of anything suspicious on board sir, so we passed a line between the boats and let them go.'

'Right. You couldn't have done anything more as they are in their own waters. We have to help them if they're in trouble but it is a blessed waste of time. Right, Officer of the Watch – set lever 80. Half ahead both engines, please!'

Out on the boat deck Micky Goble is watching as the Pacific is winched back aboard. He then turns to look as the two Albanian powerboats linked by a length of rope disappear into the sea mist.

'Nah, they're up to somethin'! I ask you – pleasure boats comin' out here on a day like this? Look at it – overcast, the sea's all over the place and he's out for a blinkin' joy ride? Do me a favour! He's been carryin' guns or refugees or somethin' I'll bet. And now they're jus' takin' the flamin' piss askin' us for petrol to get home. That other geezer will probably tow him back in a minute to ask for his Green Shield stamps . . .!'

It is **1020**. Up on the bridge Russ Harding is overseeing the hand-over of Area Ethel to *Brilliant* from the Dutch warship *Olfert Fischer* whilst James Rapp climbs down the companionway from One Deck to Two Deck rubbing his left eye which is now watering badly.

Since waking up this morning he has felt some discomfort at the back of the eye which he has tried to ignore, but watching the Albanian powerboats through his binoculars seems to have aggravated it. Holding his left hand over the weeping eye he walks down the Two Deck passage towards the stern. He stops at a door marked 'Sickbay' and knocks.

Surgeon-Lieutenant Richard Newton opens the door.

'Oh, hello sir. Got a problem?'

'Left eye, Richard. Giving me absolute gyp,' says the captain.

'Come in sir, and let's have a look.'

'Thanks Richard.'

James Rapp enters the small but well-equipped surgery and sits on the consulting bed. Newton swings over an Anglepoise lamp and starts investigating the reddened surface of the severely bloodshot eye.

'It's certainly very pink and inflamed on the surface sir, and the pupil is very small. I just want to take a peek at the back of the eye.'

The doctor picks up his ophthalmoscope and looks through the captain's inflamed eye deep into the retina.

'Is it just itchy or does it actually hurt?'

'Well, it itches like the devil but it is beginning to hurt. Perhaps that's because I keep rubbing it.'

'Hmmm,' says the doctor, standing back from the captain and considering the symptoms.

'Just stand here, sir. Face that way. Now, using your good eye only, read that optician's chart on the wall from left to right.'

The captain holds his hand in front of his left eye and reads:

'P, T, U, N, X, F ,T, H, T, N, U, P, D, S, A, X, N, F, D, H, N, T, P, U, Z, A, D, X, F, B, H, T, A, Z.'

'Good. Now sir, read with your bad eye. Read it again, but this time from right to left in case you remember the sequence.'

'U, T, P, H, T, er P, X, S, O, P . . . now I'm starting to struggle . . . O, N . . . no, it's getting pretty blurred.'

'Right, sir. The most common cause of red eye, which is an infection in the outer layer of the eye, is acute conjunctivitis. But I think you may have something here which is a little more uncommon – anterior uveitis which is an inflammation of the front part of the eye.'

'Is that serious?' asks the captain.

'No, not if we catch it in time and treat it carefully. I'm going to give you some drops that will dilate your pupil together with some steroid drops that will dampen down the inflammation. Now, this might affect your ability to blink involuntarily, so to stop all the dust and specks from getting into your eye I'm also going to give you this . . .'

It is **1105**. James Rapp returns to the bridge and walks self-consciously to the commander's seat on the right of the main control console. He says nothing but everybody on the bridge stares in amazement at the melodramatic black patch now fixed firmly over his left eye. It has given his already stern features a distinctly crazed and piratical look that at first astounds but then starts to amuse. The yeoman, the quartermaster, the officer of the watch, the navigator, the bo'sun, the duty signalmen and the bridge-wing look-outs all turn their heads towards some distant point on the horizon and bite their lips hard as they sensibly decide that hysterical or uncontrolled laughter at this moment would not greatly advance their promotion prospects.

Russ Harding is the first to approach the captain with a sympathetic enquiry.

'Not good news then, sir?'

'Don't know yet Russ. Doctor's going to keep an eye on it, so to speak, and see if it gets any worse. If it does deteriorate I might have to hand over conduct of the ship to you. On the other hand the Nawab of Pataudi managed to play test cricket with one eye didn't he!?'

'I'm sure you'll be alright sir.'

'We'll see. Meanwhile I'm stuck with this blessed Captain Pugwash patch so they're all going to see me coming now.'

'I think it looks rather becoming actually sir.'

'It fits the part doesn't it?' grins Rapp.

'It certainly does. You'll frighten the life out of any ships we have to board.'

It is **2356**. The main lights along the passageway on One Deck have been switched off for the night. Only the red emergency lights remain on. Nobody is around and it is all quiet except for the constant low buzz of the air-conditioning system and the distant sound of the doctor playing his trombone in his cabin. Then, from the shadows just outside the regulators' office, a dark figure emerges and moves silently and slowly towards the main notice board, which displays a typed biography of the captain next to an official 10 x 8 inch colour photograph of him in full uniform.

It is in front of the photograph that the silent figure stops. . .

It is **2358**. The passageway on One Deck is deserted. The mysterious night-walker has disappeared. Everything is quiet. Everything is normal – or so it seems. An astute eye might recognize that the photograph of Captain James Campsie Rapp RN is not as it was two minutes ago. On the proud, chiselled face of the four-ringed high-flyer an indelible black marker has irresistibly added a gigantic black eye-patch, and, on his right shoulder, a maniacal beaky parrot.

DAY *Monday*	**DATE** *10*	**MONTH** *October*	**YEAR** *1994*
PLACE	*Area Ethel, Otranto Straits – near Albania*		
POSITION	*Classified*		

DISTANCE TRAVELLED midnight to midnight *171.03 nautical miles*

SHIPS LOG. Continued Ethel patrol. Boarded merchantman Klooga from Estonia carrying ballast and the Volgo-Balt 218 from the Ukraine carrying raw magnesite. Weather remains reasonable but noticeably fresher than when last in Area.

It is **0905**. The operations room is buzzing as usual. Although all three 'environments' [surface, sub-surface and air] are being monitored it is the surface picture of approaching shipping which is of most operational interest whilst in Ethel.

Around the room, the scanning, luminescent arms of a dozen radar screens constantly describe with absolute precision the tell-tale distribution, speed and heading of every ship within a 96 mile radius. At the central console Bob Hawkins is plotting the course of several ships at once.

Whereas in Area Iceman to the north the *Brilliant* helped to provide a ring of steel around Montenegro against the dedicated embargo violator as well as monitoring Yugoslavian naval and air activity, down here in Otranto the job is to sanitize all the shipping coming through the straits – the choke point of the Adriatic. All vessels coming through them are monitored to make sure they go where they say they are going, and any ship heading for Croatia or Slovenia is considered a potential violating vessel [PVV] and automatically stopped, boarded and searched to verify the cargo. Although the majority will be innocent carriers of things like cars, sheep, flour, gas, oil, citrus fruit and bananas there is always the danger that a few will try to conceal contraband such as arms and ammunition within their officially declared cargo.* Most boardings prove to be benign but there is always a latent threat to the boarding teams that carry out the searches. For this reason the *Brilliant* carries a Royal Marine protection party [RMPP] which consists of six highly trained marine commandos who are the first to go on to any ship being boarded. Their job is to secure that ship and to protect the naval search parties that will follow.

It is **0917**. James Rapp walks into the darkened op's room and over to Bob Hawkins who is still poring over his radar.

'Quiet night then, Bob,' says the captain squinting at the radar through his good eye.

'Yes sir, pretty quiet really. Although we heard of one incident over the radio when an Albanian craft, a certain powerboat of our recent acquaintance, got into trouble and required assistance.'

'Oh no. Not again!'

' 'Fraid so sir. Two ships in line went over to have a look as well as a maritime patrol aircraft. It actually left us wide open in this part of the straits. In the end a ferry called *San Sovino* picked up the stranded crew and is now on its way to Corfu with them. And that's not all sir. When we first located the powerboat it was in Albanian territorial waters but then it went into international waters and then it

---

* Eighteen months earlier the merchant ship MV *Jaguar Express* was boarded by Italian customs officials and arms were discovered. She was diverted to Brindisi and weeks afterwards they were still opening containers of rocket-propelled grenades, thousands of rounds of ammunition and other significant military hardware.

was blown into Greek territorial waters where it is still drifting and the USS *Deyo* has declared it a navigational hazard.'

'God, they're a menace those small boats.'

'Certainly are sir. How's the eye today sir?'

'Bloody painful. The doctor's going to have another look at it later. What have you got on the screen at the moment?'

'Well, right now we've got two PVVs. On track 5224 we've got the *Neptune* which is going to be boarded by *Wandelaar* and on track 5172, about 30 miles to our south, we have the *Klooga* on route to Rieka and declared to be in ballast. She's coming our way, sir so we've been asked to have a look at her when she gets here.'

'Fine. What's the ETA?'*

'I should say at around 1020, in about an hour. So hands to boarding stations will be announced at about 1005 sir.'

'Right. It's still looking a little rough out there so I'll make up my mind about whether we go over by Lynx or Pacific nearer the time . . .'

It is 0933. Richard Newton knocks on the door of the captain's cabin.

'Come in.'

'Good morning sir. How's the eye today sir?'

'Still hurts. Sort of stinging pain. Gritty.'

Newton gently removes the eye-patch and examines the still reddened eye with his ophthalmascope.

'It's still very red on the surface, sir, but I can't see any evidence of damage at the back of the eye. I'm going to do what I did yesterday and dilate the pupil as well as putting some steroid drops in, so just put your head back a bit sir.'

'I love this bit!' says the captain with grim irony as he looks up at a loaded glass eye-dropper poised immediately over his inverted but rapidly blinking left eye. Newton, carefully squeezing the rubber bulb of the pipette, tries to synchronize the drops with the blinking rather in the way machine guns on the front of First World War fighter planes were timed to shoot through spinning propeller blades. Though not with as much success.

'Seen a picture of myself in the main passageway,' says the captain with eye-drop liquid trickling in rivulets down his chin. 'Quite entertaining really, although I'm told the master-at-arms is less amused. It's a picture of me with that wretched eye-patch on and a blessed parrot on my shoulder . . . !'

---

* Estimated Time of Arrival. For more acronyms, see The Wonders of Naval Abbreviation, page 218.

It is **1024.** Leading Radio Operator Richard 'Eric' Gates presses the transmit button on the bridge VHF radio and talks urgently into his microphone:

'*Merchant vessel Klooga, merchant vessel Klooga this is Watchman Nine Zero,** Watchman Nine Zero calling you on channel 16, over.*'

Gates pauses but hears only the rasp of empty static in his headphones. He transmits again:

'*Merchant vessel Klooga, international call sign Three, Echo, Charlie, Echo, Six. This is Watchman Nine Zero calling on channel 16, over . . .*'

The radio crackles but does not answer and Gates turns to the captain, who is looking out to sea with his good eye pressed to one side of a pair of binoculars.

'Not having much luck raising the *Klooga* sir.'

'Well I can see her alright so she must be able to see us. Just give them a minute and then try again. Some of these chaps have been boarded so often and they are so fed up with it that sometimes they just try and ignore our calls. I don't know whether they think we're just going to go away.'

'Yes sir,' replies Gates, 'and the other thing is that channel 16, being the VHF channel, is always packed solid with maritime radio traffic so I don't know how well they can always hear us. We could try them on channel 73 . . .'

At that moment a distant voice breaks through the interference on channel 16:

'*Watchman Nine Zero . . . thees ees Klooga, thees ees Klooga, over.*'

'Excellent!' says Captain Rapp. 'OK, LRO,** tell them what it's all about.'

Gates presses 'transmit' and delivers the routine challenge.

'*Klooga, Klooga. This is Watchman Nine Zero. I intend to send a boarding party to examine your manifest and cargo in accordance with United Nations Security Council resolution eight, two, zero. No harm will be done to your vessel or your crew or your cargo, over.*'

'*OK. OK. You are coming now on board for checking by the British navy. Zank you, zank you.*'

'*Merchant vessel Klooga. This is Watchman Nine Zero. Please have the following documents on the bridge: your deck logbook, ship documents, cargo manifest, bill of loading, general plan of the ship, and your crew documents. Over.*'

'*Yes understood, yes understood . . .*'

Captain Rapp takes a final look at the sea state and then turns to four men standing attentively behind him: Russ Harding, the ubiquitous first lieutenant;

---

* The *Brilliant's* call sign in Operation Sharp Guard. 'Watchman' is a general name given to all ships in the operation whereas 'Nine Zero' is from the *Brilliant's* own pennant number – F 90 – which she has painted on her sides.
** Leading Radio Operator. For more acronyms, see Who's Who (Official Job Titles), page 216.

Lieutenant Jerry Barnbrook, the flight commander; Lieutenant Kevin Easterbrook, the Royal Navy boarding officer and Lieutenant Steve O'Neill the officer commanding the Royal Marine protection party.

'Right. There is a bit of a swell but I don't think it's too rough to go over in the Pacific, so Jerry, you can sit this one out. I expect we will need to go over in three sticks. Obviously you will go over with the first stick of marines, Steve. And then you and your men in the next two sticks Kevin. OK?'

'Yes sir,' reply the two boarding officers, already moving out of the bridge door on their way to the quarterdeck at the stern of the ship.

The captain looks across to the Estonian cargo ship now in the middle distance and makes a quick mental calculation before turning again to Gates at the radio.

'OK. Bring her course round to two four zero and reduce her speed to five knots.'

'*Merchant vessel Klooga. This is Watchman Nine Zero. Please make your course two four zero degrees and reduce your speed to five knots . . .*'

It is **1101**. The Pacific rigid inflatable pulls away from the quarterdeck with six Royal Marine commandos on board. Resplendent in flak jackets and camouflaged combat gear, popularly described by sailors as 'you can't see me suits', and grasping fully loaded SA 80 assault rifles, they brace themselves for a fast sea-skimming ride over white, breaking wave crests to the waiting merchant vessel *Klooga*, now positioned about 300 yards off the *Brilliant's* starboard beam.

It is **1104**. The Pacific, now hovering alongside the Estonian cargo ship, is being hurled violently by the sea swell against her rusting sides, but one by one the marines, waiting for exactly the right moment in the rise and fall of the water, hop on to the wooden-slatted rope ladder that has been thrown over the side for them.

It is **1108**. With an armed marine at every strategic entrance and exit in and around the bridge Lieutenant Steve O'Neill, happy he has secured the ship, calls up the *Brilliant* on his radio:

'*Boss to Mother. Boss to Mother. Ship secured and safe.*'

It is **1121**. The Pacific is returning to the *Brilliant* after completing two more trips to the *Klooga* to deliver a full naval search party of twelve sailors and the boarding officer, Kevin Easterbrook. Like the marines they are also in combat gear and fully armed. Even after a ship has been secured the risk of violent reaction by the crew cannot be ignored – especially if contraband of any description is found.

It is **1128**. Two marines with darting, ever-watchful eyes guard the bridge where Kevin Easterbrook is checking the ship's log and bill of loading with the *Klooga's* master – a plump, smiling man with thick spectacles and long grey unmanageable hair whose favourite English words are 'thank' and 'you'.

'Yes, zank you, zank you – thees ees log of today and also, zank you, before today and thees ees papers of cargo where we come from and where we go to in Rieka. Zank you sir, Zank you so much. You like vodka perhaps . . .?'

Easterbrook, checking carefully through the papers, looks up to decline the kind offer but the smiling master has already moved over to one of the more uncompromising looking marines to see if he might fancy a tot.

'Soldier, soldier, zank you soldier sir, you like vodka, yes?'

The marine's eyes narrow into slits as he gives a curt shake of the head and tightens the grip on his assault rifle.

'Thank you Master,' says Easterbrook quickly taking the Estonian captain by the arm, 'we are not allowed to drink whilst on duty. But thank you very much for asking. You are very kind.'

'Oh zank you, zank you so much!' says the master, smiling more widely than ever.

It is **1141**. Apart from the master and the first mate who remain on the bridge, the entire *Klooga* crew has been corralled in the main dining hall down below. This is partly so that their identities can be checked against their passports, but mostly so that they can be kept in one place under armed guard whilst the ship is searched. Twenty-eight Estonian sailors sit and wait in nervous silence, watching Petty Officer Kiwi Belben methodically sift through their passports whilst three marines, fingers on triggers, stand at the door – two facing in and one looking out.

The dining hall is depressingly stark and devoid of decoration except for a ragged and curious collection of pin-ups stuck to one of the bulkheads – pictures of smiling women modelling thick cardigans and winter woollies torn from a Russian knitting magazine, clearly the nearest thing to pornography the Estonian seafarers could find.

'Not exactly *Reader's Wives* you got up there mate,' quips Kiwi Belben as he gives the chief engineer his passport back.

The chief engineer looks blank but smiles politely.

It is **1158**. With the passport inspection finished a few of the *Klooga* crew have been released from the dining hall to accompany the search party around the ship.

THE ROYAL MARINES

The marines' predecessors are the soldiers who, from the earliest days of the navy, were a part of a ship's company. Their role was two-fold: in battle they used their muskets to shoot at the enemy on the upper deck and their halberds to repel boarders; in peacetime they assisted the master-at-arms in imposing harsh discipline.

It was this latter task that brought them firmly into conflict with Jack and started a long history of mutual antagonism.

In 1664 a marines regiment of 1200 men was raised from the City of London and the Royal Marines still retain the freedom of the City with the right to march through the square mile with drums beating, colours flying and bayonets fixed. It was first called The Duke of York and Albany's Maritime Regiment of Foot and then the Lord Admiral's or Admiral's Regiment. Its uniform was a sumptuous yellow coat, hat bound in gold braid, red breeches and stockings. In 1701 six regiments of 'marines' were raised to fight an amphibious campaign against the Spanish. Engagements at Cadiz and Vigo were followed by the capture of Gibraltar in 1704. This successful attack brought in its turn an epic siege by the Spanish which saw 200 marines defeat an attack by 1000 Spanish at the Round Tower. Gibraltar was secured and to this day remains the sole battle honour displayed on the corps' colours.

As a result of this success marines were constantly employed around the world. Some were in sea service on board warships and others in regiments that were deployed to fight infantry-style battles. The latter fought with great distinction in the early Napoleonic wars and in 1802 George III described the marines as the country's 'sheet anchor' and decreed that they should henceforth be styled the 'Royal Marines'. Their uniforms were altered to have dark blue facings.

The 'Royals' remain a breed apart and woe betide any matelot who tries to use 'their' pubs around Stonehouse barracks in Plymouth. Although the Parachute Regiment may be the Royal Marines' true *bête noir*, and their ship-policing role has gone, they often keep Jack at arms length – just as the sea soldiers did 500 years ago.

Leading Weapons Engineering Mechanic Tony 'Lucky' Knowles, accompanied by the ship's navigator, a tall blond man with sad eyes, is checking the cabins on Three Deck.

'Zis vun is mine,' says the navigator proudly, opening a door into a time warp. The small, neat cabin is a museum of antiques, kitsch and religious paraphernalia. To the left, on shelves over the bunk, is a comprehensive library of leather-bound books written in various Eastern European languages. Underneath hangs a huge gilded crucifix surrounded by framed pictures of the Madonna and Child. On a beautiful, mahogany table under the single porthole there is a collection of valuable looking china and silver placed carefully around old, black-and-white family photographs.

On the opposite wall, behind some hanging, plastic ivy there is an extraordinarily varied collection of postcards and posters.

Knowles walks up to it as if he were a visitor at an art gallery. In the middle there is a 1950s world map. Next to it, on one side, are dozens of postcards, mostly of ships, footballers and wild animals. On the other side, incongruously, is a dog-eared 1960s poster portrait of the Beatles entitled 'Psychadelia'.

The tall man with sad eyes taps on Tony Knowles' arm and points with intrigue to another picture, half concealed by a flannel dressing gown hanging on a hook by the door. Pulling back the dressing gown he reveals a *Playboy* centre-page pull-out of Miss February 1975 in all her considerable glory.

On a ship where knitting pattern models represent all that is steamy and decadent this is treasure indeed.

'Zat is my own pornography,' says the navigator with conspiratorial pride.

It is **1214**. Kevin Easterbrook radios back to the *Brilliant*.

'Boss to Mother, Boss to Mother. The search of the accommodation has now been completed. The holds have been checked and are clear. The engine-room has been checked and is clear. All other compartments have been checked and are clear. Recommend this vessel can be cleared.'

DAY *Tuesday*	DATE *11*	MONTH *October*	YEAR *1994*

PLACE	*Area Ethel, Otranto Straits, near Albania*

POSITION	*Classified*

DISTANCE TRAVELLED midnight to midnight *166.34 nautical miles*

SHIPS LOG. Remain on patrol in Area Ethel. Boarded MV Sigulda by helo during forenoon after fun and games with one of their crew on deck. Weather very fresh.

It is **1005**. Surgeon-Lieutenant Richard Newton and senior medical assistant Petty Officer Clive Wilkinson look on as MAQ Jacqui Quant nervously prepares the captain's eyedrops.

'Do I have to take over putting his drops in sir?' she asks the doctor.

'It'll be fine Jacqui. It's some extra responsibility for you and I've written it all out on a little schedule of what you have to do. Now, which medicines are which?'

'These ones are the steroidal ones and these ones are the medicated ones.'

'Right, so how often do you put them in?'

'Steroidal, five times a day. Medicated, three times.'

'Good.'

'I would feel fine if it wasn't the captain. S'posing I hurt him?'

'You won't hurt him. Just be nice to him, be natural. He's only a person after all.'

'Yeah, that's right,' breaks in PO Wilkinson. 'He's just another patient. I've got used to them over twenty years. I treat 'em just the same 'cept I call 'em "sir" rather than "mate" and I jab the needle in a little harder!'

It is **1015**. The captain has had his medication successfully administered by the young medical assistant although, worryingly, the eye does not yet seem to be responding to treatment. Nevertheless, Quant, relieved it is all over, has gone back to sickbay for a restorative cup of tea whilst Rapp has returned to the bridge to oversee another boarding – this time of a Latvian steel-wire carrier called the *Sigulda*. Because of the rough sea state this boarding will be done by helicopter with all the attendant risks, so he is pleased to hear from Petty Officer Dave Standen, the communications yeoman, that the Latvian master is both friendly and amenable.

'I told him we're going to board by helicopter, sir. He is very happy with that and seems quite used to it by the sounds of it. Said he would prepare everything for us.'

'Splendid. Check crew numbers and whether he has any women or children aboard.'

'*Merchant vessel Sigulda. This is Watchman Nine Zero. How many people have you got on board and how many of those are women and children? Over.*'

'*Hello Watchman Nine Zero. I greet you again. I can see you. I have twenty-four crew people. Twenty-three mens and one womans. I don't have no childrens. Over . . .*'

'He has twenty-four sir. One woman.'

'OK. Get him to muster them.'

'*Merchant vessel Sigulda. This is Watchman Nine Zero. Please have two crew on the bridge. Two in your engine room and all the remaining crew in your crew room. My boarding party will land on your stern in one zero minutes, ten minutes, over . . .*'

'*Yes please . . . we help your helicopter . . . over . . .*'

'*Merchant vessel Sigulda please have the following documents on your bridge . . .*'

As Petty Officer Standen completes his document request Russ Harding, who is watching the *Sigulda* through his binoculars, turns to Captain Rapp.

'You know sir, a lot of this chap's English is by rote – standard replies. I wonder just how much he really understands.'

'Yes. You've got a point . . .'

It is **1029**. Bright Star is on the flight deck with rotors turning. Inside, six armed marines are waiting to be dropped on the Latvian cargo ship currently lying about 300 yards off our starboard bow. They have now been waiting for nearly ten minutes. Meanwhile, on the bridge, Captain Rapp has been forced to take the radio himself.

'*Merchant vessel Sigulda. I will not let my helicopter leave my ship until all your men are inside your ship as we requested. Do you understand? Your men must leave the deck. It is dangerous!*'

'*I can see you, I can see you, over . . .*'

'*Sigulda, I repeat your men must go into the ship, into the crew-room. They must leave the stern of the ship. As long as they stay there my helicopter will not come over.*'

'*I see, I see, over.*'

'I can see some men moving now sir,' says Harding. 'I think he's finally got the message.'

' 'Fraid not sir,' says Dave Standen. 'There is still one man walking aft on the port side.'

Captain Rapp rolls his eyes, or at least one of them, in frustration. 'Oh dear, this is impossible. Give me the radio again, Yeoman . . . *Merchant vessel Sigulda, this is Watchman Nine Zero! You still have one man on the upper deck. He must move. I repeat. He must move. It is dangerous for him to stay there because my helicopter will come to that position. Do you understand? Over.'*

'*I understand you, I understand you . . . over.'*

'But he's still there! He's standing on the stern. No he's not! He's sitting down now. I don't believe it – he's sat down . . . !'

'*Watchman Nine Zero. All my men are inside ship now. One man only waits to greet your helicopter. You are welcome now please.'*

'Oh, I see,' says Russ Harding, 'it's a politeness thing . . .'

'*Merchant vessel Sigulda,*' perseveres the captain, '*this is Watchman Nine Zero. Thank you very much but your man should not greet us. My boarding officer will greet you on your bridge. Your man must go below . . . Sigulda, do you understand? Over.'*

'Eureka!' shouts Russ Harding. 'He's going, he's going . . . he's gone!'

'*Watchman Nine Zero. My man is gone below . . .* ' says the master of the *Sigulda* in a crestfallen voice, '*. . . now there is no person to greet you, over.'*

Captain Rapp sits back in his seat with relief. 'I know he was only trying to help but his English is so limited . . . but then I suppose my Latvian is nothing much to write home about.'

DAY *Thursday*	**DATE** *13*	**MONTH** *October*	**YEAR** *1994*

PLACE	*Area Ethel, Otranto Straits – near Albania*

POSITION	*Classified*

DISTANCE TRAVELLED midnight to midnight *205.84 nautical miles*

SHIPS LOG. Continued to patrol Ethel. Major RAS and VERTREP with Fort Austin. Tons of stores successfully brought over – very satisfying professionally. Boarded Magellan Rex. Captain away for most of day so first lieutenant had conduct. Continued patrol overnight.

It is **0710.** The captain had another restless night with his inflamed eye and early this morning called the doctor, Richard Newton, to his cabin. A brief examination confirmed a further deterioration, which prompted Newton to suggest another and more drastic course of action. It is for this reason that Russ Harding has been sent for.

'Russ, as you know my eye has been a problem for about six days now.'

'Yes sir.'

'Well, after due consideration the Doc and I think it best that I go ashore and have it looked at. He's managed to get me an appointment later today at Taranto hospital in southern Italy. It's a bore to say the least, but I'm sure he's right.'

'Absolutely, sir. You can't take chances with eyes.'

'Yes, and Richard would feel a lot happier this way as well. He's young, on his first trip to sea and readily admits he only did two weeks ophthalmology training during his qualification to be a doctor. So, he would be grateful for some specialist support.'

'When are you going sir?'

'The forward logistic people in Grottaglie are sending a Sea King to get me around 1000. If all goes well I hope to be back sometime this evening but until then you will have conduct of the ship.'

'Very well sir.'

'Of course, it would have to happen on the day we're having a big RAS* and VERTREP** but I've got to sort this out once and for all. I hope it all goes smoothly for you Russ.'

'Thank you, sir. I'm sure it will. Just you get that eye better . . .'

It is **0940.** The ship's tannoy system bursts into voice with an urgent directive:

'Clear lower deck, clear lower deck. All hands not on watch muster immediately in the main dining hall.'

Nobody except officers is exempt from this call, known as 'general muster', so the dining hall is soon buzzing with over two hundred people. Chay Robertson, the master-at-arms, stands outside in the passageway making encouraging noises to the latecomers.

'Come on you lot! Get a bloody move on! Get in here and get yourselves sat down. On the double! Move yourselves. There's a RAS in twenty minutes!'

---

* Replenishment at Sea [stores, fuel or ammunition passed from an auxiliary stores ship].

** Vertical Replenishment [stores, fuel or ammunition taken on board from a helicopter]. For more acronyms, see The Wonders of Naval Abbreviation, page 218.

It is **0945**. Martin Atherton, the supply officer, stands in front of the assembled ship's company and waits for them to settle.

'Good morning everybody. Right, today, as you know, we have a stores RAS. This is no ordinary RAS however. It is with the *Fort Austin* – one of the latest fleet replenishment ships* and is likely to be a much bigger event than most of you will have experienced before. We will be taking on food stores, that is frozen, dairy, fresh, NAAFI, dry and beer as well as general naval stores and transit stores. We will also be back-RASing by sending over all our various empties – such as oil drums and beer barrels. We will also be carrying out some VERTREPing with our Lynx picking up stores from *Fort Austin's* flight deck.

'What I want from you is plenty of energy, enthusiasm and flexibility.

'Everybody has got to muck in as we have tons of food coming over on the heavy jack stay and I want to get it into the larder very quickly – especially the frozen goods. Watch out for yourselves and each other as a big RAS like this is not without its dangers. Remember, the stuff coming over is in the end yours so it is in your interests to get this right. Think of it as Christmas coming early. OK . . . ?'

Atherton pauses to look at the expressionless faces of the sailors and Wrens sitting silently in front of him. He knows and they know that a stores RAS involves sinew-snapping, back-breaking hard labour.

'. . . Right. Carry on,' he says in the least ominous way he can.

Everybody rises and moves for the doors.

'Oi! 'Old on a minute you lot!' barks Chay Robertson. 'Before you all leg it just listen to me for a sec. When you're workin' on the upper deck stay away from any movin' ropes, coils or bites. Do not go near the dump points unless you're in the dump party – in which case wear your life jackets. And anybody that's goin' to be workin' with ropes take your rings off – it's not very nice walking around with only four fingers and it makes a terrible mess of the deck – any questions?'

It is **1010**. The captain and the doctor, winched up to a Sea King helicopter ten minutes ago, are now speeding towards the western horizon and southern Italy. Russ Harding, with conduct of the ship, is on the bridge overseeing the final approach to the gigantic 24 000 ton *Fort Austin* on our port side. As always, it is a tricky manoeuvre requiring great precision, concentration and skill.

'Range, two cables.'

---

* The Royal Fleet Auxiliary Service is the specialist front-line support force for the Royal Navy and replenishes warships at sea with fuel, stores and weapons. It is unique in that all the navy's major auxiliaries are civilian-manned but with everybody trained in operational skills. Vessels are fitted with close-range small-calibre self-defence weapons and decoys manned and maintained by RFA personnel.

'Affirmative. Steer zero six zero. Log speed to two zero.'

'Range, one and a half cables.'

'Steer zero, sixty two. Log speed to two one.'

'Stand by on the levers . . . set both levers ahead . . . one six.'

'Set levers one six, sir.'

'Log speed two zero, one eight, one six, one four.'

Within minutes the two ships are successfully positioned in close parallel to each other and the RAS is ready to start. Harding gratefully accepts a cup of tea brought up by one of the stewards and takes it out to the port bridge wing. From here, temporarily but proudly in command, he watches his ship prepare for a massive maritime shopping spree.

It is **1030**. *Fort Austin* is disgorging barrels, cannisters, boxes, cartons, drums, crates, kegs and packages in their hundreds. Most are coming across to the *Brilliant* in bulk loads lashed together on pulleys and suspended on the thick ropes of the heavy jack stay.* Some, however, are being picked up in a giant net slung under the belly of Bright Star which Jerry Barnbrook and Nick Cooke-Priest are flying continuously between the two ships.

Once a load arrives it is untied, broken down and passed straight to the 'dumping' areas to be sorted into type. From there the various commodities are passed along human chains that stretch the entire length of the ship on both the port and starboard upper decks.** Once they have reached the end of the horizontal chain they are either passed down the 'vertiflow' lift to the storage spaces in the depths of the hull or simply carried down by hand.

Everybody is lifting, carrying, pushing, pulling or passing something.

It is **1050**. It is a warm day and for each of the links in the human chain it is getting warmer with every load. Shirts are being discarded and overalls are being pulled down to the waist – much to the dismay of the Wrens in the chain gang.

'It's not fair,' says Roni Whittaker to Micky Goble as he passes her a 50 lb sack of potatoes, 'you blokes can go topless and nobody minds!'

Micky Goble looks over at the attractive, full-figured Wren and is about to voice the obvious reply when another sack of potatoes is thrust into his gut.

'Hmmmmph!' he splutters.

---

* The means by which two ships, steaming at some 14 knots, are connected by a rope and pulley of considerable strength which is used for the transfer of stores and ammunition. It can support a pallet of up to 2 tons in weight and is mechanically supported by winches.

** Frozen and fresh foods are passed along the chains, then long-life products, then non-consumables.

It is **1100**. Martin Atherton, dressed in white overalls and a protective hard hat, walks around the upper deck ticking off items from the wodge of lists on his clipboard. For him, as supply officer, this RAS is the biggest logistical challenge of the trip and the culminaton of a great deal of planning and management.

'One of the great lessons of the Gulf War was the necessity of constant replenishment. Running a warship is not only about fighting and showing her teeth but keeping sustainable. RASing is hard work, but if the ship's company want British beer and sausages they know that this is the only way they're going to get them and that is a highly motivating factor. But it's more than that as well. For me this is what the navy is all about – working together as a unit and achieving an end that everybody can be proud of.'

For Martin Atherton the true significance of today's RAS is more symbolic than practical. For him its great challenge is to help organize people of different skills and backgrounds into a functioning team with a common purpose and, most importantly, to do so without coercion.

'In the Royal Navy we are at our weakest when we rely on the rank structure. Obviously, in time of crisis or war you have to consent to it and have faith in it and obey it without question because there is no time for a forum. But at other times we must always remember that the rank structure is underpinned by a network of real human relationships which, because they acknowledge that structure, make it more complete, more workable, and more truthful. There is no reason at all why I, as a lieutenant-commander on the *Brilliant*, can't turn to an able seaman and openly learn from him, because anybody who tries to subsume others by brandishing rank does so at their peril. An admiral and a stoker are still more remarkable for their similarities as people than their differences as naval personnel. I have been given the responsibility to manage people because that is what my talents, such as they are, enable me to do. That's the way I fit into this organization and everybody who works for me, or to me, has the right to expect management of me. It doesn't automatically confer status on me other than the status they consent to give me. It's the same with respect. I have to earn status and respect but if I fail in a particular requirement then I have let them down just as much as they would if they failed in a task I set them.'

It is **1148**. Atherton is standing near the central dump on the boat deck looking pleased with the progress being made when the master-at-arms taps him on the shoulder.

' 'Scuse me sir. I think we've got a bit of pilferin' goin' on.'

'Oh no. What is it this time?'

'Yorkie bars sir. Forty-eight of them. Apparently, a box of them accidentally fell over the side . . .'

'Oh not that old chestnut!'

'Exactly, sir. I've been finding empty Yorkie bar wrappers all over the place . . .'

It is **1210**. The great Yorkie bar mystery has taken on the dimensions of a Hercule Poirot murder case. Chay Robertson's investigations have taken him from the main store dump, via the Sea Skua magazine to the for'ard Sea Wolf missile deck where, his information suggests, the missing chocolate bars were last seen wrapped. The sailors in this vicinity, however, are tight-lipped.

'Ain't seen nothin'.'

'What Yorkies?'

'Wasn't here at the time.'

'I don't even like chocolate . . .'

But Robertson perseveres and is ultimately rewarded with a tip-off.

'Well, I'm not sayin' I saw anythin' but then I'm not sayin' I didn't . . . try the bootnecks' mess.'

It is **1304**. The heavy jack stay is down and the *Fort Austin* is pulling away. Over 50 tons of stores have been taken on board in record time and only the last few items of general stores remain to be taken down below. This has been a textbook RAS and as Martin Atherton waves to the crew of the departing supply ship he is smiling with delight at the effort everybody put into it

There is no doubt that this effort, and indeed the spirit that went with it, is in large measure due to the great goodwill the ship's company feel for the quietly spoken lieutenant-commander with a background in English Literature. Whether he realizes this or still sees it as something to strive for is impossible to know.

It is **1305**. Micky Goble walks into the billowing steam of a crowded for'ard shower room and waits in line for one of the cubicles to become vacant.

'Hey, Micky!' says Sid 'Doggy' Barker joining the queue behind him, 'Guess who took the Yorkies?'

'Last I heard was they were lookin' for an overweight HGV driver without his lorry!'

'Nah. It was the booties. We just saw the Joss* havin' a go at 'em on the boat deck. He wasn't pullin' his punches neither.'

---

* Master-at-arms. For more naval slang, see Jackspeak, page 212.

Bob Hawkins climbs back aboard.

Hands to bathe!

Captain Rapp in
his patch.

The Royal Marine
Protection Party leaves
Brilliant for a 'board
and search' in the
Otranto Straits.

HMS *Brilliant* intercepts a merchant vessel *en route* to the former Yugoslavia.

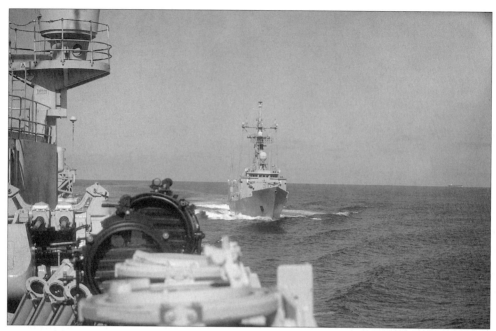

The Spanish ship SNS *Victoria* tails HMS *Brilliant* during manoeuvres.

Returning by light jack stay from a CROSSPOL with SNS *Victoria*.

The 'Lost Boys' mess performs its version of 'Relight My Fire' during the SODS Opera.

Jacqui Quant, Medical Assistant.

Roni Whittaker at Harbour Stations.

Relaxing in the Wrennerie.

'Really?'

'Yeah. I 'ope they really get it in the neck this time. They think they can walk on water them bootnecks.'

'Dare you to say that to their faces Doggy!'

It is **1955**. Russ Harding picks up the microphone for his routine evening sit. rep.

'Good evening. First Lieutenant speaking. Well done to everyone involved in today's RAS with Fort Austin. It went extremely well and you all have every right to be very pleased with yourselves. Most of you will know that the captain departed shortly after 1000 this morning. His eye became slightly worse last night and the medical officer's opinion was that he should see a specialist ashore in Taranto. He got ashore at 1130 and saw the specialist early this afternoon. I have heard from him on the radio and happily his eye is alright. He has been given some different medication but is fit for sea duties. I'm expecting him back tonight around 2100.

'Once again, well done to everyone for today's RAS. It was a very tight evolution but we got everything over we intended. More beer for everyone and, at last, some British sausages. That's all.'

DAY *Sunday*	**DATE** *16*	**MONTH** *October*	**YEAR** *1994*

PLACE	*Area Ethel, Otranto Straits – near Albania*

POSITION	*Classified*

DISTANCE TRAVELLED **midnight to midnight** *164.01 nautical miles*

SHIPS LOG. Continued Ethel patrol. Busy day with three boardings: MV Osor from Croatia carrying citrus fruit, MV Entella from Italy carrying gas oil and MV Brittak from the Lebanon carrying ballast. Weather mild and sea state calm.

It is **0700**. The Royal Marine protection party have been doing unarmed combat drills on the for'ard Sea Wolf missile deck. After an hour of boxing, karate and ju-jitsu they are stripped to the waist and finishing off with a rapid circuit of twist sit-ups, wide-armed press-ups, trunk curls, squat jumps, tricep dips, high knee raises and gridders*. The six men, supremely fit and focused, work at the punishing schedule with total concentration, pausing only to shout words of encouragement to each other.

These men are a distinct and separate unit on the ship. Highly motivated and supremely self-confident, they take themselves and their 'can do' philosophy very seriously. This proudhearted self-belief often jars with the sailors around them who, with their traditionally more relaxed and self-effacing attitude to life, are quick to dismiss marines as arrogant, haughty, conceited and imperious.

Lately, there has been an unmistakably heightened tension between the marines and the rest of the ship's company and this is the main topic of conversation as the six hot and sweating men start to warm down and stretch out their aching muscles.

'They're all so bleedin' pleased we got done for the Yorkies – that's what gets me!'

'They're jealous, that's what it is. Sailors always are of bootnecks.'

'Who'd be a bloody matelot?'

'Too right! You know the other day in Crete when Chippy and me met that old bootie and his missus – well that's what being a marine is all about isn't it. Sticking together. Belonging to the group. Being one of the lads. Even at that age he was one of us – a Green Beret.'

'The other thing that gets me is the way they want us to do all the bloody scrubbin' and cleanin' around the ship. And, like the other day, humpin' all those stores around. I mean we're a protection party on twenty-four-hour duty not a load of skivvies . . . !'

'And you know what? I get really pissed off when I see 'em wearin' those "I've been to Bosnia" T-shirts as if they've been over there with the troops when all they've been doin' is sailin' up and down the Adriatic in a nice safe warship. Mind you, I would hate to be in one of these things if it got hit. Must be 'orrible.'

'Some of the younger sailors are alright – I've invited Taff Morris to my wedding next year – but the older ones just look at me like I'm a fruit cake, a real piss head . . .'

The upper deck tannoy interrupts the marine's flow with an all too familiar announcement.

'*Hands to boarding stations. Hands to boarding stations . . .*'

'Oh no here we go again! I hope this one is by helo. I'm sick of gettin' soaked in the rubber boat . . .'

The marines' heartfelt antagonism towards the sailors is partly to do with the

---

* Sprinting hard and repeatedly between two points.

tiredness and exhaustion that everybody on the ship is beginning to feel after a long and active deployment, but it is also to do, quite simply, with the long-standing antipathy that has always existed between bootneck and Jack.*

It is **1959**. The officers file into the wardroom for Sunday dinner. As they go in they take their table napkins, rolled up in silver-plated napkin-holders, from a shelf over the counter and choose their places at one of the two long dining-tables. The table furthest from the door is generally considered to be the senior one and is where Russ Harding sits together with the heads of department, although this is more a convention than a rigid rule of the wardroom. The table nearest the door tends to attract the younger officers and is consequently louder and a little more unruly, although excessive noise is quickly silenced by a glance from the first lieutenant.

Hovering by the serving hatches from the wardroom galley, Petty Officer Steward Tony Lilley waits for the officers to settle down. Once he is satisfied he gives the order to his team of steward ratings to serve the first course. Leading Steward Andy Conway, Able Seaman Steward 'Lurch' Nethercott and Wren Steward Viv Worrall move forward in a phalanx to collect the steaming bowls of vegetable soup that are being pushed through from the galley by Petty Officer Cook Galpin.

Wardroom dinners are nerve-racking for stewards as there is so much to attend to and, potentially, so much to go wrong. Serving three-course, silver service dinners (including soup and peas) on a rolling sea to high-ranking officers in formal dress is a feat to challenge the brave, but Royal Navy stewards seem to be blessed with the balance of tight-rope walkers.

Tony Lilley darts around anxiously, making sure that all the officers are served and that there are enough jugs of iced water on the tables. He responds immediately to an indication from Jerry Barnbrook that one of the salt cellars is empty, reacts instantly to a dropped soup spoon under Martin Atherton's chair and momentarily responds to a beckoning wave from Russ Harding.

'Yes sir.'

'I think we'll have a couple of bottles of red on this table tonight, Petty Officer Lilley.'

'Yes sir. On whose tab?'

'Put one down to me. No fines outstanding are there?'**

---

* See The Royal Marines, page 119.
** Many Royal Navy wardrooms operate a system of fines whereby any officer breaking mess rules, by being late for meals, for example, or wearing a cap in the wardroom, must forfeit a bottle of wine. The first lieutenant, as president of the wardroom, is always the final arbiter.

'No sir. 'Fraid not sir.'

Lilley, a stocky little man with friendly, smiling eyes and an uncanny resemblance in looks and manner to Norman Wisdom, takes his job as senior wardroom steward very seriously.

'I consider these officers to be my 'gentlemen'. I look after them. See to their needs. Get to know their little ways. Some people say this is all wrong them having this special service and that it's too "upstairs, downstairs" but I don't agree. I reckon officers deserve a little better. It's their right. If we go to war we look to them to do right by us so they should get the rewards in peacetime.'

The second course is now being served. Tonight, as every Sunday night, it is roast beef, Yorkshire pudding, roast potatoes, peas, carrots and gravy. With apple pie and custard to follow, the 'Sunday roast special' is regarded as the pick of PO Cook Galpin's considerable repertoire. The only person not given a generous helping of prime, rare fillet of beef is Lieutenant Liz Hall, the resident wardroom vegetarian, who has, instead, a freshly made Spanish omelette.

Tony Lilley pours the rich, steaming gravy into the central well of the first lieutenant's Yorkshire pudding and then over the top of his vegetables, just how he likes it. Russ Harding looks around to see that everybody else has been served, picks up his knife and fork and nods once. This is the signal for everyone to start their favourite meal of the week. Everyone, that is, except Lieutenant-Commander Bob Hawkins . . .

It is **2025**. One deck up Bob Hawkins peers into his radar in the darkened op's room. Unlike everybody else, he is still having to work a Defence Watch routine of seven hours on and seven hours off* 24 hours a day. Alternating with fellow officer Paul Metcalfe, he has to mount a permanent lookout for PVVs as well as maintain a high level of battle readiness in all three threat environments [surface, sub-surface and air]. Hawkins has worked this unforgiving routine for nearly six months without stop.

'Running an op's room is a very punishing and very focused occupation. It is also, by its nature, very isolating – something I find particularly difficult to cope with being a gregarious sort of bloke. At the moment I feel like I'm living in a vacuum. I get up, read the latest signals, come on watch, come off watch, have a quick sandwich, go back on watch, come off watch, have a late supper on my own, go to bed for four hours and then I get up again and do it all again. Day in,

---

* The normal Defence Watch shift is six hours but Hawkins and Metcalfe decided to make their shifts one hour longer to allow themselves time for administrative work outside of the op's room.

NAVY COOKS

Napoleon said an army marches on its stomach but that lesson escaped the Royal Navy for a millennium. By the fifteenth century a ship's cook was regularly appointed to warships but he would usually be skilled in anything but cookery. All meals were strikingly similar. The ship's cook lit a fire between decks and would boil salted beef, known as 'junk', which had previously been allowed to steep and soften. This almost inedible food would then be divided and issued to mess cooks who were responsible for dividing it in their own messes.

By the late eighteenth century, the ship's cook was invariably a Greenwich Hospital pensioner who would receive but 35 shillings a month pay, 11 shillings and 8 pence pension and whatever profit he made from the sale of slush. This slush, which gives rise to the term slush fund, was the fat skimmed off the top of the cauldrons used for boiling salt beef. It was much prized by seamen for making 'duff' or puddings. It was not supposed to be sold since its oily properties were used in the preservation of rigging but, sailors being sailors, the fat flowed.

Attempts to head off scurvy through healthy eating were often frustrated by the ineptitude of the feeding system, and it was not until the latter half of the nineteenth century that the establishment of more professional pursers, and more caring doctors and officers, led to better catering. Tinned food, beef screens on the upper deck and the availability of steam and ultimately electricity gave rise to new standards of cooking that, by 1914, were almost adequate. Livestock was kept aboard some older ships until 1945 and ship's cooks were supplemented by butchers and bakers – and by candle-makers who used the salt-beef fat to make their wares as late as the 1920s.

The availability of cool and cold rooms, fridges and an understanding of proper diet brought the impact of well-trained cooks to the fore and modern standards finally arrived in the 1960s with the introduction of central cafeteria-style dining rooms where all the ship's company could select and eat their meals away from the mess decks. For a while, cooks trained with the army at Aldershot, but they are now back in the Naval Supply School at HMS *Raleigh* at Torpoint.

day out. Tonight I feel particularly hard done by because it's roast beef night which everybody enjoys. It's not just the food though, it's the opportunity to relax and let off a bit of steam. It's good to have a laugh once in a while. Communal mess life is very good for morale . . . I seem to remember.'

It is 0056. Bob Hawkins slides open the door to a deserted wardroom. He walks wearily over to the dining-table on the far side of the room, sits down at a place set for one, and waits for the duty steward to bring in his supper.

'It's all beginning to wear a bit thin now. At this stage in the deployment I feel like I've had enough and just look forward to getting home . . .'

Able Seaman Steward Stuart Conder brings in a plate of warmed-up chicken curry from the galley and puts it down in front of the exhausted principal warfare officer. Hawkins can hardly keep his eyes open but forces himself to eat.

'I have to admit that sometimes I feel like I'm reaching the end of my tether, but then I force myself to dig deeper into the reserves. I know that no matter how fatigued I may be I've still got to lead my team in the op's room. The PWO's the guy to set the standards and we've still got a lot of work to do. At the moment we are boarding an average of three or four ships a day. They don't stop coming and you never know what you're going to find or if one might bite back.'

Hawkins puts down his knife and fork, pushes his chicken curry to one side and gets up to pour himself a cup of coffee from a thermos flask left by the galley hatch.

'I might complain sometimes but I wouldn't do anything else. The navy is my life. It allows me do something I fundamentally believe in and, at the same time, it lets me live out my dreams – as it has done for the last seventeen years.

'I come from a working class family. We lived in a council estate just off the North End Road in west London and my dad was a greengrocer in Covent Garden, so being an officer in the Royal Navy wasn't the most obvious choice for me. In fact, when I left Wandsworth Comprehensive without even bothering to finish my A levels in the late seventies I had decided to join the navy as a sailor. But my father, who'd been a signalman in the navy during the war, persuaded me to go to the recruiting office and ask about entry as an officer. I didn't really want to but I went along for his sake and was incredibly impressed by all the bullshit they gave me. A few months later I was at Dartmouth . . .'

Hawkins reaches into his inside pocket for a small wallet of photographs which he proceeds to leaf through.

'. . . One of my great sources of inspiration to do well and succeed in the navy is to make my family proud, my father in particular. I remember when I got promoted to lieutenant in November 1982 and had my uniforms changed to two stripes. I came back with them from the tailors and hung them in the hallway still in their cases. Then a little later I was coming out of the kitchen and saw my father unzip one of the cases, take out one of the sleeves and stroke the gold braid with a big smile on his face. Then he carefully put it back and zipped up the case again. He didn't see me looking and I never said anything but that moment will always be very special to me. And I know that he has loved everything that has followed: my being promoted to lieutenant-commander; my appointment as op's officer on the *Brilliant*. One day I hope to tell him I have my own command . . .'

DAY *Monday*	**DATE** *17*	**MONTH** *October*	**YEAR** *1994*

PLACE	*On passage from Area Ethel, Otranto Straits, to Brindisi, south-west Italy.*

POSITION	**At 0600** *Classified* **At 1600** *40°01′N 17°58′E*

DISTANCE TRAVELLED midnight to midnight *190.1 nautical miles*

SHIPS LOG. Final day in Ethel. Early morning boarding of MV Kelme from the Ukraine carrying ammonium phosphate. Handed over duties to ITS Perseo before leaving Area. Closed up for ADEX in Western Adriatic. Entered Brindisi for dusk and berthed at central position right in town centre.

It is **1415**. On full power and swerving evasively the *Brilliant* rips through a heaving sea at nearly 30 knots. The ship's radars have detected four aircraft closing at speed in a highly aggressive attack profile. Everybody is bracing for an air assault.

In the op's room Bob Hawkins, preparing to engage the aggressors with Sea Wolf missiles, speaks anxiously to his air trackers and upper deck gun batteries on the command open line:

'What speed are they closing at?'

'*500 knots on 23 zero 45. Now at 60 miles.*'

'Port and starboard batteries . . .Air threat warning White!'

The gunners on the upper deck, wearing white flash gear and helmets, frantically scan the distant horizon from behind the two twin GCB 30 mm cannons and the two Gambo single 20 mm guns.

Hawkins looks over to Captain Rapp on the other side of his console.

'They're coming in on a direct course sir.'

'What do you recommend?'

'I propose to engage with the for'ard launcher first and if we require to radiate I'll then use aft as a filing system.'

'I concur . . .'

'They've split sir! They're coming at us from different directions . . . !'

'One aircraft now south at 30 miles.'

'Air threat warning Yellow!'

The computer-guided Type 910 aircraft tracking system has already locked on to the incoming aircraft and is automatically priming the Sea Wolf missiles in their for'ard and aft launchers with the relevant coordinates.

'Aircraft approaching bow at 16 miles . . .'

'Air threat warning Red! If it flies it dies!'

'Tango, tango at 5 miles, tracking north at speed.'

'Low target.'

'Fire and engage. Take it out!'

'Tracker locked on . . . missile fired!'

'Second bandit at two three zero. One mile . . .'

On the upper deck all guns are aimed with deadly intent on the attacking fighters that are now clearly visible and closing fast. As two come in low towards the starboard bow the 30 mm cannon on that side immediately swings round on its electrically driven mountings to meet them. Following their path as they scream over the foc'sle the gunner, aiming manually, keeps his finger on the firing button that activates 600 rounds of anti-aircraft shells per minute. The two rocking aircraft clear the ship and pull up sharply into steep, spiralling climbs.

Within seconds two more sweep in from the south, this time on the port side, and almost skim the radar mast before banking away in a tight, curving trajectory towards the horizon. The gunners continue to train their sights on the glowing, white-hot afterburns. . .

It is **1444**. One of the four attacking vertical take-off fighters draws up to our starboard bridge wing in a dramatic, deafening hover. Riding the enormous power of his vectored-thrust Pegasus engine the pilot waves to Captain Rapp standing at the bridge door. The captain returns the wave with a smile as he watches the fighter rise, turn slowly on its axis and soar into the Mediterranean sky.

It is **1505**. Russ Harding clears his throat and presses the transmit button on the microphone:

'*Good afternoon. First Lieutenant speaking with an earlier than usual sit. rep. Well done everyone who was involved in this afternoon's air defence exercise with the Sea Harriers from HMS Invincible. The computers show that the exercise was very successful with all four attacking aircraft destroyed by Sea Wolf misssiles on their initial approach to the ship.*

'*So, it's been a good day but a long one for all of us. After a crack-of-dawn boarding at 0520, the seventeenth in eight days incidentally, and the fifty-ninth since we joined Sharp Guard, we handed over Ethel to the Italian ship Perseo at just before 0900 and then made good time crossing the Adriatic to meet up with the Harriers for the ADEX. We are now continuing towards the port of Brindisi in Italy where we should arrive at around 1700 to start a well-deserved three-day run ashore before going back into Iceman for the last time . . .*'

Chapter Six

FOR ONE NIGHT ONLY

DAY *Friday*	DATE *21*	MONTH *October*	YEAR *1994*

PLACE	*Area Iceman, Eastern Adriatic*

POSITION	*Classified*

DISTANCE TRAVELLED midnight to midnight *184.4 nautical miles*

SHIPS LOG. Sailed from Brindisi very early this morning. Went straight to Action Stations for reloading then reduced to Defence Watches before approaching Montenegro waters. Assumed duties in Area Iceman. Weather very poor with cold wind from east-south-east.

It is 0615. At dawn, under a steely, stormy sky, the *Brilliant* leaves the pizzas and piazzas of Brindisi to head back to the strictures and deprivations of Defence Watches in Area Iceman. It had been a fairly typical run ashore, not as memorable as Souda Bay, but diverting and relaxing for a few days and not without its moments: marines Chippy Norton and Spider Webb had a run-in with the master-at-arms after being found drunk and disorderly in the city centre fountain; the gunners' mess, discovering one of their number in an alcoholic stupor, shaved him bald and painted him orange; Dave 'Clubs' Mynett surpassed himself with a rendition of 'You're the One That I Want' in front of the entire lower deck at a local karaoke bar; and the doctor woke from another blissful night of intoxication with the unmistakable outline of a fully erect male phallus drawn on his forehead in indelible ink.

Now, however, the mood of the ship, faced with another patrol inside the Serbian missile envelope, is deteriorating as fast as the weather.

It is 1150. With the coast of Italy now far behind us the *Brilliant* plunges her bow determinedly through the swollen, rolling waves of an Adriatic whipped up by strong easterly winds. On the upper deck, sea-soaked and sullen, the gunners and weapons engineers struggle to reload the ship's guns and missile launchers. Down below, in equally solemn mood, the duty watches prepare for the ship's arrival in Iceman, sustained only by the knowledge that it will be for the last time.

In the communications room Bob Hawkins reads secret signals about a recent big build-up in Serb military exercises, reminding him of just how real a threat the Yugoslavians would pose if their will-power matched their fire-power. Next to him, leaning on one of the cryptodecoders used for transmitting and receiving coded information, Nick Cooke-Priest checks through the latest meteorological data coming in through the laser fax.

'October the twenty-first today, Bob,' says Cooke-Priest, looking over to the principal warfare officer.

'Absolutely!' reacts Hawkins immediately. 'Trafalgar Day – the most important day in the naval calendar and we can't celebrate it because we'll be on Defence Watches. Crying shame I call it!'

'Never mind Bob. Join the aviators for a bash on Taranto Night* instead!' laughs Cooke-Priest.

'Watchit, you bloody WAFU,'** says Hawkins with a grin, but warming to a subject dear to his heart. 'Don't knock the memory of Lord Nelson. He's one of our greatest national heroes.'

'Of course, but Trafalgar was a long time ago. Taranto was only fifty-four years ago,' says Cooke-Priest only partly playing the devil's advocate.

'The battle of Trafalgar was the single most important naval victory in all our history.'

'Oh, I'm not so sure about that . . .'

'Listen. The only thing stopping Napoleon from sending 130 000 troops across the Channel was the channel blockade fleet. And the only thing capable of defeating that was a combined French and Spanish navy of about thirty-three warships. Nelson with only twenty-eight ships annihilated them in four and a half hours.'

'Yes, but the battle of Taranto virtually knocked the Italian Fleet out of the Second World War . . .'

'I'm not saying it wasn't important . . .'

---

* The Fleet Air Arm's epic night attack on the Italian naval base at Taranto. The men of Taranto and their celebrated feat are remembered on the anniversary of 11 November 1940 wherever FAA gather around the world. (See also The Fleet Air Arm, page 52.)
** General service nickname for a member of the Fleet Air Arm, or anything to do with the FAA. The acronym is popularly thought to mean 'Wet And [Flipping] Useless', which indicates the healthy rivalry that has always existed between the FAA and other naval specializations. Divers, for example, have made FAA abuse an art form, viz: 'Fly navy. Divers need the work!'

'. . . someone said after Taranto – one of the sea lords I think – that it proved the Fleet Air Arm was the most devastating weapon the navy possessed.'

'Well, if it hadn't been for Nelson you'd be talking French now!'

'Yes, well . . . that is a bonus I suppose,' concedes Cooke-Priest.

'You know, it is extraordinary when you consider that the French are meant to be our natural enemy and that the Royal Navy has spent more time fighting them than every other nation combined that we still go and build a tunnel under the Channel. It horrifies me.'

'Not half as much as it would horrify Nelson . . .'

It is **1950**. Russ Harding picks up a familiar microphone.

'Good evening. First Lieutenant speaking. We are now back on patrol in Area Iceman for the next seven days until the twenty-eighth of October when we will be relieved by the Canadian ship HMCS Toronto. I know we are all beginning to feel the tension of a long and hard deployment but it is important to keep up the pressure, especially during this, our last time in Iceman. We are in an environment considered medium threat but that could increase to high threat at any time so remain vigilant at all times.

'Just two more points to make. Firstly, the supply officer has asked me to point out that the ship's company dining hall is rapidly running out of cutlery. You are all asked to search your mess decks and respective workspaces and return any cutlery as soon as possible. The next step is fingers!

'Finally, let me draw your attention and your energies to that most important of events – the SODS Opera. It is planned to hold this feast of "heavenly" entertainment on the evening of the twenty-eighth of this month – weather permitting, on the flight deck. I know there are a lot of ideas for acts from the different messes, but ideas are not enough without application and rehearsals – so get a move on. Remember, this event is for your enjoyment and it does allow you a degree of freedom of comment on the ship, the command and the deployment thus far. It's a way in which you can let your hair down, tell it how it is, and give your messmates a laugh at the same time. So, remember, SODS Opera is on the twenty-eighth of October . . . for one night only! That's all.'

SODS Opera is a bizarre tradition unique to the Royal Navy. To the uninformed an evening with the 'Ship's Operatic and Drama Society', which the word SODS is supposed to stand for, might suggest a harmless presentation of monologues, recitals and sea shanties. Nothing could be further from the truth. What is actually offered is a series of completely uncensored and full-blooded entertainments put on by the lower decks that taunt, mock, ridicule and deride anybody and everybody on the ship – with complete impunity. The most popular targets are the captain, the master-at-arms and the officers but anybody is fair game. The theory is that SODS Opera provides a social pressure-release for a community with no escape from itself. By giving everybody a night of amnesty to do and say what they want old scores can be settled and the air cleared. That is the theory.

From now until 28 October all the messes have the licence to devise, write and rehearse the most depraved and diabolical skits, songs, and satires they can think of. Bad taste, outrage and insult will be the order of the night.

It is **2215**. In the Wrennerie, the mess deck for the seventeen women ratings on board, a group of Wrens have just sat down for a cup of tea. They all look exhausted and are gratefuly escaping into an episode of *Inspector Morse* when Ginny McHale comes back from her watch in the op's room.

'Hey you lot, I've just been listening to some of the lads chatting on the comms. I didn't hear everything but you know some of them are planning to have a real go at us in the SODS Opera?'

'Oh, let them!' retorts Alison Bevan. 'I'm sick of worrying about what they say about us.'

'Why don't we do something ourselves?' says Fiona Sloan. 'We could have a go at them.'

'Like what? SODS Opera is just an excuse to be filthy and insulting. Why should we degrade ourselves just because of what they all do?'

'I'm not saying we have to degrade ourselves, just that we should put something on together as the Wrens. It would show solidarity. You know how the blokes are always trying to bring us down.'

'You're right Fi,' says Amanda Roberts. 'All they'll do is take the piss. We could really say something. Make a stand.'

'Yeah!' replies Sloan. 'We could really give them a taste of their own medicine. We won't be seeing half these lads again after this deployment.'

'Never mind the lads,' says Alison Bevan. 'I don't even want to see another ship once I've got off this one!'

This has been a long deployment for everybody, but nobody more so than the Wrens. The policy of sending women to sea* is still in its infancy and by no means fully accepted or appreciated by every sailor in the navy, or even every sailor on the *Brilliant*.

---

* The decision to send Wrens to sea was taken in February 1990. The Navy Board's original target for integration was to have 8000 women available for sea by the year 2010 although the number has now been revised to around 6000. The first ship to have Wrens was, in fact, HMS *Brilliant* which took fifteen Wrens in October 1990 and consequently to the Gulf a few months later. See also Women at Sea, page 145.

During this exercise in Operation Sharp Guard some sailors, both junior and senior rates as well as some officers, have come to the firm conclusion that a warship is no place for a woman. Some have kept their feelings to themselves. Others, however, have made it perfectly clear to the seventeen Wrens of the Wrennerie that they are not welcome. The Wrens on this ship are well-qualified, well-trained and well-adjusted young women but after six months the pressure of pioneering for their gender in the face of some committed opposition is beginning to take its toll.

It is 2250. The Wrens have abandoned the plot of *Inspector Morse* and been drawn into a heartfelt debate on their position in what is still widely perceived as a man's world:

'The lads say we wouldn't be able to cope emotionally in a war situation,' says Roni Whittaker [Radar] with feeling, 'but they don't know – we've never been in one. A lot of the men crack up under the pressure, so who's to say we might not do better. I think it's a matter of personality not sex. The other thing is they try and knock us by saying we haven't got the physical strength for the job but half our jobs don't involve physical strength. I sit in the op's room looking at a radar not carting it around on my shoulders.'

'Well, I'll tell you what gets me,' interjects Leading Wren Alex Sparrow [Radio Operator]. 'Because I'm engaged to someone on this ship all the lads give us both a hard time saying that if the ship got hit then we would only be concerned for each other. Well, if we were hit by a missile or something my first concern would be for Jason, I admit that, but surely that would be the same for brothers at sea or fathers and sons at sea. They're allowed to serve together so what's the difference?'

'You're right,' says Clare 'Dutchy' Holland [Weapons Engineering Mechanic}, at eighteen the youngest person on board. 'And you know if there's a fire you're meant to be able to shut the hatch on your oppo in case it spreads. The blokes say we would never be able to do that, you know, actually let someone die. Well, maybe they're right. I'm not sure I could but that's not because I'm female 'cos I don't think half the lads in the same situation would be able to do it either. I mean you live with your mates, work with them, spend near enough twenty-four hours a day with them – it's not something that would come natural to anyone.'

'It's going to take a long time for men to get used to us coming to sea,' says Whittaker, 'and the situation isn't helped by the bad press we get, is it? All the media is interested in is stories about affairs between Wrens and sailors and the pregnancies. I mean, there have been two or three pregnancies out of four thousand of us and yet that is all you ever read about!'

'They've branded us all slags which is so unfair,' responds Alex Sparrow. 'They don't go on about the lads and what they get up to ashore because everybody thinks that's what sailors should do. I've been to parties back home where there's been matelots' wives or girlfriends, and as soon as they found out I was a Wren they completely ignored me. One even attacked me once just for being a Wren, do you remember Fi?'

'Yes. We've become social outcasts haven't we?'

'I went to a do shoreside when I was on my last ship,' recalls Whittaker, 'and a few of the sailors' girlfriends came along. Well, of course I didn't go along in my Eights and steaming bats.* I did myself up – you know, hair up, make-up, the works. Anyway, so one girl turns round to me and says "Oh, I was under the impression that all Wrens were dogs." That's what her boyfriend had told her. She had asked him some question about working with Wrens at sea and he had said, "Don't worry, they're all pig ugly and fat." You've heard that haven't you Alex?'

'Oh yeah. You know I used to be really proud of being a Wren but now I feel like it's a dirty word. Sometimes when I'm ashore I'm frightened of telling people I'm a Wren so I lie and tell them I'm a secretary. That's really sad.'

'Well, I'm not frightened to say it's the worst thing I have ever done in my life joining the Wrens and coming to sea,' says Alison Bevan. 'It's a tragedy for me because I think it's a great job, a great opportunity for the right girl. I'm just not the right girl. I can honestly say these have been really bad times of my life and I hate it. I don't think it is a life for a woman! We don't get treated the way we should!'

'I actually like it at sea,' says Fiona Sloan. 'But I think it is going to take time before we are accepted without question.'

'There is one really great thing about it,' says Ginny McHale. 'I've made some of the best friends I'll ever have amongst Wrens both on this ship and my last one. It's because we have to depend on each other at some of the lowest times in our lives.'

'Well, that's exactly why we ought to stick together now,' says Fiona Sloan quickly. 'We really should do something for the SODS Opera. Something that the lads won't expect. Something they'll remember . . .'

---

* Tough, steel-capped and rubber-soled black boots worn at sea. For more naval slang, see Jackspeak, page 212.

DAY *Tuesday*	DATE *25*	MONTH *October*	YEAR *1994*

PLACE	*Area Iceman, Eastern Adriatic*

POSITION	*Classified*

DISTANCE TRAVELLED midnight to midnight *212.6 nautical miles*

SHIPS LOG. Much calmer day in Iceman. Chased, challenged and boarded MV Dajti, a chrome-ore carrier from Albania – an unusual event for this area. Fuel RAS with USS Kanawa in late afternoon. Quiet patrol overnight

It is **0742**. 'Merchant vessel Dajti, merchant vessel Dajti. This is Watchman Nine Zero, Watchman Nine Zero calling you on channel sixteen, over . . .'

The *Brilliant* is speeding to intercept an Albanian merchant vessel that is ignoring all attempts to communicate with her. She is still out of view over the horizon and, although we have her firmly in our radar sights and are closing in rapidly, her steadfast refusal to respond to any calls (from us or any of the other NATO ships in the area) has already necessitated the launching of a German maritime patrol aircraft (MPA) from the Italian coast.

The communications yeoman, Petty Officer Dave Standen, perseveres in his attempts to contact the Albanian ore carrier on different VHF channels:

'Merchant vessel Dajti, merchant vessel Dajti. This is Watchman Nine Zero, Watchman Nine Zero calling you on channel ten, over . . .'

On the flight deck Jerry Barnbrook and Nick Cooke-Priest are in the Lynx with rotors running, waiting for the order to take off and investigate the silent and suspect merchant vessel.

In the op's room Bob Hawkins is briefing the captain:

'She's not answering our calls or responding to our challenges at all, sir.'

'Where's she come from?'

'She came up through the areas overnight from the Albanian port of Durezz. The German ship *Karlsruhe* was going to board her last night but it was too rough so we were contacted and asked to board her this morning, but she is just not responding to calls.'

'Was she given a rendezvous point to meet us at?'

WOMEN AT SEA

Like so much in the Royal Navy women at sea are nothing new. Even in Nelson's day up to a dozen women were on board the greatest of first rate ships of the line in a variety of roles. Some accompanied their warrant officer husbands, some were seeking a man and eked out an existence cooking and cleaning, some simply lived out their lives in the company of a great many British Tars. Babies were born at sea and very often took the name of the ship in which they entered the world as their own. In action women carried powder or water for the guns or the dying or were slaughtered with as much savagery as the men. Some women helped the surgeon tend the wounded in the dank hole that was the sickbay. One woman even petitioned Nelson for wages after a particularly gruesome voyage where she nursed and saved many wounded after the Battle of the Nile.

By the end of the nineteenth century, women had all but disappeared from naval service save in unofficial capacities in far flung stations. They reappeared in the guise of the Women's Royal Naval Service (WRNS) as Wrens in 1917 to replace men required for active duties afloat. In the two years before the service was disbanded it grew to some 7000 strong with women working not only as telegraphers and writers, but also as boats' crew. In 1919, however, peace saw the WRNS discarded until April 1939 when it was reformed. By the outbreak of the Second World War there were 1000 drivers, cooks, writers, communicators and WRNS officers. At its peak in 1944 there were 74 620 Wrens doing duties such as frontline aircraft maintenance and weapon handling . . . anything except service at sea.

After the war the WRNS was retained and in 1949 it was incorporated into the Royal Navy, although its members were not subject to the Naval Discipline Act until 1978. This was the start of the move by the Royal Navy to give the WRNS equal opportunities and by 1990 women had gone to sea. The following year saw the adoption of Royal Navy ranks and badges and finally the abolition of the WRNS altogether. Today the Royal Navy no longer describes itself as having women at sea, simply people at sea, and females have a career structure designed to give them the same chances as their male counterparts of reaching the top of their profession.

'One was transmitted to her last night but she has not gone to it, sir. At the moment there should be a maritime patrol aircraft flying over her and we have Bright Star on the flight deck ready at Alert Five to take off and prosecute contact.'

It is **0810**. The *Dajti* has been sighted. Ahead of us, about 6 miles on our port bow, a small, rusting cargo ship is moving slowly on a northerly heading. No more than 200 feet above her, a twin-engined maritime patrol aircraft is making long, low passes in an attempt to divert her from her course. Dave Standen continues to transmit:

'*Merchant vessel Dajti, merchant vessel Dajti. This is Watchman Nine Zero . . .*'

On the other side of the bridge James Rapp and Russ Harding are watching the scene through their binoculars.

'The MPA is going in pretty low, sir.'

'Yes, it's quite extraordinary. The *Dajti* is just ignoring everything.'

'She must be fully laden judging from her water-line.'

'Look, someone's come out on the bridge wing . . .'

'Three men, sir. They're just looking up at the MPA with their arms crossed.'

'It's unbelievable.'

It is **0825**. With the Albanian cargo ship now only 500 yards off our starboard bow Captain Rapp has decided to drop a Royal Marine security team on her stern by helicopter. Their task will be to overcome any resistance, secure the ship and find out why she has repeatedly ignored all attempts to contact her.

It is **0834**. Everybody on the bridge of the *Brilliant* watches with apprehension as Bright Star heads in a large arc towards the *Dajti*. Once over the stern they see her come to a hover and drop the boarding-rope. Immediately, six Royal Marines 'fast rope' to the deck and then proceed in a rapid crouching run towards the ship's bridge, covering each other with their assault rifles as they go. Captain Rapp trains his binoculars round to the bridge wing where he sees the three men who emerged earlier still standing, arms crossed, and watching the marine commandos advancing towards them.

It is **0838**. 'You're kidding!' says Captain Rapp, talking through the radio-telephone to Marine Lieutenant Steve O'Neill on the *Dajti*. 'A broken radio! Why on earth couldn't they have made signs or something rather than just stand there with their arms crossed? OK, now we've got them we'll search them. Stay there. We'll send over the search parties in two sticks by Pacific . . .'

It is **0839**. Micky Goble, looking at the yellow blip on his radar that is the *Dajti*, bursts into helpless laughter.

'Poor, bleedin' buggers!' he splutters. 'They must have thought the Third World War had started.'

'It was their own fault for havin' a knackered radio,' says Ginger Lowden.

'Yeah, I know, I know, I know . . .' says Goble with eyes watering, 'but there they were, just sailin' along, mindin' their own business . . . when a bleedin' great MPA starts dive-bombing 'em . . . then a fuckin' great British warship comes hurtlin' over the horizon like a sleek messenger of death and practically runs 'em down. Then, if that ain't enough, a friggin' helicopter swoops out of the sky and drops six trained killers on their stern dressed in battle fatigues and flak jackets and pointin' high velocity assault rifles at anyone that moved. And all for havin' a dodgy cat's whisker . . . !'

It is **1800**. Nick Cooke-Priest and Jerry Barnbrook look around furtively before knocking on Richard Newton's cabin door.

'Come!' says the doctor from inside.

The two flight officers walk in quickly and sit down. Seconds later, there is another knock.

'Come!'

The door slides open and Keith Blount steps in, followed by Kevin Easterbrook.

'Right!' says the doctor. 'Now we're all here let's get started. Nobody's got any second thoughts I hope.'

The four other officers look at each other quizzically.

'They'll probably string us up,' says Easterbrook.

'Yeah!' agrees Barnbrook. 'They don't take prisoners on the night – especially officers.'

'Look, no one's going to bottle out now. We'll play it straight. Just some good barber shop stuff. Now here's the sheets for 'Goodnight Sweetheart' – Kevin, you lead. Jerry, you take the high part. Keith and me'll take bass and Nick, you harmonize . . .'

'If they don't like something they hurl beer cans you know,' says Blount.

'Yeah! Probably full ones,' says Easterbrook.

'OK on three,' says the doctor. 'One . . . Two . . . Three . . .'

It is **2110**. The darkened op's room continues the quiet but intense business of surveillance by scanning Iceman for unannounced vessels and the Montenegrin coast for infringing Serb aircraft. Bob Hawkins, concentrating on his radar screen, starts as Leading Seaman (Missile Man) Steve Lewis taps him on the shoulder.

'Sorry to bother you sir,' whispers Lewis.

'Go ahead.'

'Just to let you know, sir, you'll be playing a Devonport slapper.'

'Oh, right. I love wearing women's clothing!'

'Yes sir, I've heard.'

'Where do I get the gear?'

'I'll get you a wig and a skirt. You have a word with the girlies and ask for some lipstick and a blouse. Make sure it's nice and big 'cos you should have an enormous pair of jugs.'

'I wouldn't have it any other way Leading Seaman Lewis!'

It is **2220**. Weapons Engineering Mechanic Kevin 'Gladys' Gladman is sitting down in his mess with Paul 'Sharkey' Ward and sipping thoughtfully at his tea.

'. . . so you lot will all stand there in black, alright? And you'll all be carryin' clubs or truncheons or somethin' and wearin' shades. We'll have really low light except from underneath so we all look seriously heavy and I'm goin' to call myself "the grim reaper". I'll do the whole thing in verse and I tell you what, there ain't goin' to be nobody gettin' off lightly. I'm goin' to have a bleedin' bash at the whole fuckin' ship . . .'

It is **2300**. In the Wrennerie Fiona Sloan is humming a tune to some of her messmates. It is the well-known soul classic 'I Will Survive' by Gloria Gaynor.

'You all know it don't you?' she says. 'Well, that's the one to hit them with. Now we've just got to come up with some new lyrics . . .'

It is **2330**. Micky Goble creeps into his gulch and climbs into his pit as quietly as he can.

'Is that you Mick?' whispers Dave Mynett from the pit above.

'No. It's Captain Rapp! Who d'ya think it is you prat?'

'You doin' anythin' for the SODS Opera?'

'Oh, I dunno'. Chief Franklin's asked if I'd like to be the master of ceremonies. I said I'd think about it . . .'

DAY *Friday*	DATE *28*	MONTH *October*	YEAR *1994*

PLACE	*Eastern Adriatic, on passage to Istanbul*

POSITION	At 0600 *Classified* At 2359 *39°02′N 19°30′E*

DISTANCE TRAVELLED midnight to midnight *273.3 nautical miles*

SHIPS LOG. Handed over Iceman to HMCS Toronto. Fast passage out of Montenegro. Fall out from Action Stations for unloading to Cruising Stations. R/V with SPS Victoria for passage to Istanbul.

It is **1400**. The *Brilliant* has been relieved from duty in Iceman by the Canadian ship *Toronto*. The upper deck weapons have been unloaded and we have joined with the Spanish ship *Victoria* for our passage to Istanbul. Normally, coming out of Defence Watches into Cruising Stations would mean a more relaxed time for everybody but today is the last full day for SODS Opera rehearsals so the ship is a hive of creative activity. Everywhere, people are rehearsing songs, dances, routines, acts, melodramas, revues, sketches, skits and mimes – some of them controversial, many of them insulting and most of them vulgar. Nobody knows exactly what the Wrens are putting on for the show but everybody is talking about it and rumour is rife.

In the wardroom Russ Harding and Bob Hawkins have just sat down for a cup of tea.

'I expect the Wrens are going to have a go at the blokes,' says Hawkins. 'Get the boot in for all the flak they get.'

'I'm so sick of this ridiculous attitude to women at sea. It's so misinformed and ignorant.'

'Russ, you can't say that. A lot of people have genuine problems with the idea of women at sea.'

'Only old dinosaurs who can't move with the times.'

'Well, I think I'm as forward-looking as the next person but I have a big problem with the whole issue.'

'Such as? I thought you rated your women in the op's room.'

'Oh, I do. Absolutely. Some of the women I've had working for me have been amongst the best radar operators I've ever had. They are conscientious and able to concentrate better and harder than a lot of the blokes. No, it's not a professional thing. It's a personal thing. My argument is that the business of a warship is to be aggressive. And I think that a warship with women on board is less aggressive and has a different, softer flavour to it. As a warfare officer my view is that such a ship is less able to do its job as a warship. I sincerely believe that Russ.'

'I will admit that in the beginning I had severe misgivings too. But I have now come round completely. I mean a lot of people go on about the fact that girls aren't strong enough to cope with life at sea, don't have the upper body strength. Well, that's utter rubbish. Look at me. I'm not exactly Arnold Schwarzenegger. It completely depends on what job you're doing. You don't need a 16 stone prop forward to look at a radar or be a medical assistant or even to be a PWO.'

'I agree with all that. I can appreciate all the logical arguments for having women at sea. My problem is the moral issue of sending women to war. I know it's an old-fashioned view but I see women as the life givers not the life takers – they should not be sent into a war zone. And, what is more, I think that any government that makes a policy decision to send women to war is morally bankrupt.'

'You're being too emotional Bob,' says Paul Metcalfe from the other side of the room. 'The RAF has now got a front-line woman fighter pilot and, as we know, the US Navy has two women helicopter pilots working out here. I think that is progress and we've got to give change a chance. When we first put women to sea it was never going to work overnight. I reckon it has to be seen as a ten-year plan at the minimum because we won't have a true evaluation of women at sea until women have reached the highest levels. And I don't just mean as officers but as senior rates as well.'

'But Paul, the career structure for women can't be the same as the one for men.'

'Why on earth not?'

'Because women, quite naturally, want to take time out to have a family. That will always be disruptive to the continuity of their career.'

'You're overstating the case Bob!' says Harding, now raising his voice slightly.

'Women in the Royal Navy are now firmly established as seagoing. No government is ever going to change that. The only thing that will change is peoples' attitudes as they get used to the idea. There has been a lot in the press about women who have been forced to leave their jobs in one of the services because of pregnancy. That is changing. That has got to change. In the future, when one of our wives has a baby, whether she's in the navy or not, we will be allowed to take time off as paternity leave because the rule for one must be the rule for the other. That is equality. I see that very clearly.'

'Well, you're lucky Russ,' says Hawkins. 'You've obviously been able to sort all this out for yourself. I'm still struggling with my conscience about the whole thing. As I said, this is not a professional problem for me – it's purely personal. But, I'll tell you something. It's my belief that a very substantial proportion of this ship remains firmly against the idea of mixed manning and that is from their professional point of view.'

'Go and talk to the POs and the chiefs. A few of them used to be committed anti-Wrenners but they've come round.'

'Not all of them Russ, and certainly not some of the younger chaps.'

'That's a male tribal thing. Listen, there's still a great deal of ignorance about because the men haven't got used to the idea yet. On this ship less than ten per cent are women so our girls don't stand a chance of swaying mass opinion when they're such a small minority. Wait until we are getting twenty, thirty, forty per cent female crews. That's when opinions will start to change. Meanwhile it's up to the converted to keep the faith . . . and the Wrens to keep the courage.'

DAY *Saturday*	**DATE** 29	**MONTH** *October*	**YEAR** *1994*
PLACE	*Southern Ionian Sea, on passage to Istanbul*		
POSITION	At **0600** *38°14′N 20°04′E* At **2359** *37°07′N 23°48′E*		

DISTANCE TRAVELLED midnight to midnight *314.4 nautical miles*

SHIPS LOG. A morning of passage exercises with SPS Victoria. Started with CROSSPOL. Light jack stay to return personnel. In the evening perfect clear skies and warm weather for SODS Opera on the flight deck. Continued passage through southern Aegean overnight.

It is **1000**. Sailing in convoy with the Spanish frigate *Victoria* we have come into the busy shipping area south of the Peloponnese. We will proceed through the Kitherai Channel into the Mirtoan Sea and then up to the Aegean on our way to the Dardanelles and Istanbul.

Earlier today we took advantage of sailing with the *Victoria* by doing 'officer of the watch' manoeuvres, a series of complex, close quarter evolutions involving high speed turns, weaving loops and formation cruising. For 120 minutes the vessels danced an elaborate tango for two frigates before stopping to 'crosspol' – the naval procedure of swapping personnel between ships for a few hours. Normally carried out between ships of different nationalities, it is a diplomatic exercise designed to encourage understanding and friendship between navies.*

Today the *Victoria* and the *Brilliant* swapped five personnel, including Captain Rapp, by the Pacific rigid inflatable.

It is **1500**. The *Brilliant* and the *Victoria* have lined up side by side to 'recover crosspol' – that is, to give each other's sailors back. Today, everybody will be hoisted by light jack stay, a pulley and rope system rigged between the ships.

The first 'Brilliantine' to come over is Petty Officer Yeoman Dave Standen. Suspended in his harness from a running block, he is pulled slowly across the thick hemp rope that stretches between the two warships. Dangling no more than 30 feet above a deep-swelling and fast-running sea, his passage is very smooth – until about half way. From that point on, however, naval tradition demands that he has as rough a ride as possible. To everybody's great amusement Standen is bounced repeatedly, lowered tantalizingly to the wave tops and swung violently backwards and forwards before being hoisted in – or nearly. His progress is halted once again, about 5 feet from the ship's side, when Kiwi Belben runs forward to hurl a full bucket of cold water over the hapless, pendulant PO.

'That's me friggin' baccy ruined you bastard!'

Everybody laughs the louder.

The next three jack stay customers get the same treatment. But now it is the turn of Captain Rapp. He comes over smoothly all the way. As he approaches the side of the *Brilliant* Kiwi Belben, now fully warmed to his task, edges forward with his bucket of water. Everybody watches aghast.

Belben, hiding behind a torpedo tube, waits until the captain is in exactly the right position and then, trembling with excited expectation . . . puts the bucket down.

'Not a good career move,' he says with a sudden rush of wisdom to the head.

It is **1930**. The *Brilliant* maintains her heading through the southern Aegean Sea under a gleaming, canopy of Mediterranean stars. From the bridge Russ Harding gives his routine evening address.

---

* Crosspols are popular with sailors from 'dry' navies, like the US Navy, who go to spend a few hours on a ship from a 'wet' navy like the Royal Navy. Their departure is invariably more wobbly than their arrival.

'Good evening. First Lieutenant speaking. The SODS Opera will begin in approximately one hour. The chiefs have been working hard to set up the stage on the flight deck. For those of you who haven't been on the upper deck yet, fate has smiled kindly on us. It's a beautiful, warm evening with stars as bright as I've seen. Let's all enjoy this evening – I know people have put a lot of work into preparing entertainments. The humour, I know, will be as sharp as ever and, in the best naval tradition, scathing and biting. As you know there are not really any rules tonight although I would ask you not to aim it personally or take it personally. Let's all have a good time. That's all.'

With an hour to go people are still frantically getting ready: Bob Hawkins is attempting to stuff two blown-up condoms down his blouse whilst Liz Hall helps him to put on his lipstick; the doctor is busy practising his baritone 'doo wops' whilst the flight commander is still trying to hit the soprano 'ooh wahs'; 'Gladys' Gladman is sharpening his tongue ready for a scything performance at his cutting best; Micky Goble, the night's compere is wondering if it is too late to sit down and write some sort of script; and the Wrens are behind closed doors.

It is **2030**. The flight deck of the Type 22 frigate has been transformed into an end-of-pier vaudeville theatre. A massive red curtain is draped across the entire hangar and adorned with a huge gold anchor and enormous letters proclaiming the name HMS BOLLOCKS. Underneath, in only slightly smaller letters, is the captain's name, complete with his middle initial of C exaggerated for effect: CAP-TAIN J. C.RAPP. The ratings, in loud Hawaiian shirts and Bermuda shorts, crowd round the elevated stage with cans of beer to hand while the captain and his officers, in full dress uniform, sit in their traditional front row seats.

The lights go up and the audience applauds appreciatively as the the round and familiar figure of Leading Seaman Micky Goble rolls on to the stage. Wearing baggy shorts, T-shirt and a multicoloured Turkish skull-cap, he takes the microphone and the first of many liberties by winking seductively at Captain Rapp.

'Right! Good evenin' and welcome to SODS Opera 1994. We've got a lot of acts to get through so we'll get straight down to the scorin' procedure. Over here on the right we have the famous clapometer. You'll see no expense has been spared and we've used the best cardboard in its construction. It's really very simple – how it works is that when you applaud, the indicator, actually worked by PO Clive Wilkinson on the end of a piece of string, will rise up this scale. Starting at the lower end of the scale you've got Dog Shite, then movin' up to slightly better you've got Dog's Breath. Above that you've got the dizzy heights of Dog's Knob, and then you reach the zenith of Dog's Bollocks. Alright? I know it's complicated, so just you clap like fuck and leave the high tech stuff to us . . .'

It is **2138**. As expected, the evening is becoming increasingly offensive, anarchic and obscene. It actually started fairly innocuously with 'Doc and the Monotones', heavily Brylcreemed and Raybanned, singing their much rehearsed 'Goodnight Sweetheart' and 'Come Back My Love' which scored a less than generous Dog's Breath' on the clapometer.

Then Bob Hawkins amply demonstrated his commitment to crossing rank divisions by taking part in a sketch with the gunners that involved pouting suggestively while dressed up as a Devonport prostitute. An approving audience delighted Hawkins by awarding them an unequivocal Dog's Knob.

Now a combined mess of gunners, seamen and radio operators, called the 'Lost Boys', gyrate hip-swingingly and pelvis-thrustingly to Take That with their version of 'Relight My Fire'. Dressed as devils dancing in hell, they look hilarious but their message is deadly serious: if the Admiralty implements its proposal to amalgamate weapons operators and maintainers many will lose their jobs and be condemned to unemployment on Civvy Street. To a roar of sympathetic cheers the Lost Boys' finale is to offer the Admiralty a collective, personal message. All five of the devil chorus turn round, bend over and expose ten bare buttocks, each with a letter lipsticked on to it: KI SS MY AR SE.

It is **2201**. Micky Goble is back on stage filling time whilst the next act gets ready:
'. . . and here's one for all you Trekkies. How many ears has Mr Spock got? He's got a right ear, a left ear and . . . a final front . . . ear!'

'OK, OK, that's the last clean joke of the night I promise you. Right, I have just been told we are ready for the WEM's mess and "Gladys" Gladman who is goin' to read you one of his poems. Keats – eat your heart out . . .'

Leading Weapons Engineering Mechanic Kevin 'Gladys' Gladman appears as the grim reaper, flanked by vicious looking 'bodyguards' carrying baseball bats. To the backing of a pounding, electronic rhythm he spits out a sneering epic poem that scatters insult, offence and ridicule like bullets from a machine gun:

> Welcome to the *Brilliant's* SODS Opera
> Are you having a good time, by the way?
> Fuck off. I'm about to offend you –
> This is your own Judgement Day
> No stone will go without turning,
> So I hope you're not holier than thou.
> If you can't handle public humiliation
> You should leave the flight deck right now.

Good evening men. Jimmy here.
An evening sit. rep. I will make.
This will only take an hour
So no need to book a shake.
The old man makes me do these pipes,
It's not a matter of choice,
So please don't let it be said that
I love the sound of my own voice.

We serve aboard the *Brilliant*,
A ship so fine and stealthy,
I have never known a ship quite like it,
For its morale is oh so healthy
We volunteer for everything,
And even more if we could.
We are the only ship in NATO
That would board a piece of fucking driftwood.

We have a bunch of Royals on board,
The marine protection teams.
All day they mince round Two Deck
Like a fucking bunch of queens.
We have a bunch of Royals on board,
All in green with stony face.
Can someone please tell me their job on board.
They're a fucking waste of space.

We are oh so glad for Wrens at sea,
They are not lamb dressed as mutton.
But when it comes to PMT
Don't let 'em near the fire button.
They spend all day soaked in cheap perfume,
The smell really is quite rank.
It's amazing how much time off they get
With the offer of a soapy tip wank . . .

And what about Alfie and Cathy
For Christ's sake what is the score?
I suppose that she's saved you a fortune,
Well you don't have to pay for a whore.

155

I know I'm in shit for my verses
But I can handle DQs.*
I don't care if I have offended some people.
I don't give a shit, a stuff or a hoot.
I have been vetted from the first day of joining.
That is life in a fucking blue suit.

It is **2235**. Micky Goble is leading up to his final introduction of the evening.

'. . . and what do you call a collection of Wrens? What do you think of a "complaint" of Wrens, or maybe a "moan" of Wrens. No, I think the best one is a "wriggle" of Wrens . . . ! Actually, I don't know why people have such a problem with havin' Wrens at sea. It's much better than havin' men when you think about it. Men are so bleedin' aggressive – I mean if we can't fuck it we kill it, that's our attitude. No, personally I think we should have women in all the top military and political positions. There wouldn't be any wars that's for sure. Just intense negotiations every twenty-eight days . . . !

'Ladies and gentlemen, please welcome direct from the Wrennerie our very own wriggle of Wrens.'

To a mixture of jeers and cheers, a group of twelve Wrens walks out to centre stage. Lit by a single spotlight Fiona Sloan steps forward to speak:

'Gentlemen, before we entertain you with a song I have a few words to say by way of introduction.' She pauses.

'I would just like to say thank you for the superb welcome and hospitality you gave us when we arrived on the ship . . . NOT!'

Some sailors at the back of the audience start to hiss.

'You have at all times treated us not as splits** but as equals . . . I DON'T THINK!'

The hissing gets louder.

'Your kindness, tolerance, and lack of prejudice has not gone unnoticed. THANKS FOR NOTHING ONE AND ALL! This song's dedicated to you . . .'

A section of the audience has now broken into a chorus of hisses, jeers and catcalls. The officers in the front row look uncomfortable.

Over the loudspeaker come the familiar opening bars of Gloria Gaynor's stirring anthem of defiance: 'I Will Survive'. The Wrens tap their feet in time to the rhythm and wait for their cue to sing . . .

* Detention Quarters. For more acronyms, see The Wonders of Naval Abbreviation, page 218.
**Wrens. For more naval slang, see Jackspeak, page 212.

First when we joined we were petrified.
Kept thinking we could never live with you side by side
But then we spent so many nights thinking how you did us wrong
And we grew strong, we learnt how to get along
And so we're back . . .

The audience: YAAA! GET EM OFF! GET EM OFF! GET EM OFF! BOOOO!

So there you go, walk out the door,
No turning round now,
'Cos Wrens aren't welcome anymore.
Weren't you the ones who tried to break us on this trip,
But you didn't win,
'Cos we took all of your shit . . .

HISSSSSSSS! BOOOOO! OFF! OFF! OFF! OFF! OFF . . . !

We will survive,
As long as we've got Action Stations
We know we'll stay alive,
We've got all our charts complete,
And we're in the driver's seat,
We will survive. . .

OGGY OGGY OGGY! OI, OI, OI! OGGY OGGY OGGY OI, OI, OI . . . !

It has now become a contest to see who can sing or chant loudest. The sailors are settling into the rhythm of a football chant in an attempt to shout the Wrens off stage. The Wrens respond with a new determination and are now belting out the song at the tops of their voices.

HEY look at US,
We're PEOPLE TOO,
We're not just some LITTLE GIRLS
Who should BOW DOWN to all of YOU!

GET YER TITS OUT, GET YER TITS OUT, GET YOUR TITS OUT FOR THE BOYS . . . !

So you felt like drafting us
Thinking we would just agree.
Well we're SICK of all this SEA TIME,
You can SOD your life at SEA.
So here we GO,
Walk OUT the door.
Don't turn around now, we're NOT WELCOME anymore.
Weren't you the ones who tried to break us with 'Goodbye'?
Did you think we'd crumble?
Did you think we'd break down and cry?
Oh no not us, WE WILL SURVIVE . . . !

It is **0000**. SODS Opera has finished. The flight deck is empty and the British warship continues on her path with poise and equanimity.

For one night only the strict order of a naval society was openly dismantled and replaced with active disorder. This was not an anarchic act of mini-mutiny, but a bizarre way of actually confirming and strengthening the very order that was dismantled. Tonight's disorder was part of a greater order, and the discord part of a wider harmony. Ironically, SODS Opera underpins the ultimate control that guarantees continuity and solidarity. Everything is normal and as it should be.

Tonight some home truths have been told. Tonight some people have been upset. Tonight some scores have been settled.

Tomorrow it will be business as usual.

DAY *Sunday*	**DATE** *30*	**MONTH** *October*	**YEAR** *1994*
PLACE	*Northern Aegean Sea, on passage to Istanbul*		
POSITION	**At 0600** *37°52'N 24°30'E* **At 2359** *40°40'N 27°28'E*		
DISTANCE TRAVELLED midnight to midnight *250.1 nautical miles*			

SHIPS LOG. Continued passage to Istanbul. Passed through the Dardanelles in late afternoon. Slow passage through Sea of Marmara overnight.

It is **1045**. A small crowd is congregating in the main galley for the Sunday church service. Tracie Lovegrove and Nick Cooke-Priest, who is to conduct the service, are still photocopying the hymn sheets so several people are taking the opportunity to talk about the events of last night while they wait.

'The Wrens had real balls to do that. I admire them for it and I've told them so,' says Bob Hawkins.

'They did themselves a lot of favours,' agrees Norman Boyes. 'I've written them a letter congratulating them for their courage and telling them to ignore all the oiks.'

'Those blokes were well out of order,' says Chief Petty Officer Dave Gregory. 'Those girls showed 'em though didn't they. Good on 'em, that's what I say . . .'

It is **1058**. Nick Cooke-Priest steps up to the lectern to read the day's lesson:

'The reading this morning is taken from Proverbs 6, verses 7 to 19.

'A scoundrel and a villain who goes about with a corrupt mouth, who winks with his eyes, signals with his feet, motions with his fingers and who plots evil with deceit in his heart – he always stirs up dissension, therefore disaster will overtake him in an instant and he will suddenly be destroyed without remedy. There are six things the Lord hates: a lying tongue, hands that shed innocent blood, a heart that devises wicked schemes, feet that are quick to rush into evil, a false witness who pours out lies and a man who stirs up dissension among brothers. That is the word of the Lord.

'Let us pray . . .'

One deck below in the WEMS mess Kevin 'Gladys' Gladman is sitting down with a can of beer and lighting up another cigarette.

'Good last night weren't it?' he says to Sharkey Ward.

'Yeah, went down well mate. Got the only Dog's Bollocks.'

'Top bleedin' score. Brilliant!' says Gladman.

'Got any plans for Istanbul Gladys?'

'No, not really,' replies Gladman, casually blowing smoke rings up to the deck-head. 'Just have a few beers and do me best to keep out of trouble I s'pose . . .'

Chapter Seven

TURKISH DELIGHTS

DAY *Monday*	**DATE** *31*	**MONTH** *October*	**YEAR** *1994*

PLACE	*The Bosphorus, approaching Istanbul*

POSITION	*41°00'N 29°00'E*

SHIPS LOG. Sailed from Marmara Sea into the Bosphorus. Anchored at Berth One opposite Dolmabahce Palace. Full floodlighting put out on port side. In the evening an official reception for 100 guests.

It is **0900**. The *Brilliant* sails from the dark blue hues of the Marmara Sea into the sparkling waters of the Bosphorus. Hands are already in position at their harbour stations on the upper deck and all are looking towards the distant dramatic skyline of Istanbul with its domes and towering minarets. Inside the ship on the bridge flat the navigator, Perry Stowell, is holding a harbour briefing for the captain, the first lieutenant and the harbour station supervisors:

'. . . our estimated time for anchoring is 1000, sir. It's a fine, sunny day. The wind is easterly at four knots, sea state is One*, and there is no cloud cover. Visibility is about six miles. We have been given an excellent anchorage, sir, just six hundred yards offshore, and adjacent to the Dolmabahce Palace. We will anchor in a depth of thirty-seven metres so I intend to go for a running anchorage, sir, and veering the anchor to the water-line. We're in sand and mud and I propose to use the starboard anchor with six shackles . . .'**

Outside, the foc'sle party, who will be responsible for dropping the anchor, lines up at ease in front of the Exocet missile launchers. Micky Goble is amongst them and, the only one to have been to Istanbul before, is providing a running commentary to their approach:

---

*Calm waters.
** 15 fathoms (90 feet/27.5 metres) of anchor chain.

'Istanbul is actually the only city in the world built on two continents. Over on
that side, on the left, that's Europe alright? But on that side, on the right, that's
  Asia.'
  'Old in'it?' observes a voice from the back of the foc'sle party.
  'Ancient, this place,' confirms their self-elected tour guide. 'Really, really old.
Loads of history. Old King Richard came over here and tried to beat this lot up in
the Crusades. Can't see why he bothered mind, but each to his own I s'pose.'

It is 0930. The *Brilliant* sails close to the shore as she is guided through the busy,
winding straits of the Bosphorus to her anchorage. On the left is the remarkable
fortified promontory of the Golden Horn, rich in its blend of Byzantine splendour
and Ottoman opulence. Slowly, the battle-grey frigate glides past the elegant, six-
minaret Sultan Ahmet mosque, known as the Blue Mosque because of its blue tile
interior, the imposing grandeur of Suleymaniye Mosque and the magnificent
Topkapi Palace. Micky Goble is in full flow:
  'That's the Blue Mosque over there . . .'
  'Which one?'
  'That one right in front of you, you blind git!'
  'It's white.'
  'So?'
  'Why's it called the Blue Mosque then?'
  'I dunno. They ran out of blue paint I s'pose.'
  'What's that big red place Micky?'
  'That big red place is the royal palace. It's called Topcat Palace or somethin'. An'
over there is the Galata tower, that short fat stumpy one. And the other side of
that's the covered bazaar – amazin' place, full of leather and jewellery and stuff . . .
Cor, I feel like blinkin' Judith Chalmers here . . .'
  'Foc'sle party, ho!' shouts Petty Officer Ian Nurding. 'Right turn, dismiss! Stand
by to let go starboard anchor.'

It is 1730. The *Brilliant* is at anchor in the middle of old Istanbul. Just across the
water on our port quarter is the beautiful Dolmabahce Palace with its stunning
white marble facade, ahead of us is the breathtaking Bogazici suspension bridge
that links Europe to Asia and all around us the Bosphorus bustles with cargo
ships, fishing boats and passenger ferries. The evening echoes with their sirens
together with the timeless sound of muezzins calling the faithful to prayer.
  Down in the main galley Russ Harding is panicking. He is checking the catering arrangements for tonight's official reception for one hundred guests and is

worried that there are too many spinach tartlets and not enough smoked salmon canapés.

'Don't worry sir,' says Leading Cook Mark Warburton, 'I'll do a re-count and if it's still the same I can soon knock up some more canapés . . . would you like to try one sir?'

Meanwhile, the flight deck is being magically transformed into an elegant setting for tonight's party: a huge red-and-white striped canvas awning has been erected over the entire deck; the hangar doors have been opened to reveal Bright Star, washed, polished and gleaming; and on the central landing grid a working fountain is in the process of being built complete with rocks and foliage. This task has been given to the YOs – a traditional test of initiative for young officers.

Midshipman Christian 'Bam Bam' Bamforth, Sub-Lieutenant Julian Titmus and Sub-Lieutenant Dougie Auld struggle with hose pipes, sandstone rocks taken earlier in the deployment from a building site in Trieste and a dozen dwarf fig trees just delivered to the ship from a Turkish flower shop.

The hose pipe has been clamped into the grid with one end pointing upwards and the other end fed along the flight deck to a hatch going down to the quarterdeck and the nearest seawater fire hydrant.

'OK. Turn on the water Bam Bam!' shouts Titmus to Bamforth, who has climbed down to the quarterdeck.

'What?!' shouts Bamforth from a deck below.

'I said turn on the water!'

'I have!'

'Oh!' says Titmus, looking at the distinctly dry fountainhead.

'Damn!' says Auld. 'There must be a blockage somewhere . . .'

Titmus looks round. 'Er, excuse me Leading Seaman Goble!'

'Yes sir?'

'Would you mind not standing on the hose pipe!'

'Oh! Sorry sir. Didn't see it there,' says Goble with a broad grin.

The rotund radarman steps off the hose pipe which suddenly stiffens with coursing energy. Titmus and Auld dive for safety as a powerful jet of seawater explodes from the inverted nozzle, rockets into the canvas awning and sprays everything within 10 yards.

'Has anything happened yet?' shouts Bamforth from the quarterdeck.

It is **1805**. Russ Harding, cup of tea in hand, walks out on to the flight deck to inspect the water fountain.

'Well, what do you think sir?' enquires Julian Titmus.

Harding says nothing.

'It'll look better in low lighting,' ventures Christian Bamforth.

Harding raises an eyebrow.

'It's certainly a talking point,' suggests Dougie Auld.

'But . . .' says Harding at last, '. . . that isn't a fountain. It's a sort of dribbling waterfall.'

'Well sir, the problem is the water pressure. It's either this or a gusher. We can't get an in-between.'

'Well, it'll have to do I suppose,' says the first lieutenant impatiently, remembering he still has to check on the smoked salmon canapés.

'With people milling about, sir, it'll look great,' says Titmus, unconvincingly.

It is **1945**. The *Brilliant*, floodlit along her sides, looks at her elegant best from the banks of the Bosphorus. Sleek and streamlined, her silvery complexion is set off beautifully by the deep, dark blue of a Turkish night sky. She is the perfect diplomatic venue.

On the flight deck the ceremonial side piping party* prepares for the arrival of the first boatload of guests whilst Russ Harding takes the opportunity to brief the officers in the wardroom.

'The guest list for tonight is somewhat incomplete but to my knowledge there will be seventeen Turkish naval captains with their wives, some local VIPs and around sixty from the British community in Istanbul co-ordinated by the consulate. Everybody will be shuttled over on the liberty boat.** I expect the bulk of guests to arrive on the first shuttle so they'll be coming aboard thick and fast. I will meet everybody at the head of the gangway and the captain will greet them somewhere at the for'ard end of the flight deck. All of you please split up and mingle with the guests and make sure that, even though you are paying, they're supplied with drinks and finger food at all times.*** Petty Officer Lilley has a team of seven volunteers who will be serving tonight.

'One more point, gentlemen. This is a diplomatic exercise so please mingle with everybody equally. Contrary to popular opinion, pretty young women have no intrinsic need of more attention than any other category of person – at least as far as naval cocktail receptions are concerned!

---

* Historically the pipe was used to convey instructions and orders around the ship but now it is used on only three occasions. The first is to herald the approach of rounds. The second is to 'call the hands' in the morning. And the third is when the captain or other VIPs join or leave the ship during an official call.

** A vessel used to transfer off-duty personnel [libertymen] ashore and vice versa.

*** Cocktail parties on board a ship are not paid for by the Crown but through funds raised from officers.

'Right. I think it has the hallmarks of a very good do and, you might be interested to know, my sense of humour's coming back slowly.

'Carry on.'

It is **2010**. The reception is in full swing. After three shuttles of the liberty boat the flight deck is milling with high-ranking Turkish naval officers, smiling local dignitaries, elegant women in long evening gowns, mild-mannered diplomats and a heterogenous collection of laughing, back-slapping British expatriates.

As the officers perform their mingling duties various ratings, positioned strategically around the flight deck, are 'closed up to cocktail party stations': Leading Seaman Micky Goble, on ceremonial side piping duty at the head of the gangway, pipes on the guests as they arrive; Petty Officer Clive Wilkinson, on cloakroom duty, collects hats and coats on a table in front of the Lynx helicopter; Petty Officer Tony Lilley, as head steward, oversees the serving of food and drink to all the guests; and Leading Steward Andy Conway, as barman, dispenses drink with a sense of vengeful abandon.

'Andy,' says Wren Viv Worrall, coming to the drinks table with an order, 'the PWO, MEO and DWEO all want beers and FLOBS wants a gin and tonic.'

'Comin' up girl,' replies the sparky Essex boy, immediately pouring out three Budweisers. 'There you go Viv an' this 'ere's for the flight observer . . .'

Conway pours out a huge tumbler full of Gordon's Dry Gin, adds a dribble of tonic and a small slice of lemon.

'That'll blow 'is bleedin' 'ead off,' grins the leading steward, looking over towards Nick Cooke-Priest who is talking intently to an attractive brunette in a rather striking red dress.

It is 2100. As the reception proceeds on the flight deck a rather less formal gathering is taking place two decks below. Tonight is Hallowe'en and one of the messes has decided to have a wild, loud and rather boozy party of their own. The party list includes an imaginative variety of werewolves, several zombies, a Dracula, an Egyptian mummy, a human coffin, three Frankenstein's monsters, two road traffic accidents and an acid-attack victim. Dressed in their grotesque costumes, the party-goers gyrate to ear-shattering, thumping dance music whilst swigging enthusiastically from their beer cans. On the door of the mess is a notice written in blood-red ink explaining who is and who is not welcome at the party:

Men beware - Women's bits only may pass this door.

The Wrens are doing a bit of female bonding.

It is 0300. The last liberty boat has left the jetty bringing back the reception embarkation patrol,* the party die-hards are wandering off to their cabins and the Wrens have passed out in their costumes.

Having a last cigarette before going to their pits, Micky Goble and Leading Seaman George Peart lean on the guardrail of the flight deck and look across to the twinkling lights of Istanbul.

'Gonna hit the bazaars tomorrow,' says Goble.

'Yeah, me too,' nods Peart.

'Thought I might have one o' them Turkish baths and a massage too.'

'That sounds good.'

'Be a laugh anyway . . .'

DAY *Tuesday*	**DATE** *1*	**MONTH** *November*	**YEAR**	*1994*
PLACE	*Istanbul, at anchor in the Bosphorus*			
POSITION	*41°00'N 29°00'E*			

SHIPS LOG. At anchor in Istanbul. Ship was stored with fresh food. Most of those not on duty went ashore. CO attended lunch at the consulate. Weather was fine and hazy. In the evening fifty of the ship's company attended reception at the consulate.

It is 1000. It is a bright sunny day and most people are heading ashore. The liberty boat is due alongside any minute to collect the first batch of 'libertymen'. As everybody congregates on the flight deck in shorts, T-shirts and light-hearted mood the master-at-arms takes the opportunity to make an announcement on the main broadcast system:

'Do you hear there? Do you hear there? The ship's company is reminded that your best behaviour is required ashore. No sports rig is to be worn, no Union Jack shorts. Keep your money safe in your pockets and keep your identity cards separate. Before you go ashore please pick up a help card from the quartermaster. This has some useful

---

* The waters of the Bosphorus, although quite sheltered, are notorious for 'chop' – small, short waves that can make boarding or leaving a liberty boat particularly hazardous for the inexperienced, unwary or inebriated. Out of courtesy to guests, a patrol is provided to ensure their safety.

phrases in Turkish including "I AM A LOST SAILOR. PLEASE DIRECT ME BACK TO THE DOLMABAHCE JETTY" and there's a little map on the other side. Never let it be said we don't look after you. Have a good time and behave yourselves.'

Kevin 'Gladys' Gladman, the grim reaper of SODS Opera fame, listens to the announcement standing by the gangway. 'Bloody Joss treats us like blinkin' schoolkids sometimes,' he says with a smirk and then heads down to the liberty boat that has just arrived . . .

As the ship's policeman Chay Robertson has a thankless job, but this tall, broad-shouldered and bespectacled Scot from Aberdeen is more than equal to the task.

'I've become very thick-skinned doing this job. I have to apply the law and sometimes that means arresting people and helping to prosecute them in a naval court, whether held at sea or shoreside. If a sailor gets into trouble ashore, drunk and disorderly or fighting, I will go and get him from whatever local nick he's ended up in, extract him and bring him back to the ship.

'Then he is dealt with by us – probably a great deal more harshly but at least he's not stuck in some foreign gaol.

'I don't mind what they say about me. I'm doing a job that has to be done and I wouldn't do it if I didn't like it. Generally they're a good bunch of lads in the navy. There's very strong camaraderie so you find they stick together ashore and look after each other. If one has a bit too much to drink there's probably someone there to look after him, bring him back to the ship and put him in his bunk.

'They like their drink when they get ashore but that's fair enough when you consider the pressure of the job when they're at sea. Although they're allowed beer at sea, except in Defence Watches, it is strictly rationed and lots of sailors prefer not to drink until they get ashore. They'll drink here – no doubt at all. Tonight they'll get well tanked up. I just hope the locals don't try and mix it with them because then the fists start flying and that's when I get upset!'

It is **1040.** Most of the *Brilliant's* libertymen have gone to the Kapali Carsi, or the covered bazaar, in the old city. This labyrinth of streets and passages houses over 4000 shops selling a vast array of crafts and goods: ornate Turkish carpets, gold jewellery, hand-painted ceramics, embroidered skull-caps, meerschaum pipes, leather goods and an impressive range of mock designer-label fashion wear.

Bob Hawkins, Nick Cooke-Priest, Perry Stowell and Steve Boynton have wandered into The Old Bedesten, in the heart of the bazaar, which specializes in antiques and copperware. The Royal Naval officers are poking energetically through the clutter of decades in the hope of finding a treasure.

THE MASTER-AT-ARMS

Since the Police and Criminal Evidence Act of 1984 the master-at-arms has been officially recognized as the navy's service policeman. This was not always so. Five hundred years ago his duty was to instruct seamen in the practice of musketry.

By the end of the eighteenth century, he was primarily responsible for the maintenance of the king's peace and keeping order below decks. He supervised the sailors' drill, looked out for fires other than those in the galley and carried out regular tours of the ship – a task that became known as 'rounds'.

Seamen were only allowed to smoke tobacco in the galley and it was the master who enforced this rule.

His main duty, however, was to prevent petty crime. He was perpetually vigilant for drunkards and gamblers, who he would order to be chained at the mainmast to await the captain's pleasure. The master-at-arms also searched returning boats, seizing any alcohol and arresting any intoxicated libertyman.

He used informants and the nature of his duties won him few friends: it was not unknown for a master to fall down a ladder during the night hours or, occasionally, go for a silent swim with the fishes.

The reforms of the nineteenth century saw a gradual change in attitudes, but the master's tasks kept him apart from the ship's company and it is only in the last 25 years that the remit of the master-at-arms has broadened beyond his duties as enforcer of law and order. Today, as Whole Ship Co-ordinator, and the first among equals of the senior ratings, he is a vital part of the ship's management team.

He retains his policing and disciplinary role but this is often easier to discharge now that he is a full member of the ship's company rather than an imposing and draconian outsider.

Masters-at-arms serve ashore as well as at sea. They regulate naval establishments, man provost units, act as senior detectives with the Special Investigations Branch and – increasingly – they are are becoming specialists in security.

'Look at that copper pot,' says Hawkins. 'It's amazing isn't it?'

'It's fucking enormous,' observes Cooke-Priest. 'It wouldn't fit in your cabin!'

'No, no. I 'm thinking of it for home. We've got this mahogany stand in the hallway and I need a real Foxtrot Oscar pot to go on it!'

'Go for it then. At least you've got a warship to get it home for you.'

'This'll take half an hour of haggling.'

'Go on Bob, make him an offer.'

Hawkins steps towards the hugely bearded shopkeeper who is absent-mindedly fingering some exquisite ivory and gold worry beads.

'Er, excuse me. That pot up there. How much is that . . .?'

'Two million eight hundred thousand Turkish lira,' says the beard without looking up.

'Two million . . .! Fuck a duck! How much is that in real money?' says Hawkins turning to his fellow officers.

'God. I don't know,' says Cooke-Priest. 'A fiver is two hundred and fifty thousand isn't it? So two million . . .'

'Seventy American dollars,' says the beard.

'I'll give you fifty,' says Hawkins, eagerly trying to seize the initiative.

'Seventy American dollars.'

'Fifty . . .'

'Seventy American dollars. Visa or Amex accepted.'

'Aren't you going to barter with me?' asks Hawkins looking a little crestfallen.

'I will take dollars, pounds or Deutschmarks . . .'

It is 1125. At the other end of the bazaar George 'Geordie' Peart, and Dave 'Clubs' Mynett are waiting for Micky Goble who has gone to the post office to phone his father. Whilst they wait they are inspecting a wooden stall straining under the weight of a thousand pairs of 'Lacoste' socks.

'Do you think they're genuine?' asks Peart.

'It's got the crocodile logo,' says Mynett. 'Looks genuine enough.'

'How much mate?' says Peart to the stallholder.

'One dollars please sir.'

'Blimey! That ain't bad . . .'

'Watcha shipmates,' says Micky Goble ambling up to the stall. 'What's all this then?'

'Really cheap Lacoste socks,' says Mynett. 'Only a dollar and they've got the real logo.'

'Yeah!' says Goble. 'The logo's real enough. It's the socks that are bleedin' fake.'

'Hold on!' says Peart holding up a pair of socks. 'Look. They've only got a croc-odile on one sock.'

'They're half genuine then,' says Goble dryly.

'Hey, mate. Your socks have only got a crocodile on one of them!'

The stallholder shrugs his shoulders and smiles.

'You could always buy two pairs, George, and bin the two socks without the crocodiles!' suggests Goble with a grin.

'Yeah. Gi' us two pairs then pal. Nobody'll know the difference will they?'

'Hey, guess what just happened to me,' says Goble as Peart pays the stallholder.

'What?'

'I was walking through the bazaar and a bloke come up to me and said, "Are you English?" So I says "Yes" and he goes "Ah, hooligan, football hooligan!" '

'Wherever we go we get the blame for football hooliganism – especially in Europe,' says Mynett. 'It's a bleedin' cross matelots have to bear mate.'

'I blame Manchester United fans for it,' says Peart. 'They kicked off here once didn't they?'

'It was one of the big English teams wasn't it,' says Mynett. 'Can't remember which one but they've never forgotten about it over here.'

'Yeah, well it wasn't my team, that's for sure,' says Peart pulling his shirt open with pride to reveal a Newcastle United T-shirt.

'Hey, I wouldn't show that around here mate!'

'Don't worry,' says Goble grinning again. 'Nobody's ever heard of Newcastle in Europe have they George?'

'Haway man! Our time'll come. Big Kev'll get us over here.'

'Dream on Georgie!'

'Come on, let's grab a bite then we're gonna have a Turkish bath ain't we . . .?'

It is **1325**. Bob Hawkins, carrying a huge copper pot, walks into the grounds of the exquisite seventeenth-century Blue Mosque. His fellow officers have stayed in the bazaar to haggle over carpets so Hawkins has decided to take time out for reflection before resuming the mad social whirl of a run ashore. Sitting on an ancient stone seat in the tranquil mosque gardens he looks up at the six towering, rocket-like minarets and, not for the first time, contemplates life as an officer in the Royal Navy:

'There's so much about the modern navy that is changing: the nature of deployments; recruitment practices; technology; cut-backs . . . but one thing that hasn't changed, and never will, is the comradeship that comes with the job.

'Friends made in the navy are friends for life. It's to do with the specialized nature of the job, the fact that we go away together for long periods, and it's to do with the possibility that if we go to war, we might not come back. All that bonds you in a way that civilians could never understand. It's also to do with the way we socialize. We work hard but then we also play hard. If you're going to hoot with the owls you've got to make sure that you can soar with the eagles the next day . . . "We happy few, we band of brothers. For he that sheds his blood with me today will be my brother." Henry the Fifth, I think. Just before Agincourt. But still true today. So true.'

Hawkins picks up his copper pot and heads back to the old city where he has arranged to meet some of his fellow officers at one of Istanbul's famous 'water pipe' cafés where they have all vowed to try a 'Hubble Bubble'.

It is **1420**. Goble, Peart and Mynett stand at the reception of the Galatasaray Turkish Baths in the Beyoglu district of the old city.

'Yes sirs, what service is it that you would be liking today?' asks the smiling receptionist.

'Let's see,' says Goble, peering at the printed tariff. 'Right, this is the choice shipmates . . . the cheapest is a scrubbed assisted bath. Next up is the Massage *a la Turque*. It says that "you'll feel like new after this invigorating, revitalizing treatment" . . . Then there's the Ottoman service which "refreshes every sinew" it says here. And the top one is the Super Sultan's service which "is fit for a sultan and makes you feel reborn".'

'That's the one Mick,' says Peart. 'Top of the range for us mate . . .'

It is **1430**. The three sailors have each paid for the Super Sultan's service and are getting changed in private cubicles next door to each other.

'What's the deal George . . .' shouts Goble from his cubicle, '. . . do we just wrap this towel round?'

'Yeah. If it ain't big enough put the carpet on!'

'Do you keep your knick's on or off?'

'Good point. I dunno . . .'

'Off, I reckon,' says Mynett.

It is **1435**. Goble emerges from his cubicle to join his compatriots. They are wearing huge pink towels around their waists and wooden sandals on their feet.

'I don't half feel a prat!' says Goble.

'You're not far off looking like one mate,' observes Mynett.

'What happens now?'

'The bloke said someone would come and get us when we're ready.'

'I've never had a proper massage before,' says Peart.

'Me neither,' says Goble. 'My brother Russ did once. He said it was really soothin' and relaxin'. . . 'ello, someone's comin'.'

From around the corner three men appear. They are swarthy and very hairy with more then a passing resemblance to professional all-in wrestlers . . .

It is **1445**. The steam-filled massage room is a magnificent, glass-domed chamber made of solid marble. In the middle is a large, circular, granite slab on which Goble, Peart and Mynett now lie – silent, supine, and submissive. Standing over them the all-in wrestlers finish limbering up their own substantial muscles, flex their banana-sized fingers and proceed with the Super Sultan's service.

'Yeooooow!' screams Goble.

'Uuuuuugh!' grunts Peart.

'Aaaaaargh!' yells Mynett.

Each of the three masseurs starts to pummel, pound, knead, thrash and slap the luckless sailor laid before him.

'He's got hands like a fuckin' vice!' winces Goble. 'Oh, Jes'. He's beatin' me up. I'm payin' this bloke to beat me up!'

'God! He's ripping me apart this bloke,' shouts Peart. 'Oi, watchit Crusher – English legs ain't designed to bend that way!'

Mynett's all-in wrestler turns him over on to his stomach, throws a bucket of cold water over him and starts to walk up and down on his spine.

'Christ . . . look at this. He's goin' bleedin' walkies on me back . . . I'm bein' fuckin' steamrollered here!'

Goble, meanwhile, has been lathered from head to toe with soapy water and is now being tenderized with a series of fast-moving karate chops all over his upper torso.

'I think I must owe this bloke money or somethin'!'

The huge masseur starts to sponge Goble down with an enormous yellow sponge.

'I feel like I'm a car at a car wash. If he gets the hot wax out I'm goin' . . .!'

It is **1550**. Goble, Peart and Mynett emerge from the steam chamber into a cool and airy ante-room. Wearing their pink towels and wooden sandals they stand motionless under the refreshing down-draught from a revolving ceiling fan and enjoy the exquisite sensation of not being pulverized.

'It's great when it stops ain't it?' says Peart.

'I didn't know my bones could bend that far,' whispers Mynett.

'That was like a muggin',' says Goble. 'I could have stayed in Plymouth and got mugged. And it wouldn't have cost me anythin'.'

'You mean like an arm and a leg!'

'I need a drink . . .'

It is **0135**. The next liberty boat is due to leave the jetty at 0200. There are already about fifty sailors waiting and more are coming back all the time – only a few are walking in a straight line.

The duty shore patrol of five uniformed ratings busily guides everybody to a waiting area and makes sure everything remains peaceful and quiet. Most of the returning sailors have been to the British Consulate where a reception was thrown for the ship's company tonight. Drink was free so everybody is pretty merry.

Micky Goble, merrier than most, wanders up with Pincher Martin. They have just bought some kebab rolls from a street vendor, and whilst Martin eats Goble is busy inspecting the dubious contents.

'I reckon I've got the remains of some domestic pet in this roll!' he says with a conviction born of beer.

'Shut up and eat Goble,' says Martin. 'Whatever it is it'll soak up some of that ale inside you.'

'Hey, it was good to get some real English beer at the consulate wasn't it?'

'Nobody else got the chance mate. I think you sunk the lot.'

'Rubbish. It was free flowin'.'

'You got so sozzled. You know what you said to the vice-consul's wife when she asked who you were, don't you?'

'What?'

'You only went over and introduced yourself to her as Michael Goble, the ship's gynaecologist!'

'Ha, that's me. Dr Goble – cervix with a smile . . .'

Suddenly, the quietness of the early morning is shattered by an explosion of car horns, revving engines and screeching tyres. All around the waiting sailors cars and trucks are being driven at breakneck speed, hurled into tight skidding curves and slammed into screaming, rubber-burning halts. Hanging out of the windows men in masks shout, yell and punch the air. Some make obscene gestures whilst others unfurl and wave huge flags. The cars then accelerate away, flashing their headlights, only to return after a quick circuit of the jetty car park.

The sailors, suddenly sobered, stand in line ready to face their mysterious taunters.

'Steady lads. Steady now,' says Leading Cook Mark Warburton, one of the duty shore patrol.

'Settle down. We don't want any trouble with this lot.'

'Who the fuck are they anyway?' asks Andy Conway.

'They're Turkish football fans,' says Warburton. 'The Turkish team, Galatsaray, were playing Aston Villa tonight in the second leg of a European Cup tie and we were told their fans might come up and have a go at us if we won the game or goad us if we lost.'

'So what are they doing – havin' a go or goadin'?'

'It was a one-all draw but they won two–one on aggregate.'

'Sod it!'

It is **0200**. The liberty boat pulls out from the jetty with nearly a hundred sailors on board and heads out for the floodlit *Brilliant* floating in the blackness of the Bosphorus.

From the shoreline Turkish football fans flash their headlights in a random morse code of hostility and menace.

Micky Goble and Pincher Martin, still a little wobbly on their feet, stand in the bow of the liberty boat and gaze out to the illuminated British frigate. She looks reassuringly serene and poised.

'You know Pincher,' says Goble, his words slightly slurred, 'if that had kicked off there the news would have been "British thugs on rampage in Istanbul", "British football hooligans start trouble again . . ." The *Sun* and the *News of the World* would have lapped it up.'

'Yeah, they were just dying for us to react. But there was no point was there? If we had flashed we might have given 'em a hidin' but then we'd be in the slammer. Lose pay. Lose leave. Lose rank.'

'Yeah, but it really guts me that Jack ashore is always considered fair game. Know what I mean Pincher?'

'Yeah. Sure do Mick.'

'Look at that, Pincher!' says Goble, pointing with pride at the looming warship. 'What you got there is British sovereign territory. A little piece of England that no one can take away from us.'

'They can't touch us on there Mick.'

'They can't Pincher. You're right, mate. People moan about it, people drip about it but it is a little bit of England. And that . . .' says Goble, turning unsteadily on his feet and pointing towards the shore, '. . . is all foreign land. But this bit here is England . . . hic!'

It is **0215**. The last of the returning libertymen troop up the gangway towards the flight deck of the *Brilliant*. The ship is buzzing with the news that somebody has been hurt in a fight.

'One of the petty officers got beat up apparently.'

'Which one?'

'Don't know. I just heard that there was a fight and a PO got clobbered.'

'What, by the Turkish football crowd?'

'No, no. Apparently it was by a junior rating.'

'You're kidding!'

'Straight up.'

'Who!'

'The word is it was LWEM Gladman.'

'Gladys!'

'He's for the chop then . . .!'

Chapter Eight

CAPTAIN'S TABLE

DAY *Friday*	**DATE** *4*	**MONTH** *November*	**YEAR** *1994*

PLACE	*On passage from Istanbul*

POSITION	At **0800** *41°00'N 29°00'E* At **2359** *38°21'N 24°50'E*

DISTANCE TRAVELLED midnight to midnight *242.9 nautical miles*

SHIPS LOG. Sailed from Istanbul at 0800 then made fast passage (21 knots) across Sea of Marmara to the Dardanelles. Continued at 17 knots towards Corinth Canal on passage to Straits of Otranto for last time!

It is **1000**. The *Brilliant* vibrates gently as her twin Tyne gas turbines drive her steadily through the southern Dardanelles at 14 knots. We are cruising back to the Straits of Otranto for one more week of boarding duties before at last heading for England and home. With only three weeks of the deployment left to go the mood of the ship's company is palpably lighter than it has been for some time. For one person, however, the prospect of an imminent home run is little relief or consolation for the dire circumstances he finds himself in.

On an ordinary morning 25-year-old Leading Weapon Engineering Mechanic Kevin 'Gladys' Gladman would be checking the electrical circuits on the Exocet missile launchers. But not on this Monday. For despite being nearly 2000 miles from home a British court is about to sit. A court which has the power to imprison, detain, fine or castigate those whom it convicts. It is a duly constituted court under the laws of the United Kingdom. A court whose ancestry goes back 3000 years. A court that vests in one person the power to determine matters of fact, consider submissions of law and, should it be required, pass sentence. On board Her Majesty's Ship *Brilliant*, that embodiment of justice is in one man, the commanding officer, Captain James Campsie Rapp RN.

Dressed in the ubiquitous dark blue woolly-pully and, unusually below decks, a white Gieves and Hawkes cap brimmed with the gold lace signifying a senior officer, Rapp returns the salutes of the little group who have assembled in the forward cabin flat to orchestrate his court – known as the Captain's Table.* Rapp himself is unaware of the details of the incident involving Gladman which he is about to try. He knows only that this young Essex boy, whom he has met on several occasions around the ship and seen taking a leading and controversial role in the Sods Opera *en route* to Istanbul, is accused of striking a superior officer contrary to Section 11 of the Naval Discipline Act, 1957. He is also aware, as is Gladman, that the maximum penalty for this offence is two years imprisonment. It is clearly a serious matter, both for the discipline of the ship and for the immediate future of the alleged pugilist.

Neither Rapp nor Gladman, however, are without guidance. Rapp has been trained for this role. He has attended jurisprudential seminars and courses, witnessed hundreds of summary trials and sat at courts martial. He has in front of him the navy's bible of justice, BR11, the *Manual of Naval Law*, whose authors [lawyers who serve regularly at sea] have sought to prepare advice for every contingency. Beside him is the supply officer, Lieutenant-Commander Martin Atherton, who is an expert in legal procedure, and who assumes a role similar to that of a magistrate's clerk serving experienced lay Justices of the Peace. Atherton must ensure that all the statutory details are upheld and is also tasked to advise his captain should a matter of law arise: his is a second neutral mind directed towards fair play.

Five hundred leagues from Blighty, Gladman does not have the opportunity to see a solicitor. He does, however, have an experienced adviser in his divisional officer, Lieutenant Kevin Easterbrook, the deputy weapons engineering officer. Easterbrook has been trained for this role, is aware of the legal pitfalls and procedures and, as he learnt at Dartmouth, knows he must represent Gladman 'independently, fearlessly and courageously mindful only of his duty not to mislead the court'. It is a point of honour for those given the responsibility of a division that they should properly advise and assist their people, not only when times are good but especially when they are in difficulties. A divisional officer's failure to walk the third mile for one of his troops would soon lead to a total breakdown in trust; and it is on trust, respect and co-operative leadership, rather than coercion that the modern Royal Navy tries to maintain discipline – largely with success.

It was not always so: when nearly 300 people are confined in a small, austere and continually noisy environment that only the most hardy hermits might find

---

* The actual captain's table is a fold-up lectern that carries the ship's crest. It is also used for 'requestmen' – the hearing of requests for advancement, redress or recognition following success in academic or sporting matters – usually a happy occasion, in contrast with its use in matters of discipline and crime.

homely, frictions are bound to emerge. Historically, ructions were discouraged through harsh, even draconian punishments in a regimen that was common to all navies dating back to the earliest Phoenician merchant warriors.* In times gone by Gladman, if found guilty of striking a superior officer, could have been ducked three times beneath the ship tied to a weighted barrel or, even as late as 1915, been given the death sentence.**

Today the Royal Navy's aim is that every person accused of an offence should not be disadvantaged in any respect as against his civilian counterpart.Quite how successfully that aspiration works in practice, Gladman is about to discover. Having settled himself, Captain Rapp nods to the master-at-arms, Chay Robertson, to start the trial.

'LWEM Gladman!' shouts Robertson in a manner and tone born of healthy authority. 'Sir!' comes back the not entirely so wholehearted reply and Gladman attempts to march through the narrow doorway into the cabin flat, avoiding tripping over the dwarf bulkhead and retaining an air of dignity. He comes to a presentable halt two or three paces in front of the table. He has been carefully pre-briefed to stop at that point. Captains sometimes fear that in extreme cases the accused might take a swing at them if they come much closer! There follows the traditional symbol of a disciplinary court coming into session as the master-at-arms gives the order applicable only to Gladman, 'Off cap!'.

Chay Robertson then turns to Captain Rapp and reads out the charges. A tape recorder whirs in the background so that a transcript of proceedings can be made at a later date.

'Sir, the date is Friday the fourth of November at 1003. Leading Weapons Engineering Mechanic Gladman has three charges against him.

'The first charge reads that on the first of November, nineteen ninety-four, he was drunk on shore at the Sherlock Holmes public house, Istanbul.

'The second charge reads that he did on the same date behave with contempt to Petty Officer David Wibberly, service number Delta 214, 886 MIKE, of Her Majesty's Ship *Brilliant*, his superior officer.

---

* Naval Discipline, page 183.
** Stern and repressive measures were the means by which the navy of the 'good old days' controlled the lower decks, but it was always hoped that they achieved their end through deterrence rather than practice. The early ordinances of naval discipline were copied out on to parchment and nailed to the foremast of each ship. Since most of the rank and file were quite unable to read, however, it became the custom to read out the ordinance once a month at a muster of hands. Today, the Queen's Regulations for the Royal Navy require the contemporary Articles of War to be read out to the ship's company at the first opportunity after commissioning and to be displayed in a prominent position. In HMS *Brilliant*, they are on the main notice board next to the routine office, for all to see.

'The third charge reads that he did, on the same date, use violence to Petty Officer David Wibberly, service number Delta 214, 886 MIKE, of Her Majesty's Ship *Brilliant*, his superior officer.'

Captain Rapp nods his head and turns to the serious-looking weapons engineering mechanic who stands facing him rigidly at attention.

'Stand at ease LWEM Gladman. Do you understand those three charges?'

'Yes sir.'

'Master. Outline the facts.'

Chay Robertson rifles through a thick wodge of papers, pulls out a single type-written page and clears his throat.

'Sir, these are the facts of the case for the prosecution. On the first of November, nineteen ninety-four, Petty Officer Wibberly returned from night leave and made a report to the officer of the day. He stated that he had been struck by LWEM Gladman. I carried out an investigation sir, and collected statements from witnesses at the Sherlock Holmes pub in Istanbul which are presented in evidence. In short sir, on the night in question LWEM Gladman was ashore with other members of the ship's company. He went to the Sherlock Holmes pub in Istanbul and was seen by at least two other petty officers. They state that in their opinion he was drunk which substantiates the first charge. It seems that LWEM Gladman started a conversation with Petty Officer Wibberly which became heated and which involved the use of contemptuous behaviour towards the senior officer, sir. It was during that conversation that LWEM Gladman is alleged to have struck PO Wibberly with his right hand on the right side of the face, sir. Those are the facts appertaining to the three charges placed in front of you sir.'

'Thank you Master,' says the captain looking sternly at the stony-faced sailor. 'LWEM Gladman I consider that if proved these charges would probably result in at least a disrating. Therefore, because of the possible seriousness of the consequences, you now have the right to be tried by court martial at a later date when we have returned to Devonport if you so desire. Alternatively, you could decide to be tried summarily by me. It is your choice LWEM Gladman. You have twenty-four hours to make your decision. Do you understand?'

'Yes sir.'

'Dismiss.'

It is 1955. Russ Harding presses the transmit button on the main broadcast system.

'Good evening. First Lieutenant speaking. We have made good time through the Dardanelles. Tomorrow we will head down towards Piraeus and then line up on a

westerly heading for the entrance to the Corinth Canal. For those of you who haven't been through the Corinth Canal before it's one of the most extraordinary examples of late nineteenth-century engineering. Opened in 1893, it joins the Aegean and Ionian seas and is just six miles long and twenty-six feet deep. It is extremely narrow and will give us only fifteen feet clearance either side but it will save us over a hundred miles. Once through the canal we'll begin the passage through Patraikos and then, turning right, proceed to the Otranto Straits where we will take over duties in Area Ethel for one final period of boarding duties before we go home.

'A word about morale and attitude at this time. It is difficult not to start feeling excited about the trip home after such a long and arduous deployment but I must remind you that we still have a job of work to do in Operation Sharp Guard. We are required to play our part in the enforcement of the arms embargo for one more week so we must remain vigilant and maintain our usually high standards. I don't want to see people slacking off and falling victim to the curse of demob happiness. Firstly, that is not good for morale, secondly, it is not good for your own sense of self-respect and thirdly, it is what can cause accidents to happen. Keep up your concentration.

'That's all.'

DAY Saturday	**DATE** 5	**MONTH** November	**YEAR** 1994

PLACE   *Ionian Sea, on passage to the Straits of Otranto*

POSITION   At 0600 37°30'N 24°13'E At 2359 39°00'N 19°59'E

DISTANCE TRAVELLED midnight to midnight 283.23 *nautical miles*

SHIPS LOG. Overnight passage past Athens towards Corinth Canal. Completed successful transit then made slower passage past Patras towards southern Adriatic. Weather very variable – very calm and sheltered in the canal but 50 kilometre winds on the other side. Continued passage to Area overnight.

It is 0910. A Greek tugboat pulls the *Brilliant* gently along the straight, narrow course of the Corinth Canal that separates the Peloponnese from the Greek main-land. This man-made waterway forced through towering limestone rock deposits is so dramatic that virtually the entire ship's company have come out on to the upper deck to witness the transit. The British frigate is only feet from jagged rock-face on either side as she glides slowly towards the Ionian Sea already visible to the west.

One person who is not on the upper deck, however, is Gladman. He is too busy polishing his shoes and pressing his uniform to be worried about examples of nineteenth-century canal engineering. In one hour he must report again to the Captain's Table and give his decision: court martial or summary justice. As he irons his tunic his friend Paul 'Sharkey' Ward comes in from the upper deck.

'It's amazing that Corinth Canal Gladys. You ought to go and have a decko before we're out of it.'

'Can't mate. Gotta get ready for the skipper's table.'

'What have you decided to do?'

'I don't know mate. I just don't know what to do. Really I think I should go for a court martial when we get back so then I can get a barrister and really put up a good defence. I mean I'm bein' really stitched up here as far as I'm concerned. You know, I 'ad a bleedin' shoutin' match wiv' the geezer but he's the one who says I put one on 'im. I'm sayin' I never touched the bloke. There's no witnesses who saw me 'it 'im is there? There's only people who saw us arguin'.'

'So, it's only your word against his.'

'Yeah. But he's a PO ain't he, so what good is my word against his? An' also, if I choose to be tried by the skipper his decision is final. That's why I think I'd have a better chance at a proper court martial when I could get hold of a proper brief.'

'You've got more to lose at a court martial 'cos the punishment could be greater if you do go down.'

'I know, but at the Captain's Table I reckon you go in guilty 'til proved inno-cent. They'll do me alright – it's just a matter of what they do me with. I know my divisional officer will be able to put up mitigatin' factors like my work record an' that but I still reckon I'd get done. I wouldn't mind a fine but I can't handle a dis-ratin'. If my money goes down because of a loss of seniority I won't be able to afford me mortgage and so I'll lose me house. I'm only just managin' now. That's why I got into the argument in the first place with Wibberly 'cos he was goin' on about all the extra money he earnt as a young PO compared to a leadin' hand like me. Fuckin' prat!'

'So, what are you going to do?'

'Oh, I don't know. I'll probably just decide on the spot . . .'

It is **1000**. Kevin 'Gladys' Gladman stands outside the forward cabin flat where the Captain's Table is always held. He is smartly turned out according to all the uniform regulations with a particularly impressive buff on his boots. The only slightly individual touch to his appearance is the addition of a Remembrance Day poppy stuck into the silk around his cap. The master-at-arms walks up from the regulating office to brief him on procedure before the captain comes down from his cabin.

'Right, when you hear your name being called shout out nice and loudly "Sir!". March in through the door like you did last time and come to a halt one pace away from the table. Do nothing else. I will then tell you to take your cap off. The captain will then ask you whether you want a court martial or a summary trial by him. If you decide to go for court martial the captain will still carry out a preliminary investigation to see if your case warrants a court martial. He could still change it if he felt your case was too weak and then try it himself. That is his right. Do you understand?'

'Yeah.'

'If you decide to go for summary trial and plead not guilty to any or all of the charges, then cautions and warnings will be read out. The prosecution will present their witnesses and then your divisional officer will start to call any witnesses for the defence. Understand?'

'Yeah, I understand.'

'Now, if at any time you're unhappy with things or not clear about something you can request a standover. Happy with that?'

'Yeah, happy.'

'Right, on completion of the whole thing you put on your cap smartly, right turn and march out. But don't leg it, 'cos I want you back to put the captain's table away against the bulkhead.'*

It is **1010**. Captain Rapp stands behind his table. To his right is his secretary, Lieutenant Liz Hall. To his left is his first lieutenant, Russ Harding, and Lieutenant-Commander Martin Atherton, his legal adviser. Opposite them is Chay Robertson, the master-at-arms, Pincher Martin, the leading regulator, and Lieutenant Kevin Easterbrook who is Gladman's divisional officer.

On the order Gladman marches into the confined space and faces his captain.

'LWEM Gladman,' says the captain, 'you've had twenty-four hours to consider how you wish to be tried on the three charges that you face. Have you come to a decision?'

---

* On a Type 22 frigate the captain's table is usually stowed behind straps in the for'ard cabin flat, near the wardroom on Deck One. The accused, whether found innocent or guilty, is responsible for setting it up and taking it down.

'Yes sir.'

'And how do you wish to be tried?'

'By you sir.'

'Right, and you understand the charges?'

'Yes sir.'

'On the first charge of being drunk ashore how do you plead?'

'Not guilty, sir.'

'Duly recorded,' says the master-at-arms.

'On the second charge of behaving with contempt, how do you plead?'

'Not guilty, sir.'

'Plea is recorded sir.'

'And on the third charge of using violence against a superior officer, how do you plead?'

'Not guilty, sir.'

'Very well, let us proceed . . .'

It is **1020**. As the summary trial proceeds in the for'ard cabin flat on One Deck Gladman's fellow WEMs are in their mess on Two Deck. They are busy organizing a sweepstake:

'Come on you lot. Quid a go!'

'OK! I reckon he'll go to the slammer.'

'No. Put me down for a fine – £500.'

'Personally, I think he should get a bleedin' medal.'

'I think he'll get off it. You know what old Gladys is like.'

'Yeah! Slippery!'

'No. He'll be done. Put me down for detention and hard labour . . .'

One of the particularly challenging aspects of living on a warship like the Brilliant is that everybody knows everybody else. The ship's company is a small, intensely vibrant community in which it is vital for everyone to get on with each other if the ship is to function effectively in its tasks, whether at peace or war. Comradeship is, therefore, particularly highly valued and is something that seems to develop strongly and naturally out of naval society. It follows, of course, that should two people fall out personally and have an argument or fight then it is consequent on the wider community to contain and control the ruction before it starts to create dangerous shock waves. This is especially important if the personal difference occurs between people of different ranks. One of the formal and official devices for maintaining control is the system of summary trial and punishment which is unique to the armed forces and differs from shoreside civilian courts in

NAVAL DISCIPLINE

The history of naval law goes back to the Phoenician seafarers of two millennia ago. Their sea-law was incorporated in an ordinance of Richard the Lionheart in 1190 when he gave instructions for his fleet before it set out on the Third Crusade. He banned:

Murder for which the seaman was to be tied alive to the corpse of his victim and hove into the ocean.

Drawing a knife for which the seaman was to lose a hand.

Striking another for which the offender was to be ducked.

Robbery and theft for which the seaman was to have boiling pitch poured on his head and feathers shaken over him to mark his crime before he was cast ashore at the first point of land.

Insubordination which carried between three and 300 lashes.

In 1652, the first Articles of War were issued and a basic court martial procedure was set up to try offenders. The articles were to be displayed at the mainmast and read to the ship's company at each commissioning. The same public proclamation is used today but nothing else remains of the draconian punishments the first Naval Discipline Act of 1661 established: twenty-five of the thirty-seven articles carried the death penalty.

In 1757 Admiral Byng was tried for negligence following the fall of Minorca and, despite a recommendation for clemency from the court martial, he was shot on the quarterdeck of HMS *Monarch* 'to encourage the others'.

The number of capital offences was reduced after this harsh case but, as late as 1915, striking a superior officer could be penalized by 'death or other such punishment as the court shall deem the offender to deserve'. At a less severe level, flogging was suspended as peacetime punishment in 1871 and finally disused in 1897 although it remained a theoretical wartime option until 1948.

Since then, procedures for the apprehension, arrest, interviewing and trial of suspects have been changed to coincide with civilian practice except where the exigencies of ships at sea so demand. At courts martial naval officers who are qualified barristers defend all accused and all concerned with the administration of justice have been trained in law. Proper appeal procedures are used and serious trials are reviewed by judges.

two fundamental ways. Firstly, everybody involved, from the prosecuting and defence counsel to all the witnesses and the defendant, will be known to each other. Secondly, the captain has vested in him the power of being both judge and jury. The potential for allowing this system to be abused is so enormous that it actually ensures the highest level of pragmatism and a complete sense of propriety. On a warship there is only one thing worse than having to call a Captain's Table and that is to execute the table badly or unfairly. In the case of Gladman the table was conducted with great precision and an unerring sense of justice and fairness. All parties including witnesses were questioned and cross-examined until the full extent of the circumstances was understood – as far as is possible when it is ultimately a case of one man's word against another's:

It appears that on the fateful night of 1 November in Istanbul, Gladman had been out to a casino where he won 23 million Turkish lira (about £400). This, along with his identity card, was later stolen from his back pocket at the same casino. He then went along to the Sherlock Holmes pub, a favourite haunt of the British community in Istanbul, where his shipmates offered to buy his drinks. This led to a comment from PO Wibberly about relative pay grades to which Gladman, already upset by the theft of his hard-won money, took great exception. A heated argument ensued which was allegedly concluded with a series of fast right jabs to the head. There were plenty of witnesses who said they saw the argument but nobody who claims to have seen the punches. Only two people will ever know for certain whether any punches were actually thrown, but from the point of view of Captain Rapp sufficient is now known to help conclude the affair.

It is **1235**. After a final consultation with Martin Atherton Captain Rapp once again calls in the defendant to face him at the table.

'LWEM Gladman. I've heard the case for the prosecution of these three charges and the evidence. I have therefore decided to dismiss the charges as read but replace them with a lesser charge. Master, please read out the new charge.'

'Yes sir. The new charge reads that LWEM Gladman did, on the first of November, nineteen ninety-four, without reasonable excuse use provocative behaviour likely to cause a disturbance.'

'LWEM Gladman, do you understand this new charge?'

'Yes sir.'

'Do you plead guilty or not guilty to that charge?'

'Guilty sir.'

'Right. I'm content that I've heard enough evidence already with respect to the other three charges that we heard earlier. Before I pass sentence I invite you,

Lieutenant Easterbrook, as LWEM Gladman's divisional officer, to offer any miti-
gating circumstances.'

'Yes sir,' says Easterbrook, taking a step forward. 'LWEM Gladman regrets the
incident. He was very upset on the night in question because he had a considerable amount of money stolen, sir. His relationship with his girlfriend recently
broke up and that has left him with a large mortgage so he feels any loss of money
quite hard. He has assured me sir, that this incident will not happen again.'

'How has LWEM Gladman been performing at work?' asks the captain.

'He's quite a sound chap sir. Works well and his senior rate recommends him.'

'Apart from his loss at the casino, does he have any other financial constraints?'

'Just his large mortgage sir.'

'Right,' says Captain Rapp, looking once again at Gladman. 'LWEM Gladman
we have spent a long time looking into this incident. I am satisfied that on that
evening you did use provocative behaviour likely to cause a disturbance. I'm also
well and truly satisfied that a disturbance occurred but I am not clear exactly what
that was according to the evidence given at table. That said, I would point out to
you in the strongest terms that I expect everybody on this ship to behave responsi-
bly. You are part of this ship's company and therefore a member of this ship's society, and that means behaving accordingly. And you didn't. Right?'

'Yes sir.'

'Right, you want to get yourself sorted out sailor. Everyone's got to live together
on this ship and if you meet ashore you are to do so in the spirit of camaraderie
and enjoyment. Right?'

'Yes sir'

'If you do harbour any disliking for people deal with it. Sort it out. Right?'

'Yes sir'

'I hope you've learnt from this incident otherwise you are not worthy of wearing a hook on your arm.* Fined one hundred and fifty pounds . . .'

It is **1320**. Gladman is back in his mess and talking to his messmates.

'It was great. They kept reducin' the charges 'til I thought they were jus' gonna
accuse me of buyin' him a drink or something.'

'So there was no charges for the pump-action shotgun then Gladys!'

'No. I wiped me dabs off that, see,' replies Gladman laughing.

'Well, it's buggered up the sweepstake. I had you down for the cat-o-nine tails!'

'Yeah. Not bad is it – hundred and fifty quid for attempted manslaughter . . .'

---

* A leading hand wears a badge on his sleeve showing a small, fouled anchor known as a 'killick'.

Chapter Nine

HOMEWARD BOUNDERS

DAY *Monday*	**DATE** *7*	**MONTH** *November*	**YEAR** *1994*

PLACE	*Straits of Otranto, Area Nancy*

POSITION	*Classified*

DISTANCE TRAVELLED midnight to midnight *180.7 nautical miles*

SHIPS LOG. Moved from Area Ethel to Area Nancy for one day. Relieved HMS Nottingham and had an excellent sail past. Quiet patrol for rest of the day. Weather beginning to deteriorate – heavy thunderstorms and increasing wind.

It is **1024**. The *Brilliant* is on full power and set on a head-to-head collision course with a destroyer that is also on full power and aimed directly at us. Overhead a helicopter from the destroyer is buzzing us repeatedly in a series of intimidating swoops. At first sight it looks as though we are preparing for a suicidal ramming of a hostile warship which is intent on doing exactly the same to us.

In fact, this is no act of war and no belligerency is involved. Far from it – this is an example of warships at play and is the build-up to a famous naval ritual.

The destroyer is the HMS *Nottingham*, a Type 42 destroyer who we are relieving in Area Nancy so that she can start her journey home to Britain. She has been deployed in Operation Sharp Guard for about seven months – about the same length of time as the *Brilliant* – so this is a big day for her. That is why, according to tradition, we are giving her a sail past which is the naval way of saying good luck, goodbye and Godspeed.

A good sail past involves ship-to-ship hose fights, a great deal of shouting and often extremely loud music played over the main broadcast systems. There is usually an element of competition involved to see which ship can outdo the other in noise, commotion and general hullabaloo.

The *Brilliant* and the *Nottingham*, with flags and pennants flying from every halyard, meet at a combined speed of about 55 knots. As they pass close on each other's port beam both simultaneously open fire with powerful fire hoses but the looping white jets of seawater refract harmlessly into the wind creating an immense curtain of spray and a dozen dancing rainbows. At the same time, the *Nottingham's* Lynx helicopter tries to seize the initiative by performing a spectacularly acrobatic flying display over our heads. The *Brilliant* strikes back with a volley of surprise effects: clouds of bright orange smoke billow from her funnel; a giant pair of hands fixed to the for'ard Seawolf missile launcher starts to wave inanely as the launcher is activated into rapid backward and forward movements; the *William Tell* overture is played at an ear-splitting volume over the upper deck tannoys.

At the same time both ships busily flash each other morse code messages from the signal lamps on their respective bridge wings.

Brilliant to *Nottingham*: 'Have a good trip home. We will be following close on your tail.'

Nottingham to *Brilliant*: 'Thanks for a fantastic sail past. See you in Blighty.'

Bob Hawkins, who has come out on to the bridge wing to watch the proceedings, is delighted and moved by the spectacle.

'That looked fantastic. Two warships travelling at speed towards each other like that is one of the most exhilarating things you can imagine. The sail past is a great naval tradition which shows warships up in all their finery and splendour. How can anybody wonder that we refer to our ships as "she" when they look as beautiful as that – sleek and proud.

'One of my big grouses is the way some of the younger ratings and even some of the younger officers insist on calling a ship an "it". A ship is a "she"! A ship has always been a "she". A ship has always been thought of as a woman. A beautiful woman who looks after us as long as we look after her. I know the feminists are outraged by this idea but they shouldn't be. They should be proud because a ship represents all that is best about womanhood. Like a mother a ship protects us against the threat of the elements and the violence of the enemy. Just because we now talk about things like action data automation, magnetic anomaly detection and computer assisted command systems does not mean that we have to depersonalize everything about our navy including the very ships we sail on.'

He waves proudly at HMS *Nottingham* now in the distance and heading for England.

'Five more days and that'll be us,' he says with a smile.

DAY *Thursday*	DATE *10*	MONTH *November*	YEAR *1994*

PLACE	*Straits of Otranto, Area Ethel*

POSITION	*Classified*

DISTANCE TRAVELLED midnight to midnight *175.8 nautical miles*

SHIPS LOG. Handed over Nancy duties to HS Hydra then moved back to Ethel and took over from FS Anquitile. Final fuel RAS with FS Meuse. Then had NBCDX1 in afternoon.

It is **1435**. Surgeon-Lieutenant Richard Newton and his medical assistants, Clive Wilkinson and Jacqui Quant, are overrun with patients in the sickbay. Newton is attending to a marine with a deep, bloody headwound, multiple lacerations and a shattered femur, Quant is concentrating on a stoker with a crushed rib cage, severe contusions to the lower abdomen and a fractured skull whilst Wilkinson is busy with a gunner in severe shock who has a piece of jagged shrapnel embedded in his upper thigh.

'Is that white bit a piece of bone sticking out of my leg sir?' asks the marine.

'Yes. Your femur's practically totally disintegrated.'

'Really?'

'So don't fiddle with it, there's a good chap. All those bits might come away.'

'OK sir. Can I go now? Just got time for a cup of tea.'

'Yes. Just mind you don't drip blood all over the place.'

'Okey dokey sir.'

'How are you doing Clive?' asks Newton, going over to his petty officer medical assistant.

'Fine thank you sir. Nice bit of shrapnel in here.'

'Oh yes. That's excellent,' says the doctor peering over the PO's shoulder. 'How does that feel to you?' he asks the blood-spattered gunner.

'Really good, thank you sir, except all the blood's tricklin' down me leg into me shoes.'

'Just try not to get it all over the floor, that's all I ask.'

'Sir,' says Jacqui Quant turning round to the doctor. 'Is this guy in enough shock? Or shall I give him some more?'

'Yes, he should be looking paler than that with those injuries. Slap some more white on him.'

'Clive!', calls Quant. 'Can I borrow your white?'

'Yes. I'll swap it for some "deep bruise" blue . . .'

The medical department is preparing the first of a number of 'victims' for an imminent major damage control exercise known as NBCDX1 – Nuclear, Biological, Chemical Defence Exercise. Today's scenario is that the *Brilliant* will be hit by two missiles launched from shore and then attacked by fast patrol boats. Although it is an exercise everything is made to appear, feel and sound as real as possible: explosive charges will be dropped over the side to cause loud explosions when the missiles 'hit'; smoke bombs will be let off all over the ship creating dense clouds of choking, suffocating fumes; selected ratings and officers will be 'killed' without notice; severely wounded personnel will appear at any time and at any place; pre-selected officers will become hysterical and will lose their ability to command.

It is under these conditions that the ship's company is regularly tested in their ability to control damage and maintain a defensive or fighting integrity.

It is **1530**. The first missile hits the ship on the port quarter causing extensive flooding and fire in the aft engine spaces. Several casualties and many wounded. First aid parties and damage control specialists fight through thick billowing smoke to get to the affected areas. The damage control centre (HQ1) directs operations by VHF portable radios and immediately marks up the damaged areas of the ship on a huge diagram on the bulkhead.

It is **1531**. More explosions in the engine spaces and a fire breaks out in the aft Seawolf missile magazine. At least five more killed including a first aid party. HQ1 redirects some of the damage control groups to the ammunition magazine.

It is **1534**. Widespread flooding in all the engine spaces. Three people have drowned and two more are missing. The radar trackers in the op's room warn of a second incoming missile.

It is **1535**. The second missile hits the ship causing severe damage to the upper deck and the op's room. Several gunners have been killed. One ammunition loader, hysterical and badly wounded, bursts into the bridge and needs to be subdued. The PWO is dead.

It is **1538**. Fast patrol boats are attacking the *Brilliant* on the starboard side. Shellfire has strafed the upper deck. Two Wrens are dead.

It is **1544**. Fire has spread into the wardroom galley and is threatening the wardroom itself which has been turned into an emergency room for casualties. The captain has been badly wounded.*

It is **1550**. The fire-fighting parties have most of the main fires under control. All flooding has been stopped and the *Brilliant* is once again secured for action . . .**

It is **1958**. Russ Harding clears his throat:

'*Good evening. First Lieutenant speaking. Well done everybody in today's NBCDX1. Your reactions were excellent and we repaired all major damage to the ship within twenty minutes of the first attack before returning to Action Stations. There were one or two minor points to pick up on for those people in the for'ard repair parties – mainly questions of technique – but overall your efforts were commendable. Clearly we must always be ready for any eventuality so even though we are nearing the end of a long and gruelling deployment, exercises such as today's are never redundant.*

'*Clubs has asked me to remind all prospective Rock Racers that our visit to Gibraltar draws near and that the race to the top of the rock will take place on our second day there. He urges everyone to train hard as it is not a wise undertaking for anybody who is not totally fit. My own view, for what it's worth, is that anybody who does the Rock Race is not only unwise but also completely barmy. That's all.*'

DAY *Friday*	**DATE** *11*	**MONTH** *November*	**YEAR** *1994*
PLACE	*Straits of Otranto, Area Ethel*		
POSITION	*Classified*		

DISTANCE TRAVELLED midnight to midnight *181.6 nautical miles*

SHIPS LOG. Penultimate day in Ethel and on patrol. Visited by CSNFM for farewell. Conducted evening boarding on MV Preslav. Weather continues to deteriorate.

---

* During battle the captain and his second-in-command, the first lieutenant, will stay as far away from each other as possible. This is to reduce the chances of both of them being killed at the same time.
** A warship has three command priorities: float, move and fight. At Action Stations the main priority is to fight. If she is damaged, the priorities might change towards saving her from sinking or moving her out of danger. Once the ship has been secured the priority will return to 'fight'.

It is **0900**. A Lynx helicopter called 'Bad Girl' lands on the flight deck. The rotors slow, the side door opens and a tall, gentle-looking man in a Dutch naval uniform climbs out to be greeted with a warm handshake from Captain Rapp. The visitor is Commodore Van der Lught, the Commander of Standing Naval Forces Mediterranean, who has come to say goodbye to the *Brilliant* on the eve of her departure from Operation Sharp Guard.

It is **0930**. After a cup of tea and a piece of PO Cook Galpin's famous ship-made shortbread the Dutch commodore addresses the ship's company over the main broadcast system from the captain's cabin:

'Good morning. Commodore Van der Lught speaking. Tomorrow you will leave Operation Sharp Guard and your long deployment in the Adriatic will be ended. Then your very valuable contribution to the important work going on out here will be history and you will undoubtedly be looking forward to your return to your own country and to a celebration of Christmas with your loved ones.

'I know that when you have left this theatre of naval activity and when you are back home you will look back on these days and ask yourselves, "Did it all do any good?" and "Why did we spend seven months patrolling boxes of water in the Adriatic?" I want you all to know that this operation is one of the things we can do to make life a little better now for all those people who live on the eastern side of the Adriatic, and hopefully a great deal better in the future. Be assured that your routine duties that were so demanding and sometimes, I'm sure, very boring, were of immense value to this multi-nation task force. As a deterrent you will never know how many arms you prevented from being taken into the countries of the former Yugoslavia and therefore you will never know how many lives you saved.

'Thank you for letting me come and talk to you on your proud and capable ship. Our ways are about to part so I very much wanted to pay you one more visit to say thank you and goodbye. I am proud of Brilliant. It was both a pleasure and a reassurance to have her around. I wish you a safe journey home and a well-deserved rest with your families.

'That's all.'

DAY *Sunday*	DATE *13*	MONTH *November*	YEAR *1994*

PLACE	*On passage to Cagliari, Sardinia.*

POSITION	At 0600 *37°49′N 15°47′E* At 2359 *39°00′N 10°58′E*

DISTANCE TRAVELLED midnight to midnight *339.5 nautical miles*

SHIPS LOG. Transit of Messina Straits in early morning then fast passage to R/V with HMS Cumberland for ADEX with German Tornados. Excellent performance by the op's room in very good conditions. Continued passage to Cagliari overnight.

It is **1030**. The *Brilliant* is cruising smoothly at 20 knots through a cluster of volcanic islands in the Tyrrhenian Sea just north of Sicily. It is a bright, warm day and visibility is good allowing spectacular views of the famous Stromboli with its smoking, steaming crater. The entire ship's company, except those on watch, is congregated on the flight deck for a special Sunday service to be taken by Bob Hawkins, the principal warfare officer. He is standing at a lectern in front of a huge White Ensign that has been hung from the hangar doors. In his hand is a typewritten sheet which is headed:

A SERVICE FOR SHIPS WITHOUT CHAPLAINS
SUNDAY 13 NOVEMBER 1994
REMEMBRANCE SUNDAY

Hawkins steps forward and reads the opening prayer.

'On this day of remembrance, O God, as we recall those who died in the service of their country, we pray for the peace of the world. Guide the leaders of the nations and give them true understanding of your righteous will; that the tragedy and horror of war may be averted for the coming generation . . .'

It is **1040**. The congregation has just finished singing 'Onward Christian Soldiers' and as Captain Rapp walks up to the lectern to give the address a gentle breeze blows in from the north and ripples through the hanging ensign.

'For many of us our thoughts this Remembrance Sunday will have been refreshed by the extensive coverage of the D-Day ceremonies that involved so

Lieutenant-Commander Martin Atherton in his cabin.

Master-at-Arms Chay Robertson and
Leading Regulator Nick 'Pincher' Martin.

Leading Weapons
Engineering Mechanic
Kevin 'Gladys'
Gladman.

Saying goodbye at sea.

Remembrance Sunday.

A gunner in anti-flash gear.

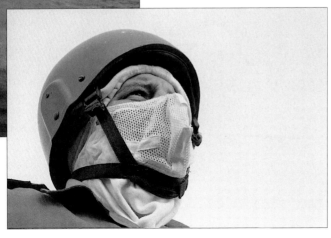

Surgeon-Lieutenant Richard Newton and Jacqui Quant, Medical Assistant, during an attack and damage control exercise (NBCDX1).

Fire fighters during NBCDX1.

Missile man in a 30 mm gun.

The gunners unload upper deck weapons.

Captain Rapp bids farewell to his officers.

Able Seaman Lirret and Leading Physical Trainer Dave 'Clubs' Mynett battle it out during the Gibraltar Rock Race.

Petty Officer Steward Tony Lilley recovers after the race.

The first glimpse of Guzz.

many naval personnel in June. The process will continue next year with the 50th anniversary of VE and VJ Day as we recall the sacrifice of those who died during the Second World War.

'There have only been two years, in the peace that followed the surrender of Japan in 1945, in which no British servicemen and women have lost their lives. For many serving today the South Atlantic, Northern Ireland and the Gulf are personal memories of operational experience. We are never far from trouble and controversy. As we stand here today on the flight deck of HMS *Brilliant*, naval personnel are serving in Bosnia and the Adriatic, in the Gulf and the South Atlantic, off the coast of Haiti and in Northern Ireland as well as on strategic deterrent patrol. Keeping and making the peace are a vital and honourable activity to which we are all committed.

'No one can justify war, for war as both concept and reality is an indefensible evil. But so many human predicaments teach us it is often the lesser of two evils. At the height of the Cold War a Jesuit priest made the following observation:

' "If I threaten to do an immoral act only in certain specific circumstances, but threaten to do so to prevent a greater evil, if I prevent that greater evil from happening was my original intention wrong?".'

It is **1100**. Hawkins reads out the Act of Remembrance:

> They shall not grow old as we that are left grow old:
> Age shall not weary them nor the years condemn.
> At the going down of the sun and in the morning
> We will remember them.

The congregation repeats the last line of the emotive verse and then, as the *Brilliant* maintains a steady course through the volcanic islands of the Tyrrhenian Sea, each man and woman on her flight deck stands silent for two minutes to ponder their inner thoughts.

It is **1102**. The silence is broken by the ship's bugler, Able Seaman Perry, who plays the Last Post.

It is **1200**. The full irony of war and inconstancy of history is put into sharp perspective by a pipe that comes over the main broadcast system:

'In one hour Sea Wolf missile teams and upper deck gun crews will close up ready for our rendezvous with HMS Cumberland and the air defence exercise against a squadron of German Tornado fighters . . .'

DAY *Monday*	DATE *14*	MONTH *November*	YEAR *1994*

PLACE	*On passage to Cagliari, Sardinia*

POSITION	At 0600 *39°00′N 18°00′E* At 1200 *39°12′N 09°10′E*

DISTANCE TRAVELLED midnight to midnight *139 nautical miles*

SHIPS LOG. *Arrived in Cagliari, Sardinia. Once alongside, divers carried out routine dive on ship's hull. The weapons engineering department changed the aerial on the foremast.*

It is **1215**. Captain Rapp walks out on to the starboard bridge wing to watch his ship's approach to Sardinia. It is a special moment for the 42-year-old commanding officer of the *Brilliant* because this could be his last few moments at sea in his own command. In three days time a new commanding officer, Captain Angus Somerville, will be flying out from England to take command of the frigate allowing Rapp to return home and prepare himself for a new and important shore-based job with the naval presentation team. It is highly likely that this change of direction in his career will be permanent so that he will never again 'drive' his own ship – at least in peacetime.

As the port of Cagliari looms on the horizon James Rapp leans on the bulwark overlooking the for'ard Seawolf missile deck and savours the moment.

'It is always an emotional time for a commanding officer when he leaves a ship. More so when it could be his last ship. A ship becomes part of you and you become part of the ship and not everybody can always understand that – especially if they're not in the navy themselves. It's true to say that there are two women in my life. There's my wife Ann at home with the children and there's this one here – my grey mistress. Circumstances are forcing me to end the "affair" but I will never forget the *Brilliant*. She will always be an integral part of my life.'

It is **1234**. Captain Rapp personally takes charge of the docking procedure and guides the *Brilliant* gently to her last berth with him at her helm.

It is **1930**. Petty Officer Steward Tony Lilley puts the final touches to the dining-tables in the wardroom in preparation for tonight's special mess dinner being held in honour of Captain Rapp. He checks that the silver service is laid correctly, the candelabras are positioned properly, the starched table napkins are folded in the right way and that enough port has been decanted into the crystal decanters.

It is **1940**. In the wardroom galley Petty Officer Cook Galpin is busy with the last stages of cooking and preparing the numerous dishes for the dinner. There is spinach and blue cheese roulade to start, fresh salmon steaks to follow with fillet of steak in brandy sauce for the main course. The pudding is a work of art: glazed sugar brandy-baskets with chocolate ice cream and caramel sauce.

It is **2000**. The officers, in full naval dinner dress, enter the wardroom, find their names on the table plan and take their seats. The starter is served with a light Chardonnay wine.

It is **2020**. The second course is served with a dry Muscadet.

It is **2045**. The main course is served with a Cabernet Sauvignon and a 1991 Chateauneuf du Pape.

It is **2130**. The pudding is served with port.

It is **2200**. Coffee is served with more port.

It is **2230**. The Queen is toasted.

It is **2240**. The captain is toasted, after which all the officers bang the table with their fists and call for their commanding officer to make a speech.

It is **2241**. James Rapp gets to his feet and asks for silence.
    'Mr President,* ladies and gentlemen. I would just like to say a few words of gratitude for all your support whilst we have been together on the *Brilliant*. It is a very special thing to be dined in one's own ship or, that is to say, one loaned by Her Majesty. I am very sorry to be leaving early as I would love to be with you all when you sail into Plymouth on the twenty-fifth of this month as I know that is going to be a very special time for everybody. Duty calls, I'm afraid, and so I have little choice in the matter . . .

---

* Russ Harding as first lieutenant is automatically president of the wardroom.

'They don't seem to give COs very long in command these days and four-ringers seem to get even less time. I have been with the *Brilliant* for sixteen months and yet it seems as though I joined only yesterday – it may not for all of you, but it does for me . . .

'We've had a busy time on this deployment. The work has been constant, unforgiving but often challenging. You all know I have a pretty merciless eye for detail and a keen desire to get it right. You will also have picked up that I can be fairly relentless in my efforts to get things done and that sometimes I have been a hammer that hits harder than we might all wish . . .

'I think there has been a great spirit on board despite the frustrating nature of the work and one or two pretty average runs ashore – although there have been some excellent runs ashore as well. I think most people enjoyed Souda Bay and Istanbul and, of course, you still have Gibraltar to come . . .

'I have become very attached to the *Brilliant*. She is a fine ship and an effective one. So, to finish, president, ladies and gentlemen, I give you a toast . . . HMS *Brilliant*.'

Everyone stands and, with glasses raised, speak as one: 'HMS *Brilliant*!'

It is 2310. The officers have retired temporarily to the bridge for liqueurs. This allows PO Lilley and his team of stewards to clear the tables of the dinner debris – and to clear the wardroom of the tables, for the officers will be returning . . .

It is **2325**. The officers are back. It is time for wardroom games – some of the most violent indoor games ever devised and a vital feature of wardroom culture. As vital as they are, the sole female officers, Tracie Lovegrove and Liz Hall, sensibly decide to leave as to stay might be taking integration a step too far.

The first of many games to be played tonight is 'war canoes' – essentially a game of 'never-say-die' tug of war. The officers split into two teams with the members of each one sitting cross-legged behind each other and holding the person in front round the waist. The two teams face each other with the two front men grasping a broom handle. On the word 'Go' both teams pull like hell and do not stop. Participants in wardroom games do not give in, give up or submit – they just fall over in a state of exhaustion or helpless laughter.

It is **2330**. Sweating and red-faced, the war canoe teams are still pulling.

Russ Harding, wearing a pink and blue jockey's cap and being suffocated by a crushing bear hug from the captain behind him, splutters indecipherable words of encouragement to his sagging team.

TOASTS

On formal occasions in the wardroom the first toast is always to Her Majesty. The officers remain seated in a gesture that either reflects the will of Charles II following the navy's part in his restoration in 1660 or, more prosaically, the need to avoid cracking their skulls on the low deckheads of wooden warships. The loyal toast takes the form of the mess president rapping the table with his gavel and saying: 'Mr Vice, the Queen.' Mr Vice is usually the most junior member of the mess and he or she responds with: 'Ladies and gentlemen, the Queen.' All present take a sip of port (or Madeira) and many add under their breath: 'God bless her.'

Other traditional naval toasts of the day are used at informal dinners and in many messes each evening at sea when there is a quorum and the ship is not on operations or exercise. These are:

Monday	Our ships at sea
Tuesday	Our men (pronounced Amen)
Wednesday	Ourselves
Thursday	A bloody war and a sickly season
Friday	A willing foe and sea room
Saturday	Wives and sweethearts
Sunday	Absent friends

The Thursday toast relates to the slowness of promotion and the need for senior officers to be killed or invalided out of the navy to make room for younger ones. In a different vein, certain philandering messes in the past are said to have added to the Saturday toast the sentiment '. . .may they never meet.'

The various branches of the Royal Navy have their own toasts, official or adapted. A Fleet Air Arm one of doubtful pedigree runs:

Here's to us in our sober moods when we ramble, sit and think,
And here's to us in our drunken moods when we gamble, sin and drink;
And when our flying days are over and from this weary world we pass,
May the fish-heads bury us upside down so the crabs can kiss our arse!

Bob Hawkins, on the opposing team and wearing an embroidered skull-cap he bought in the bazaar in Istanbul, has gone completely purple and pop-eyed with the strain of his unremitting effort.

Nick Cooke-Priest, one in front of Hawkins, yelps with excitement as he grips Norman Boyes around the waist with his arms and legs . . .

It is **0025**. War canoes ended when the broom handle broke. Now, the officers have resorted to all-in wrestling in the middle of the wardroom floor. The captain, shattered and bedraggled, has decided to call it a night. After thanking Russ Harding for arranging the mess dinner he walks over to the wardroom door, slides it open, looks back once to smile, steps out and shuts the door behind him . . .

DAY *Thursday*	**DATE** *17*	**MONTH** *November*
PLACE	*Cagliari, Sardinia*	
POSITION	*39°15′N 09°10′E*	

SHIPS LOG. CO supercession. Captain Somerville assumed command. Ship sailed at 1600 for fast passage to Gibraltar.

It is **0945**. The entire ship's company has assembled on the flight deck. They come smartly to attention as Captain Rapp comes out and steps up on to a small dais in front of them.

'Stand at ease,' says Rapp shielding his eyes from the bright Sardinian sun still low in the sky.

'I won't keep you long. I will be leaving in a short while to fly back to Britain to prepare for my new appointment so I just wanted to get together with you all one last time before we go our separate ways.

'We have almost completed a long and arduous deployment. A lot has been asked of the ship in the last seven months but she has really come through it very well and I have been very proud of how we've all done. We have all worked hard together and succeeded in our mission. We have also enjoyed some good runs ashore together as well as putting up with some pretty average ones. Above all, the spirit has remained high and that is a testimony to your own strength of character. Well done.

'This is a special time for me as it is nearing the end of my third command. If I was a gambling man I would bet that this is my last sea command as my career looks as if it is set to continue ashore. You will understand, therefore, why the *Brilliant* will always hold very special memories for me. You have all served me very well. Thanks very much for everything.'

It is **1010**. James Rapp sits at his desk with his private phone to his ear and listens to the clicks and buzzes of interference as the call to England is put through.

'Hello.'

'Hello my love. It's me.'

'Hello dear. Are you still on the ship?'

'Yes. Just doing a bit of last-minute packing. By the way, they gave me a terrific dinner in the wardroom.'

'How do you feel this morning?'

'Got a bit of a thick head, I'll tell you, but it was good fun. Excellent food. Most amazing pudding.'

'I'm glad you enjoyed it. Are you feeling a little sad now?'

'Yes. It's a strange feeling really. Just said goodbye to the ship's company. As soon as Angus gets here I'll hand over the ship and head for the airport.'

'We'll all be there to meet you darling. Seven o'clock at Terminal Two.'

'Are the girls with you now?'

'Yes, they're right here. They're blowing bubbles . . . Rachel, Hope, come and say hello to daddy.'

'Bubbles eh? What's their technique like now?'

'Very good. Rachel's just blown about twenty bubbles all around the kitchen. Here she is . . .'

'Hello Daddy.'

'Hello Rachel. Are you coming to meet me at the airport?'

'Ooooh Daddy. You just missed the biggest bubble . . .'

It is **1400**. Lieutenant Liz Hall and Sub-Lieutenant Julian Titmus, dressed in civilian clothes, stand expectantly at the arrivals gate at Cagliari International Airport. A flight from Rome landed about half an hour ago and the passengers are just starting to filter through into the main terminal. The two naval officers study each face intently whilst consulting a photograph that Liz Hall is carrying in an official Royal Navy file.

Amongst the thickening crowd of arrivals coming through the automatic doors a tall, well-groomed man of about forty, wearing a blue blazer and grey flannels, stops, puts down his suitcases and looks around. Hall and Titmus move towards him as one.

'Captain Somerville?' says Hall.

'Yes,' says the tall man.

'Hello sir. We're here to take you to HMS *Brilliant* . . .'

It is **1445**. James Rapp and Angus Somerville stand facing each other in the captain's cabin. They have completed the hand-over of all the ship's classified and secret documents and are now preparing for the moment when command of the *Brilliant* officially passes from one man to the other – a naval ritual made remarkable only by its extraordinary simplicity and understatement.

'Angus,' says Rapp, handing him a glass of champagne. 'Here's something to wet your whistle.'

'Thanks James.'

'Best of luck. You now have command of HMS *Brilliant*.'

'I have command.'

Both men sip from their glasses and shake hands firmly.

DAY *Saturday*	**DATE** *19*	**MONTH** *November*	**YEAR** *1994*
PLACE	*On passage to Gibraltar*		
POSITION	At **0600** *36°10′N 03°18′E* At **1200** *36°10′N 05°20′W*		
DISTANCE TRAVELLED midnight to midnight *166 nautical miles*			

SHIPS LOG. Arrived in Gibraltar. Weather warm and calm. Most of ship's company ashore. Painting of starboard engine carried out from paint tower.

It is **1130**. Captain Angus Somerville, the new commanding officer of HMS *Brilliant*, is on the bridge and taking charge of the ship's approach to Gibraltar.

Joining the ship so near to her return to Britain is not an easy task for this young captain on his second sea command. He is eager to get to grips with the ship, get to know her and put her through her paces but he realizes he has inherited an exhausted crew at the tail end of a grinding deployment. Wisely, he is adopting a 'softly, softly' approach to the next few days and using the time to get to know his officers and judge the character of a ship that he must make his own and on which he must eventually stamp his particular style of command. He knows that his time will come – but not just yet.

It is a fine day with excellent visibility, so many of the ship's company are out on the upper deck and looking towards the horizon and the famous outline of the Rock of Gibraltar – a beacon of welcome and symbol of merriment for British seamen since 1704. Nobody who has ever seen this gargantuan rock can fail to be impressed by its impressive stature, towering isolated above the surrounding countryside.

It is **1150**. The Rock is nearer and larger. Russ Harding broadcasts:

'Good morning. First Lieutenant speaking. We are making our final approach to Gibraltar on a fine, warm day with just a little light breeze. The weather forecast for tomorrow promises the same, so we should be in for an enjoyable run ashore. A word of warning, however. Gibraltar is not the place it used to be in the Seventies and Eighties when the border with Spain was closed and there was, shall we say, a more lenient view to the excesses of Jack. Today, that leniency has gone and for those of you who have not been here for a while, let me assure you that you will be given very short shrift by the local police if you get into any sort of trouble at all. Also, as you may know, there is a permanent naval shore patrol based in Gib and it is their job to keep their eyes on people like you. Don't give them any work to do.

'Finally, just to say, we will be in number forty-one berth opposite the clock tower, which is a perfect position for the start of tomorrow's Rock Race which will start at 1200. Clubs is hoping for a record turn-out of people to compete in the race, but those of you who are thinking better of running up a virtual mountain of 1500 feet are more than welcome to wave everybody off and then get a taxi to the top to watch the finish. Enjoy your run ashore. That's all.'

Micky Goble, waiting for the call for hands to harbour stations, sits in the sun on the foc'sle and chats to Roni Whittaker.

'Roni, just look at that huge great Everest-like outcrop stuck in the middle of the sea out there. Can you believe that some brain-dead lunatics, about eighty of them I believe, are goin' to run up it tomorrow?'

'You mean you're not Micky?' says Whittaker sarcastically.

'Why on earth would anybody want to do such a thing? There is a perfectly good road to the top and some perfectly good taxis that will go up that road. That's the way I'm doin' it, but it'll be at my leisure. It's Sunday tomorrow so in the mornin' I'm goin' to have a slow bimble down to the Donkey's Flip Flop*, have a couple of pints of best bitter, read the Sunday papers and then get a nice comfortable taxi to the summit . . .'

'And what are you going to do tonight, Mick?'

'Woman, this is Gibraltar! I'm goin' to get pie-faced, blatted, shedded, rat-arsed, handcarted, and bolloxed . . .!'

It is 1730. Practically the whole ship's company are ashore and enjoying the facilities, shops and restaurants of their beloved Gibraltar. With its Marks & Spencer, Woolworths, W. H. Smith and the densest collection of pubs in the world, it is Jack's home from home. This hallucination of England clinging to the edge of Spain is a sailor's paradise and although many complain that the mood of the place has changed with the depletion in the British naval presence and the opening of the border with Spain, it has retained much of its bizarre English charm:

A group of Wrens are having a cream tea in a tea house called the Spinning Wheel.

Some stokers are playing the slot machines in an arcade in the high street.

Bob Hawkins is standing in the street outside a television shop and watching live coverage of the international rugby match between Scotland and South Africa live from Murrayfield. He curses out loud when Van der Westhuizen scores his second try of the afternoon.

Dave Mynett is in a sports shop buying a new pair of running-shoes and a pair of blisterproof socks for tomorrow's Rock Race.

Micky Goble is in a phone box dialling his father's number in Gloucestershire to check that he is coming to meet him when the ship gets into Plymouth. He only gets the answering machine.

It is 2000. Leading Seaman George Peart leaves the ship and walks a mile down Queensway – the perimeter road of the dockyard – to a nondescript grey building with a green door. He presses a button marked with the name Tonna.

Keith Tonna is regarded as one of the best tattoo artists in the world. Sailors of many nationalities have been adorned by the needles, coloured inks and steady hand of this young and talented body artist.

---

* Nickname for The Horseshoe – one of Jack's favourite Gibraltar pubs.

It is **2005**. Peart sits in Tonna's clinical tattoo 'surgery' and in his broad Geordie accent explains what he wants.

'It's not a regular tattoo I want like.'

'It's OK. Whatever you want I can do as long as you have some art work to base it on.'

'Why aye – I've got this. I cut it out of the club magazine . . .'

Peart produces the crest and shield of Newcastle United – the team he would bleed for.

'I've decided to have this tattooed somewhere on my back. Can you do that?'

'Oh yes. No trouble with that. Just wait till I copy this and make a transfer . . .'

It is **2135**. Tonna concentrates hard as he completes the outline of the crest on Peart's left shoulder blade.

'You're a big fan then, George?' enquires the tattooist.

'All me life. There's no other team.'

'Who are their best players?'

'They're all good really. I mean there's Beardsley, Cole, Steve Howie, Lee Clark. I canna differentiate, they're all fantastic.'

'Who's the manager?'

'You mean the Messiah! That's our Kev. Kevin Keegan – "Special K". I'd even have his autograph tatooed on my back if I could.'

'Keep still George. No more talking now. I'm going to fill in the crest with the colours now.'

'Magic . . .'

It is **2230**. The naval provost and two tough-looking leading regulators on routine patrol stop their van outside The Horseshoe in Main Street. Over fifty of the *Brilliant's* company are in their favourite watering-hole. The beer flows as the singing gets louder and the laughter more raucous, but the mood remains friendly. The provost's van moves on.

Behind the bar the landlord Jimmy Wornall is pulling pints with a vengeance and a smile.

'Most people think matelots ashore are trouble – just drunken louts. But they're not. They tend to get a bit merry sometimes and they've been known to throw a punch occasionally but, on the whole, Jack alongside is just a guy who wants to have fun. For this lot coming ashore is their Friday night. Civvies get a Friday night once a week – Jack might not get his for weeks or months at a time.

'I've built a career and a business on the back of sailors so I reckon I know what makes them tick. The first thing is, don't patronize them. Accept their friendliness and their offer of a pint because it's probably from the heart. There's nobody more friendly than a sailor – I reckon it's because they all live so close together they've learnt to get on better than most of us who live ashore. Sure, they fight. Not so much with each other but sometimes with sailors from other navies or, these days, with some of the locals around here who want to see Gib given to Spain. We patch them up if they get into a bit of bother – we've had loads of bust noses and split lips over the years.

'This lot though, are great. I love having the *Brilliant* in. Her sailors are always high-spirited but never any trouble. I don't have one entry in the pub's log about any problems with the *Brilliant* ever – and she's come into Gib a lot over the years. I'm talking about the blokes, of course, but sometimes I think a ship has a character all of her own which she instills into her crew. Yeah, these lads are alright . . .'

It is **2345**. George Peart walks into The Horseshoe and is immediately surrounded by a dozen shipmates who want to have a look at his new tattoo. He pushes them back, peels off his T-shirt, gently removes a protective bandage and reveals the Newcastle United crest in all its black, white, blue and gold glory.

'It's canny, eh?' says Peart.

'It's great George,' says Micky Goble draining a pint of beer. 'But you better get it scraped off mate.'

'Eh?'

'I phoned me mate at the Clipper in Guzz and got today's results. You got done three–two by Wimbledon.'

'Oh bollocks!'

'Yeah. And my team went down as well.'

'Portsmouth?'

'Yeah. Luton did 'em two–nil.'

'Let's have a bloody drink.'

'Good idea . . .'

It is **0200**. Micky Goble leans against a convenient lamppost in Fish Market Lane. He has just emerged from the Buccaneer night-club and contains much of their beer stock. Trying to work out a few salient facts about himself – his identity, his whereabouts and the name of the planet he is on – he puts a cigarette in his mouth and searches his pockets for a lighter.

In the shadows across the road the provost and his regulators sit in their van, watch the roly-poly matelot and debate whether he is in need of 'guidance'.

Goble finds his lighter, holds it up to his mouth and flicks the igniter but it does not work. Unsteadily he squints down at the lighter, adjusts the flame-control switch and flicks it again. A searing tongue of yellow flame shoots past the astonished sailor's face and he squawks in drunken surprise.

'Fuck me!'

The provost's van draws up by the lamppost that is keeping Goble vertical.

'Evenin' mate. *Brilliant?*'

Goble nods without fully focusing on the person talking to him.

'Come on then. In yer get and we'll give you a lift back to the ship. You don't want to bump into the local police with that lighter you got there. They'll do yer for carryin' an offensive weapon mate.'

'Have you got a match?' enquires Goble wobbling towards the voice in the van.

DAY *Sunday*	**DATE** *20*	**MONTH** *November*	**YEAR** *1994*
PLACE	*Gibraltar.*		
POSITION	*36°10'N 05°20'W*		

SHIPS LOG. Quiet day in Gib. Great Rock Race. Majority of ship's company ashore. Diving on ship's hull.

It is **0950**. Eighty-three of the ship's company assemble on the jetty just in front of the ship. One is dressed up as Fred Flintstone, another as a Roman legionnaire, another as an ostrich and one as a test cricketer complete with bats and pads. Most, however, are in shorts and singlets. Everybody is limbering up for the Rock Race – a gruelling, exhausting, torturous naval tradition which involves running from the dockyard, at an altitude of 15 feet above sea-level, to the top of the Rock, at about 1500 feet. The length of the race is 3 3/4 miles and it is run almost constantly at an angle of 33 to 40 degrees.

Most of the assembled field will be happy just to get to the top and receive a certificate to say they accomplished the feat. A hard core of 'fitties', however, is running to win or drop in the process. For them the Rock Race is a serious challenge; an ultimate test of fitness and character. This select few have been training for the race for most of the deployment and their time of truth is now almost upon them. The hot favourites are Leading Physical Trainer Clubs Mynett, Petty Officer Ginger Lowden, Able Seaman Chris Lirret, Petty Officer Clive Wilkinson, Petty Officer Tony Lilley, Sub-Lieutenant Dougie Auld and Lieutenant Steve Boynton.

It is **1000**. Captain Angus Somerville climbs on to a podium, raises a large Union Jack and waits for all the runners to get into line.

'On your marks . . . Get set . . . GO!'

The crowd of runners surges ahead as one.

It is **1004**. Ginger Lowden and Dave Mynett, running together, have established a comfortable early lead. They are just coming up to the casino on the long, steep Engineer Road above the dockyard and doing their best to break the rest of the field. About 25 yards behind them is the chasing pack of Tony Lilley, Chris Lirret and Dougie Auld. The rest of the field is already stretched out far behind.

It is **1010**. Coming up towards Jew's Gate and the turn into Queen's Road Mynett has edged into a slight lead of about 10 yards over Lowden. Lilley has pulled away from the pack but is beginning to breathe hard. Lirret and Auld are still in contention. Wilkinson and Boynton are looking pained and falling behind.

It is **1013**. Running up to the end of Queen's Road and turning up into the very steep Cave Branch Road, Mynett starts to grimace and slap his leaden upper thighs. Behind him Lowden is slowly closing the gap but, behind him in turn, Lirret has made a spurt and overtaken Lilley.

It is **1017**. Mynett's muscles are screaming at him to stop as he passes the checkpoint in front of St Michael's Cave. He looks down and sees the winding roads littered with sailors variously running, stumbling, shuffling, staggering, trudging and plodding up the most famous lump of limestone in the world.

It is **1020**. Mynett has stopped running. He is walking painfully past a group of Gibraltar's renowned Barbary apes and his lungs are pumping like bellows. Closing fast is Lirret who has got a second wind. Mynett watches in dismay as the able seaman passes him and attempts to open up a lead with still a mile left to go. Mynett clenches his teeth, curses the pain and somehow kick-starts his legs into a semblance of bipedalism. The apes screech in apparent encouragement.

It is **1024**. Lirret is first into Signal Station Road which leads to the summit and the finishing line, but behind him, to the yells of encouraging supporters, Mynett puts in one last almighty effort and from somewhere finds the strength to close the impossible gap.

It is **1024 and 15 seconds**. Mynett crosses the finishing line and punches the air in glorious triumph.

It is **1024 and 32 seconds**. Lirret comes in second and to the outstretched hand of the victor.

It is **1024 and 50 seconds**. Ginger Lowden puts in an impressive sprint to finish third.

It is **1200**. Dave Mynett puts up a notice on the ship's sports notice board on Two Deck:

The Top of the Rock Road Race took place at 1000 on the morning of Sunday 20 November 1994 in perfect running conditions. It was good to see a marvellous turn-out of runners and supporters. The event proceeded smoothly and most runners had the bog-standard hangover which is all part of the fun! Altogether eighty personnel crossed the finish line. Two were disqualified for the use of a taxi. Well done LS Steve Lewis who ran as an ostrich and raised over £800 for charity.

It is **2000**. Micky Goble squeezes into the red phone box ouside Mothercare in Main Street and tries once again to get through to his father's number in Gloucestershire. The phone rings three times before it is answered.
'Hello Dad.'
'Hello son.'
'Dad, I'm in Gibraltar. Just phoning to check you'll be there when we come in on the twenty-fifth.'
'I'll be there Michael. I'm coming down with Russ.'
'That's great Dad. I've arranged a pass for your car. Just give it to the bloke at the gate and you can drive through to the jetty. Ten o'clock we're due in. Sixteen wharf in Frigate Alley . . .'

Chapter Ten

GUZZ

DAY *Friday*	**DATE** *25*	**MONTH** *November*	**YEAR** *1994*

PLACE	*English Channel*

POSITION	At **0600** *50°18′N 04°08′W* At **1000** *50°25′N 04°10′W*

DISTANCE TRAVELLED midnight to midnight *14 nautical miles*

SHIPS LOG. Sailed into Devonport bang on time. Berthed at wharf 16 in Frigate Alley. We're home!

It is **0900**. HMS *Brilliant* slices resolutely through a grey and boisterous English Channel towards a distant bright light that is flashing twice every ten seconds. It is the warning and guiding beam on top of the Eddystone Rock lighthouse, a granite tower standing some 135 feet high that is visible to mariners for 24 miles and is the first sign of approach to the Plymouth Sound.

On the upper deck officers and ratings gather to catch their first glimpse of the English coast since their departure over half a year ago. Nobody is saying very much. Most are lost in reflection.

For sailors, coming home is often a personal and private event involving powerful and opposing emotions.

Bob Hawkins stands on the starboard bridge wing and feels numb:

'It's a really odd feeling. I've been dreaming of this moment for so long and yet some of me doesn't want the journey to finish. Seeing Eddystone over there it seems as if we've never been away and yet in just six and a half months we have done so much.

'I can't wait to see Joan and the boys but coming into Devonport marks the end of my time in *Brilliant* as I will be moving on to another ship, another job. It is always sad saying goodbye to a ship.'

Micky Goble leans against the starboard bulwark on the foc'sle and looks pensively towards the flashing light:

'Once you see Eddystone you know you're home. The heart races a little bit faster 'cos you're nearly there – back in Guzz where you first started. My dad'll be there now – stood waiting with my brother Russ and some of my mates from the Clipper.

'It'll be great seein' them. Especially dad. Bein' ex-navy he loves warships and I reckon he's pretty chuffed havin' me in a blue suit just like he was when my brother was in the mob . . .'

Goble holds his hand out flat and looks up at the dark autumn clouds.

'You might have guessed it would start rainin' wouldn't you? Proves we've come back to the right bleedin' country anyway!'

Roni Whittaker stands alone on the Sea Wolf missile deck:

'I'm glad I did it. I'm pleased I've had the experience and made some good friends but I don't want to go to sea again. Maybe the lads will accept the idea of women at sea one day but it won't be for a while yet. I just want to get home, see my boyfriend and enjoy Christmas. Next year is another year.'

Dave 'Clubs' Mynett, ever smiling, is on the flight deck:

'It's been great. It's always great goin' to sea. You have a bit of adventure, bit of a laugh, bit of fun and the occasional bit of grief. I'm ready for home now though. I'm knackered – especially after the Rock Race. Yeah, my girlfriend Marianne'll be there waitin'. I expect we'll go straight back to her place . . . for a nice cup o' tea!'

Tracie Lovegrove is on the bridge and feeling excited:

'It's been hard. I've learnt a lot and I think I've done pretty well. I didn't manage to get my officer of the watch ticket this time but I'll get it next time. This is my life now and I want to prove that women can be good officers. One day there will be women captains . . . one day.'

It is 0930. The *Brilliant*, now in the Sound, heads north-east past New Grounds, then turns west to pass Drake's Island and Plymouth Hoe. Over at Devil's Point some families have gathered to wave the ship on to Cremyll Bay where she will make a sharp turn to port and head up through the narrow passage before South Yard leading towards Frigate Alley at Western Mill Lake.

She is just the latest safe return made by seven centuries of seafarers and their warships to this famous port.

Russ Harding stands proudly on the bridge wing and watches the ship's progress through his binoculars:

'The trouble with people like us is that we place very high demands on our families. My wife is expected to stay at home, look after the house, look after the children and get them educated. I miss them terribly and often feel guilty that I'm not around more but they understand that for me the navy is a vocation. It has been for the last sixteen years and it will be far into the future. That said, returning home really is the highlight of any deployment.'

It is 0952. The bow of the *Brilliant* breaks through a swirling sea fog to draw the tears and cheers of a waiting crowd of hundreds of excited loved ones on the jetty of sixteen wharf.

Martin Atherton stands quietly by the bridge door and contemplates the scene. A circle completed:

'This is the same place we left nearly seven months ago. But I wonder if we are all the same people coming back. I was a little afraid when I left the UK. I said to my family and friends that my departure marked a sort of an end but also a beginning because the Martin Atherton going would not be the Martin Atherton coming back. Living an intense, sometimes gruelling but ultimately enriching, life on a warship must change you. But I realize now that this is something to rejoice at because when we return to a place we see it not as it was but with fresh eyes.

'At this moment of homecoming I'm always reminded of something T. S. Eliot said at the end of the *Four Quartets*:

> We shall not cease from exploration
> And the end of all our exploring
> Will be to arrive where we started
> And know the place for the first time.'

It is 1000. The tenth incarnation of HMS *Brilliant* nudges gently to her final berth and the waiting, welcoming crowds.

Here she will stay until her next deployment.

The start of another circle . . .

GLOSSARY

Jackspeak

Who's Who

The Wonders of Naval Abbreviation

JACKSPEAK

(Drawn from *Jackspeak*, the definitive guide to Royal Navy slanguage by Rick Jolly; published by Palamanando.)

ADRIFT	Late, absent from a muster or duty, not with it mentally.
AMEN WALLAH	Naval padre or chaplain (also bible basher/puncher, devil dodger, God botherer/walloper, sin bosun, sky pilot).
ANCHOR-FACE	Someone, usually an officer, who lives and breathes the Royal Navy even when retired.
THE ANDREW (or the Andrew Miller)	The Royal Navy. This is derived from the infamous press gang officer active in the Napoleonic Wars. The Royal Navy is also known as 'the Mob'.
ASHORE	Anywhere other than the ship or shore establishment in which one is serving.
BIMBLE	Stroll.
BLANKET STACKER	Supplies rating.
BLOOD BUCKET	Lifeboat (synonym for blood wagon – ambulance).
BOLLOXED	Drunk. (Also handcarted, shot away, legless, newted, shedded, ratted . . .)
BOOTIES/BOOTNECKS	Royal Marines. Exact origin unknown, may derive from nineteenth-century uniform of a tunic with a leather fastener at the collar.
BOX OF	Collective noun, as in 'open another box of sailors'.
BUZZ	Rumour. (A buzz merchant is a gossipmonger, a gash buzz one that turns out to be incorrect; galley buzzes are the most common as in 'I read it in the Galley Gazette').
CLUBS/CLUB-SWINGER	Naval Physical Training Instructor (also the admiralty clown).
COMMON DOG	Common sense (CDF – Common Dog Factor).
CRABS/CRABFATS	Nickname for members of the Royal Air Force. The RAF was formed on 1 April 1918 by an enforced mar-

riage between the Royal Flying Corps and the Royal Naval Air Force. The colour of the RAF uniform is supposed to have resulted from the diversion of a huge but cancelled export order for the Tsar's Imperial Guard following the previous year's revolution in Russia. The uniform's light blue colour was identical to the greasy mercuric oxide jelly (or crabfat) which was widely issued at the time for the treatment of body lice(crabs).

CRUSHER — Nickname for a regulator (the 'chief crusher' is the master-at-arms).

DEEKS/DQs — Her Majesty's Royal Naval Detention Quarters in the Portsmouth Naval Base (can refer to any military prison for Jack/Royal).

DHOBEY — Laundry. Originally a Hindi word it has been adopted to denote any clothes washing on board ship (as in dhobey palace – the laundry room – and dhobey wallah – the laundryman).

ELECTRIC EARS — Headphones. (Electric string is insulated cable.)

FISH-HEADS — Army/RAF slang for anyone in Royal Navy uniform.

FLOAT TEST — Ditch something overboard. A euphemism for getting rid of something; an alternative is 'give it to the splash-maker'!

FLUTTERBUG — Helicopter. (Also kerosene budgie and paraffin pigeon.)

FRATTON — 'Getting out at Fratton' is Jack's expression for the coitus interruptus (withdrawal) method of contraception. This term is explained by the fact that on the railway line from London to Portsmouth, Fratton is the penultimate station before 'Pompey'!

GUNNY BUNNY — Field gunners' groupie.

GUZZ /GUZZLE — The naval base of Devonport, adjoining Plymouth. Two possible explanations are that GUZZ was the wartime signal letter group for the port's call sign and GUZZLE was what Jack did to excess on return from a long spell at sea.

HARBOUR HASSLE — The red tape associated with getting away to sea.

HATCH RASH	Forehead or shin bruising that results from banging one's head on a closed/closing watertight hatch or one's legs against the sill.
HEAD DOWN	Sleep. As in 'I'm going to get my head down'. (Also rack out and hit the pit).
HEADS	The ship's latrines. Originally a plank positioned over the leeward bow wave in the ship's head.
HOMEWARD BOUNDERS	Large or crude stitching used by Jack to sew on badges or to make repairs while homeward bound (anticipating that they would be sewn on properly by wives and girlfriends).
HOOKY (or Killick)	Nickname for a leading hand. Refers to the fouled anchor (or hook) badge that indicates their rate.
JACK	Generic term for all Royal Navy sailors. Derived from Jack Tar, the eighteenth- and early nineteenth-century matelot with his glossy black hat, carefully dressed pigtail and canvas breeches that, like his hair, were impregnated with high grade tar. (Origin of Jack the lad, Jack of all trades and Jack with bumps – a Wren!)
JAUNTY	The master-at-arms. Derived from the French 'gentil-homme a l'armes' (gentleman-at-arms). Also known as the 'joss' – joss means luck and is usually used in terms of bad joss or ill-fortune.
JIMMY/JIMMY THE ONE	The first lieutenant (also James the First/ Magnificent). In older times 'jeminy' referred to tidiness and the first officer had this as his area of responsibility and so became known as Jeminy the First or as he is now, Jimmy the One!
JESUS NUT	All-important feature securing helicopter rotor blade system on to driving shaft. Disconnection or failure of this item while in flight will result in the crew meeting the Man in person.
LIFE IN A BLUE SUIT	Resigned acceptance of the vicissitudes of life in the Royal Navy.
MANK (also drip)	To moan/complain/whinge in a repetitive manner.
MESSDECK LAWYER	Rating know-it-all who constantly quotes rules and regulation ('I know my rights'!).

NAUTICAL NAUSEA	Seasickness.
OPPO	Special friend on ship. Derived from 'opposite number' – the person who is on your watch when you're off.
RUN-ASHORE	A social visit with various shipmates to a series of pubs and clubs.
SNAKES' WEDDING/ HONEYMOON	An unholy tangle of lines and ropes on the deck.
SNOTTY	Midshipman. Derived from tradition that midshipmen had three buttons sewn on their jacket cuffs to stop them wiping their noses on their sleeves.
SPLITS	Crude, anatomically based nickname for Wrens.
STEAMING BATS	Naval issue heavy shoes with steel toecaps.
THREADERS	Very annoyed. Derived from threadbare.
TRAPPING	Seeking new friends of the opposite sex on a run ashore.
VIRGINS ON THE VERGE	Group of officers unable to make a decision.
WEBBING	Ladies' suspenders. (Also suzzies.)
WHITEHALL WARRIOR	Officer appointed to work at the M.o.D in London.

On the menu

There is a whole Jackspeak vocabulary for the all-important food served on board

BABIES' HEADS	Individual steak and kidney puddings
BITS	Baked beans in tomato sauce (also HITS – herrings, PITS - pilchards and TITS – tomatoes!)
CHEESIEHAMMYEGGIE	Ham and cheese omelette or flan
CHOKEY-NOSH	Chinese food
FIGGY DUFF	Rich suet pudding
MUCK ON A RAFT	Pâté on toast
MUCK ON A TRUCK	Take-away meals
NINE-O'CLOCKERS	Extra snacks served at 2100
PUSSER'S SNORKERS	Large sausages
SCRAN ON A VAN	Food from a dockside canteen wagon

365	Roast lamb
TIDDIE OGGIES	Galley-made Cornish pasties
TRAIN SMASH	Fried tomatoes
YELLOW PERIL	Kedgeree

WHO'S WHO

There is a vast array of acronyms for the various jobs and status titles to be found on board:

Official job titles

CO	Commanding Officer
XO	Executive Officer (First Lieutenant)
OPS	Operations Officer
PWO(A)	Principal Warfare Officer (Above Water Warfare)
PWO(U)	Principal Warfare Officer (Under Water Warfare)
MEO	Marine Engineering Officer
WEO	Weapons Engineering Officer
SO	Supply Officer
NO	Navigator
SPLOT	Senior Pilot
FLOBS	Flight Observer
OOW1	Senior Officer of the Watch
CBO	Confidential Books Officer
MAA	Master-At-Arms
CHOPS(R)	Chief Petty Officer (Operations) (Radar)
CBM	Chief Boatswain's Mate (the Buffer)
CPOMEM(M)	Chief Petty Officer Marine Engineering Mechanic (Mechanical), Chief Stoker
POCK	Petty Officer Cook
POMEM(L)	Petty Officer Marine Engineering Mechanic (Electrical)
LWEM(O)	Leading Weapon Engineering Mechanic (Ordinance)
LREG	Leading Regulator

LS(M)	Leading Seaman (Missile man)
AB(S)	Able Seaman (Sonar)

Status titles

DCO	Duty Commanding Officer
OOD	Officer of the Day
DPO	Duty Petty Officer
LHWOD	Leading Hand of the Watch on Deck
LHOM	Leading Hand of the Mess
QM	Quartermaster
BM	Boatswain's Mate
YO	Young Officer (officer under training – midshipman)

Unofficial titles

SLJO	S****y Little Jobs Officer (for example Children's Party Organizer, RAF Affiliated Units Officer, Garbage Disposal Officer)
MDSO	Malta Dog Shoot Officer (for those volunteers – and there are always some – who offer to help cull the mythical Malta Dog, little realizing it to be the sailor's name for diarrhoea).
GMCO	Gibraltar Money Changing Officer – those who are unaware that Gib is a sterling area and sign up to change two of their pounds for one 'Gibraltar' pound.
STC	Splash Target Cox'n – the innocent who volunteers to sit on the splash target, a raft streamed 500 metres astern of the ship for aircraft to shoot at. The STC begins to smell a rat when he is given a flak jacket, tin helmet and the last rites by the Buffer before being congenially debriefed!

THE WONDERS OF NAVAL ABBREVIATION

The Royal Navy uses a uniquely stylized vocabulary of acronyms that minimizes speech. A beginner's guide would include:

PSM	Please See Me (there's a problem).
ASAP	As Soon As Possible (it's a big one).
VMT	Very Many Thanks (ta).
WMP	With Much Pleasure (yes – even if it's not with much gusto).
RPC	Request the Pleasure of your Company (drinks invitation).
RDP	Run Down Period (take it easy).
PVR	Premature Voluntary Release (early voluntary retirement).
CDF	Common Dog Factor (common sense).
ROMFT	Roll On My F***ing Time (a rather *laissez-faire* attitude).
POPT	Petty Officer Physical Trainer (euphemism for 'work-shy').
DSMSMR	Don't See Me See My Relief (a regrettably laid-back attitude).
SMP	Self Maintenance Period (DIY for ship's engineers when the rest of the ship's company will be ashore getting drunk).
SOP	Standard Operating Procedure.
BZ	Bravo Zulu (well done – it's fine).
RDD	Required Delivery Date (the date we said we needed spares knowing they'd come a week later which is when we really wanted them).
GTCU	Gas Turbine Change Unit (the engine's heart).
JD	Jack Dusty (stores accountants who pretend to order spares).

AVICOS	Available In Course Of Supply (the depot has posted the item and it will turn up eventually, about a week after the RDD, see above).
WBD	Will Be Done (it will happen, probably, if I remember).
PCB	Printed Circuit Board (lots of transistors that do odd things).
U/S	Unserviceable (beyond our technical ability, anyway).
2HOTEL DG	The Diesel Generator in 2 Hotel Section.
NAAIHTO	Not Available Action In Hand To Obtain (man from depot is off on his bike to Halfords, don't hold your breath).
PPP	Piss Poor Perfomance (a disappointment).
NAMET 9/9	Lowest grade in Naval recruit's intelligence test (i.e. thick).
PSTO(N)	Principal Supply and Transport Officer (civilian manned and run stores organization which is much maligned).
NAAFI	No Ability And F***ing Ignorant (an unfair generalization).

Translate the following exchange between the Chief Stoker [CPOMEM(M)] and the Marine Engineering Officer [MEO] using the acronyms immediately above.

CPOMEM(M):	MEO, sir, you PSM'd me ASAP?
MEO:	VMT – oh, WMP your RPC – not RDP on PVR yet?
CPOMEM(M):	NEGATIVE! Too much CDF for ROMFT, I'm no POPT all DSMSMR.
	Let's move on – the SMP?
MEO:	Your SOP: BZ – RDD for DTCU OK from JD?
CPOMEM(M):	AVICOS and WBD but PCB for U/S 2HOTEL DG NAAIHTO
MEO:	PPP. NAMET 9/9 these PSTO(N)s – NAAFI.

And for the more advanced:

PIAWPO – RASON   Proceed in accordance with previous orders – remain at sea overnight.

HOOTROTDCOTUDCASDAH. SSDCUANBDCDS3CY.

Hands out of the rig of the day clear off the upper deck close all screen doors and hatches. Special sea dutymen close up assume nuclear biological chemical defence state 3 condition Yankee.

INDEX

BBC Books would like to thank the following for providing photographs and for permission to reproduce copyright material. While every effort has been made to trace and acknowledge all copyright holders, we would like to apologise should there have been any errors or omissions.

Photographs are identified by caption and the picture section in which they appear. 1st section is between pages 64 and 65, 2nd section is between pages 128 and 129, 3rd section is between pages 192 and 193.

Sue Adler: 1st section, Operations room; 2nd section, Royal Marines Protection Party, HMS *Brilliant* intercepts a merchant vessel, The Wrennerie; 3rd section, Fire fighters. Sarah Ainslie: 1st section, Lt Tracie Lovegrove, Leading Cooks Mickey Nowell and Mark Warburton; 3rd section, Lt-Cdr Martin Atherton, MAA Chay Robertson and LR Nick 'Pincher' Martin. Adrian Bell: 3rd section, The Gibraltar Rock Race. British Crown Copyright – M.o.D. Reproduced with the permission of the Controller of Her Britannic Majesty's Stationery Office: 1st section, HMS *Brilliant*, Ship's company (photographer Neil Hall, Royal Navy), Capt. James Rapp, Lt-Cdr Bob Hawkins (Neil Hall, Royal Navy), Bright Star (Neil Hall, Royal Navy); 3rd section, Goodbye at sea (Neil Hall, Royal Navy), Capt. Rapp bids farewell (Surface Flotilla Photographic Unit). Ines Cavill: 1st section, LS Micky Goble, Lt-Cdr Russ Harding, CPO 'Basher' Bates, Lt Jerry Barnbrook, Sub-Lt Nick Cooke-Priest; 2nd section, Bob Hawkins climbs back on board, Hands to bathe, Capt. Rapp in his patch, Jacqui Quant MAQ; 3rd section, Remembrance Sunday, Surgeon-Lt Richard Newton and Jacqui Quant, Missile man, PO Steward Tony Lilley, First glimpse of Guzz. Film still: 3rd section, LWEM Kevin 'Gladys' Gladman. Christopher Terrill: 1st section, Fast roping; 2nd section SNS *Victoria* and HMS *Brilliant*, Light jack stay, SODS opera, Roni Whittaker; 3rd section, Gunner, Unloading weapons. The illustration on page 16 is a pen and ink drawing of the first *Brilliant* by Van de Velde the Younger, 1696 (National Maritime Museum, London).